S0-BSQ-339

"The bitch won't die."

Jon Whispel's voice lowered as he faced the jury, "We returned to Valessa's home with a syringe that Adam filled with bleach from the laundry room. We sat in Valessa's bedroom smoking cigarettes, planning her mother's murder. She was sleeping when we entered her bedroom, but she got up and went into the kitchen in her nightgown. Adam grabbed her in a sleeper hold from behind. She tried to get away. In a choke hold, he injected the bleach into her neck. I returned to Valessa's bedroom and put my head in my hands and listened to the screaming."

"Adam entered the room and said, 'The bitch won't die.'"

Whispel coolly explained that he provided a knife, and Adam returned to the kitchen and used it to stab Valessa's mother while Valessa pinned her down.

"Adam came in holding the knife in his bloody hands." Whispel said, "Adam had blood on his hands and Valessa said, 'Babe, you need to go in the bathroom and wash your hands.' Again, we heard Valessa's mother cry out. Adam returned to the kitchen to finish her off and then returned to Valessa's bedroom, and we smoked cigarettes as we waited for her to die."

RATTLESNAKE ROMEO

JOY WELLMAN

PINNACLE BOOKS
Kensington Publishing Corp.
http://www.kensingtonbooks.com

Some names have been changed to protect the privacy of
individuals connected to this story.

PINNACLE BOOKS are published by

Kensington Publishing Corp.
850 Third Avenue
New York, NY 10022

Copyright © 2005 by Joy Wellman

All rights reserved. No part of this book may be reproduced
in any form or by any means without the prior written consent of the Publisher, excepting brief quotes used in reviews.

If you purchased this book without a cover, you should be
aware that this book is stolen property. It was reported as
"unsold and destroyed" to the Publisher and neither the
Author nor the Publisher has received any payment for this
"stripped book."

All Kensington Titles, Imprints and Distributed Lines are
available at special quantity discounts for bulk purchases for
sales promotions, premiums, fund-raising, and educational
or institutional use. Special book excerpts or customized
printing can also be created to fit specific needs. For details,
write or phone the office of the Kensington special sales
manager: Kensington Publishing Corp., 850 Third Avenue,
New York, NY 10022, attn: Special Sales Department. Phone:
1-800-221-2647.

Pinnacle and the P logo Reg. U.S. Pat. & TM Off.

First Printing: April 2005

10 9 8 7 6 5 4 3 2 1

Printed in the United States of America

INTRODUCTION

Tampa's tall, modern buildings gleam in the sun as symbols of affluence, replacing the old lighthouse that marked the port during the time pirates reigned supreme. Every year, the metropolis celebrates its past with the Gasparilla festival—staging a capture by pirates who parade through the streets, ending up in Ybor City, where cigars were made at the turn of the century.

Teddy Roosevelt chose Tampa to train his troops for the Spanish-American War, and its port to disembark from. In the last century, only the Columbia Restaurant survived without change. It caters to tourists and an upscale clientele. The old brick cigar factories now house bars with colorful names like Teddy Roosevelt's Rough Riders. The shops and galleries provide unique items, and the two new tattoo and piercing parlors add to the intrigue on 7th Avenue.

The area attracts teens and a party-going crowd. Unsupervised young people gravitate to Ybor City and the rave clubs that sprouted like mushrooms when police began to enforce laws against underage drinking by chasing teens from open fields where they used to congregate to party.

Rave clubs provide music and a place to dance free of alcohol and cigarettes. Some parents welcomed them as teen age recreation centers for children as young as twelve. Few imagined that drug dealers would fill the void and offer LSD and Ecstacy.

(A * following a name announces it is fictitious.)

CHAPTER 1

A MISSING PERSONS REPORT

One of the twenty people directing telephone calls for the Hillsborough County Sheriff's Department in Ybor City said, "Sir slow down. I know it's difficult when you're excited. Spell your name."

"Jim E-N-G-L-E-R-T."

"Who's missing?" She reached for the Missing Persons form.

"V-I-C-K-I L-Y-N R-O-B-I-N-S-O-N."

"How long has she been missing?"

"We had a date for the beach this afternoon and she didn't arrive," Jim Englert said.

The call dispatcher shook her head and stopped writing. "A few hours isn't a reason to put out a bulletin. How old is your girlfriend?"

"Forty-nine!"

You're sure she's not late shopping."

"She had an appointment to show real estate in the morning. She never misses a business appointment. Later she was to try on a dress to participate in my brother's

Joy Wellman

wedding. It wasn't just a date for the beach I'm concerned about."

"Oh, I understand. Do you suspect foul play?"

"Yes. She was afraid of her daughter's boyfriend and he was at the house, when I last saw her at 11:30 last night."

"I'll take down the information." She passed it on to the dispatch officer who took care of four different areas, 911 calls and Emergency Medical Services. Deputy Valentine Torres was covering Carrollwood, and he received the Missing Person message on his computer along with the complainant's Safety Harbor address.

MISSING ADULT [FEMALE] UNKNOWN CIRCUMSTANCES . . . 5'5" . . . BLOND HAIR . . . BROWN EYES . . . DOB 12/27/47 . . . EMPLOYED AT RE/MAX REALTY N. DALE MABRY HWY., TAMPA 33618 . . . LEFT NO NOTES, MESSAGES OR PHONE CALLS, VERY UNUSUAL ACCORDING TO BOYFRIEND/COMPLAINANT SUSPECTS FOUL PLAY.

Deputy Torres drove to Cartnal Avenue in the old Carrollwood section of Tampa. He wrote June 27, 1998 and noted the time 8:29 p.m.

Deputy Torres called the weekend Duty Officer Sgt. Jorge Fernandez and told him "I got a report about a missing woman. No one's home now. Boyfriend's afraid for her life."

"Torres, contact this guy in the morning and ask to have him meet you at her residence. Check him out. He wouldn't be the first guy to make a report after committing a crime."

"Sure, I wouldn't have thought of that," the deputy said.

"After working twelve years on homicide, everyone is suspect," Jorge Fernandez said.

* * *

Early Sunday morning, June 28, Deputy Torrez arrived at Cartnal Avenue to meet James Englert. He observed that the house appeared dark inside. There were no vehicles in the driveway. A cursory search of the property revealed no sign of foul play. The house was secure, but he found the side door to the garage was open.

James Englert arrived and told the deputy that it was normal, since Vicki had a dog who was allowed to go in and out. He expressed the fear that Vicki might be inside and unable to answer. Englert said, "Vicki had problems with her fifteen-year-old daughter, Valessa, who had made statements in the past that she knew people who would take care of her mother if she ever threatened her for any reason. I left Vicki with her and Adam Davis, a boyfriend and his friend they called Jon. Michelle, the seventeen-year-old, is away visiting her father."

Deputy Torres stared at the thin, anxious man and decided to call his supervisor for permission to enter with Jim Englert. While they waited, Jim Englert explained, "Vicki and I have been close for two years. She's wonderful and so reliable. Her only problem is her daughter, Valessa. Counseling hasn't helped. Vicki was going to send her to a place called Steppin' Stone Farm, but I don't think Valessa knew."

Two more sheriff's cars pulled up, and four men got out and walked through the house. The pink living room had heart shaped pillows on the couch and appeared immaculate. The kitchen was clean, except for a few dishes in the sink. Vicki's bed was unmade, but nothing else seemed disturbed. Michelle's room could have been in a model house and almost announced that she was away. The guest bedroom was equally pristine. Valessa's room looked lived in. The pool area was clear. Jim Englert acknowledged that Vicki wasn't unconscious in the house somewhere, and he took off, leaving the sheriffs questioning curious neighbors.

Deputy Torres filled in his report.

It stated that James Ralph Englert last saw Vicki Robinson at her home on Cartnal Avenue in Carrollwood Village Friday night, June 26, 1998, at 11:30 P.M. When Englert left, Robinson's fifteen-year-old daughter, Valessa, as well as two of Valessa's acquaintances—Adam Davis and his friend Jon—accompanied Robinson. Englert related that Robinson told Valessa to ask her friends to leave, and Valessa answered that "they wouldn't be leaving yet." When Englert called the following day, there was no answer at the Robinson house. He was unable to reach Robinson on her cell phone and business phone, as well.

Englert found the situation "unusual," as Vicki Robinson was very reliable and she would have called him in the event of a change in plans. Englert also mentioned that Robinson was afraid of her daughter.

Torres then informed Cpl. Anthony Baker of the circumstances. In order to determine whether any foul play had occurred, the decision was made to enter into the Robinson house. Torres, Baker, and Deputy John Palomino entered the house by way of the garage. They searched for Robinson, but no one was there. The officers did not discover any signs of foul play, so they secured the house and departed.

Michael Kalupa—Robinson's neighbor—reported that his wife saw Robinson's van leaving on June 27, 1998 at 5:45 A.M., but she could not identify the driver. Vicki's dog, Lady, was running in the street, so Mrs. Kalupa took her in. Mrs. Kalupa found this situation strange, because Robinson never left home so early, and Lady was never allowed to run free. Robinson's usual departure was 8:30 or 9:00 A.M.

Ed Clarey—Robinson's neighbor who lived across the street—reported that he saw the Robinson van leave at 5:15 on the same day. At 3:30 P.M., he saw the van again, but he could not identify the driver.

Englert described Vicki Robinson briefly, and Deputy Torres put out an alert via mobile computer. Robinson was entered as a missing person (locally) through the H.C.S.O. dispatcher. As it had not been established that she was endangered, she was not entered in the FGTL/NGFC computer. Englert was instructed to contact H.C.S.O. if he came into contact with Robinson. Englert also alerted Deputy Torres that a large trash can was missing from the garage, and it wasn't elsewhere on the property.

Deputy Torres returned to his office and called Jim Englert who was able to provide Robinson's license tag number of the '94 Nissan Quest. Englert repeated, "She was to have picked up a dress to wear to my brother's wedding to her best friend. That's not something a woman would ignore."

Torres obtained Vicki Robinson's driver's license and social security numbers from his mobile computer DSMV files before he responded to a call from Susan Kalupa on Cartnal Ave. He returned at 1:15 P.M. to take her statement and noticed that two newspapers had been delivered to Vicki Robinson's driveway adjacent to her property.

The blond woman gave her age and birthday. She was a year younger than her missing neighbor. Mrs. Kalupa affirmed her husband's claim that she had observed Vicki's van backing out of her driveway at 5:30 A.M. Saturday morning. She could not tell who was driving or see any occupants. "I thought it was strange that Lady, Vicki's dog, was running around and chased the van into the street. She hasn't contacted me about the dog, but I'm still taking care of Lady."

The deputy left Vicki Robinson's neighborhood and contacted her place of employment, RE/MAX Realty. The receptionist put him in touch with Robinson's manager Rebecca Eckley, who gave her age as fifty-five and her birthday as July 27, 1943. She stated, "It's out of character for Vicki Robinson not to get someone to cover her appointments or not answer her pages. She has a cell phone and is always in close contact with the office." The woman's voice raised, "She's a very responsible employee. Dependable! She simply wouldn't leave with without a word or notice." Eckley's voice moderated, "Vicki has no family in Tampa, but does have parents in another state. Her mother's name is Donna Klug. Vicki's ex, Charles Robinson, recently moved to another state, but I don't know which one. Her daughter Michelle is with him now. I don't have his number," she apologized.

Deputy Torres didn't have to ask any questions. The woman talked rapidly as if she was afraid he would hang up the phone. "Vicki had numerous problems with her fifteen-year-old daughter, Valessa, and recently found she was pregnant. She spoke of having her daughter placed in a treatment center in the forthcoming weeks and said she was afraid of her daughter's boyfriend, Adam Davis. Recently, she was very happy to learn they had a place for Valessa, but I don't know if she told her daughter yet."

Deputy Torres thanked Mrs. Eckley and contacted the on-call detective, Jorge Fernandez and advised him of the circumstances. He followed Detective Fernandez's directions and faxed all his reports to the attention of Sgt. John Marsicano for immediate follow-up. He included Valessa's boyfriend's name, Adam Davis, and the information he obtained from the computer.

ADAM W. DAVIS, WHITE/MALE, DOB 10/12/78, 5'10", 145 LBS, MED. BUILD. HAS LEFT BROW PIERCED AND HAS THE FOLLOWING TATTOOS ON HIS LEFT ARM: The deputy drew a cross. (IN

MEMORY OF K.D.). ON THE LEFT H
STAR. ON HIS RIGHT HE HAS A DOG. D
EXTENSIVE CRIMINAL HISTORY AND LIS
ROBINSON'S ADDRESS AS HIS. HIS PREVIOUS AD-
DRESS WAS ON NEBRASKA STREET. TO DATE IT IS
UNKNOWN WHERE ROBINSON'S DAUGHTER, VA-
LESSA, IS OR IF THEY ARE TOGETHER. TORRES
DID NOT TRY TO CONTACT VICKI ROBINSON'S
FAMILY AT THIS TIME.

He returned to the Sheriff's office and received another report on Vicki Robinson. He printed, KLUG,
THOMAS, YOSEMITE DR. OKEMOF, MI 488604,
6/28/98 and noted the time, 4:30 P.M.

INVESTIGATION: TORRES RECEIVED A CALL
FROM THE ABOVE LISTED SUBJECT WHO IDENTI-
FIED HIMSELF AS ROBINSON'S BROTHER. HE
PROVIDED HIS NAME AND PHONE NUMBER
SHOULD THE NEED ARISE TO CONTACT HIM.
After Cpl. Anthony Baker signed it, he faxed it to Sgt.
Marsicano.

Monday morning June 29, 1998 Torres's reports
alerted eight detectives who worked homicide to concentrate on the case. A further search of records revealed Davis was born in Little Rock, Arkansas and grew
up in Tampa, Oregon, and South Dakota. Warrants
were issued in June 1997 in Lincoln County, Oregon for
grand theft auto and violating probation for burglary.
They preceded an August complaint from an uncle in
South Dakota that Davis stole his car. Tampa records
proved Adam Davis drove his uncle's car to Tampa before he was arrested for stealing beer, cigarettes, and a
bottle of Mad Dog 20/20 from Beverage King drive
thru.

Detective James Iverson was assigned to the case and
prepared a search warrant to thoroughly examine Vicki

ROMEO
AND HE HAS
A DAVIS TED
13

...al Avenue. Detectives Walter
...sited the house with Corporal
...o had asked for the search war-
...sure no one was home. Assistant
...irley Williams approved and Judge R.
...t.

...verson, Sgt. John Marsicano, Detective Jim
Caima... ...d Detective Jorge Fernandez arrived at the
Robinson residence at 7:00 P.M. along with Detective
Chuck Sackman who came to photograph and collect
evidence. Also present was Investigator Doug Bieniek
from the State Attorney's Office.

Before entering, Detective Iverson observed what appeared to be a blood stain on the garage door. Detective
Sackman photographed it and took a number of swabs
for clinical investigation. They entered the garage and
noted the floor had recently been cleaned and faded
marks led the detectives to suspect bleach was used. One
dark stain looked like blood, but Detective Sackman
tested it and determined it wasn't. There were a number of dog bowls on the floor.

They gained access to the residence through the
laundry room. Jorge Fernandez discovered clothes in
the washer and dryer and held a few of the items up.
Detective Iverson looked at them. "I'm a father of a fifteen-
year-old girl. They're small but could belong to Vicki
Robinson's daughter, Valessa. She's missing, too."

The tall, dark haired Fernandez frowned. "I only have
a young son, but what teenaged girl leaves clothes?"

Iverson ran his fingers through his thinning hair. "One
under duress."

The detectives roamed through the house searching
for signs of a struggle or indications that a crime was
committed in the house. They found several pieces of
broken glass and a lamp lying on a bathroom floor near
an office. There were no visible signs of blood anywhere.

Sgt. Marsicano came across two names in a bedroom.

He dialed Kelli Yelloushan who described herself as a good friend of Michelle for three years and called Vicki "Mom," because she spent a lot of time at the house. "I know Valessa and talked to her on Friday afternoon the twenty-sixth and told her I was going to stop after work a little after six and pick up some clothes I left in Michelle's room. Michelle's away visiting her father. I knocked on the front door and received no answer so I went around to the pool area and saw the sliding glass door was open so I entered and took my clothes."

"Do you know where Valessa is now?" the detective asked.

"No. Vicki's been having problems with her for a year or so, but mostly over her boyfriend Adam Davis. He was arrested for helping Valessa run away."

"What's he like?"

"He's nineteen, but doesn't have a car. Neither of them were home when I was there on Friday."

Sgt. Marsicano put the receiver down and looked up as Detective Fernandez entered. "Teenaged girls haven't changed. This one described Davis as nineteen and didn't own a car. Cars still define men." He pointed to a name in an address book. "Why don't you interview the guy, while I copy my notes?"

"I'm Detective Fernandez investigating the whereabouts of Vicki Robinson and her fifteen-year-old daughter. Are you Brian Graves?"

"Yes, I'm Michelle's boyfriend. We met at Sickles High School a year ago. We're both seniors now."

"Did you know her sister, Valessa?"

"About a year, too. The last time I visited their house was the night before Michelle left to stay with her dad."

"Was Valessa in any trouble?"

"Her mother was planning to send her to some kind of a 'boot camp' some time soon."

"How about Adam and his friend? You know them, too?"

"Yes. His friend's name is Jon, but I don't know the last name. I can't help you find Vicki or Valessa."

Jorge Fernandez glanced at Marsicano. "Does his friend Jon have a vehicle?" He got a negative response and wrote "no" on the form.

While the other detectives continued to inspect each room, Detective Iverson concentrated on what he determined was Valessa's room—because it wasn't tidy and a young girl's clothes were scattered on the floor. The bed was unmade, and there were several beer cans mingled with papers in a small garbage can. The walls were covered with eyes cut from numerous magazines. He also noticed several faint writings that a black light could reveal, but his attention was drawn to her desk on the south wall of her room.

In a drawer were three letters written from Hillsborough County Jail. They had the name Jon Whispel in the left corner and the detective surmised he was the Jon who was reported to be with Adam Davis at Vicki Robinson's residence on June 26. Iverson took possession of the letters and three journals lying on a nightstand, apparently written by Valessa.

Then he noticed a butcher knife and keys on top of a dresser. He called Detective Sackman to photograph and collect them, along with the garbage can and items taken from the bedroom floor. They also took the contents of the bathroom outside Valessa's room, as well as four brushes from the master bedroom on the southwest corner that appeared to be Vicki Robinson's—in case they needed DNA.

Detectives discovered a subpoena in Vicki's home office, and James Iverson read it. It indicated that Valessa Robinson was to appear before Assistant State Attorney Carolle Hooper on July 2, 1998 to give testimony against Adam William Davis involving interference with a custody case made by the Tampa Police Department. Iverson took possession of the subpoena. He filled out the search warrant and listed all the items taken in the search, as well as property receipts. He reported that the house was secured at 8:50 P.M.

Detective Iverson now had another name to investigate. Once back at the Criminal Investigations Bureau, the computer expert found Jon Whispel's record and home address.

Jon Whispel was arrested with Adam Davis in October 1997 for stealing a taser gun from an unoccupied house in Hillsborough County. They were both incarcerated. Jon Whispel was released in December. Adam Davis had fought with other jail inmates, so he wasn't freed until April 15, 1998. The Tampa Police Department verified the subpoena and faxed the arresting officer's report.

One detective reviewed Jon Whispel's picture in the 1997 yearbook at Jefferson High School, but learned he quit school two months before graduation and never participated in sports or organizations.

James Iverson frowned when he read Vicki Robinson had Davis arrested six weeks later on May 27, 1998 for child abuse for being with her fifteen-year-old daughter, Valessa. He realized it was only the month before Jim Englert reported her missing. The girl was to testify against Adam Davis on July 2, 1998, only three days away.

Detective Iverson and Sgt. John Marsicano headed for Jon Whispel's home on Pennywell Avenue, while Detectives Fernandez and Caimano went to Jon's place of business, Papa John's Pizza on West Waters Avenue.

Whispel's house was at the end of a cul-de-sac, adjacent to a large area surrounding a canal owned by the water company known locally as Swift Mud. The sun had descended, leaving only the tops of trees silhouetted over the wild area.

When the detectives knocked on the door, the light

outside came on. The woman who answered the door
identified herself as Mrs. Tomilou Whispel, Jon's mother.
"He's not here, but he's probably with a guy named
Adam. I last saw him on Friday afternoon around three
or four. He didn't come home Friday night, nor all day
Saturday. He must have come home sometime early Sunday morning after 1:00 A.M., but I never saw him."

"How do you know that?" Sgt. Marsicano asked when
the haggard mother stopped talking.

"His mail was missing and he left nine dollars on the
dining room table for long distance calls he made. I noticed some of his clothes and his Green Bay Packers
duffel bag were missing."

Detective Iverson asked, "You didn't hear any noises
or suspect he was in the house?"

Tomilou swatted a mosquito that landed on her
shoulder, attracted by the light. "Come in officers," she
said, and closed the door after they entered. She
pointed to the couch. "Please sit down."

The detectives stood awkwardly, not wanting to
refuse the invitation, but needing continue the interview from a commanding position. "You didn't hear
your son enter?" Iverson asked again.

"I thought I heard the sliding door open and got up
but never saw Jon. I looked out of the front window and
didn't see any cars and went back to bed. In the morning, I asked my son Chris over to secure the glass door
and screw the windows shut so Jon could not get in
again. I had taken Jon's key away because of his drug
problems."

Tomilou looked up at the detectives and brushed
away a tear. "Y'all probably know Adam and Jon were arrested for stealing a car and they both spent time in jail.
Today, when I came home from work, my neighbor told
me she saw Jon walking toward the house from the area
of the nearby park." She pointed to the southeast, toward the Swift Mud Preserve. "I know someone brought

a vehicle into our garage. It ran over a can of adhesive, crushing it, leaving tire prints. I thought it was my son, Jon, but reported the incident to the Hillsborough Sheriff's Department as a burglary. He must have gained entry through the sliding glass doors again. I didn't find anything missing, but there was a beer bottle on the TV stand."

Sgt. Marsicano said, "Thank you," and started to leave.

"My son was never in trouble until he met Adam Davis, but he seems to follow him where ever he goes."

Detective Iverson thanked her for the information, too. Once outside, he observed, "She must have thought we were here because of her report."

Marsicano shrugged his shoulders. "Sometimes detectives get lucky."

"We learned one thing. A couple of our team should examine the area behind Whispel's house," Detective Iverson said as they reached the car.

Detective Iverson placed a statewide alert for Vicki and Valessa Robinson and their 1994 Nissan Quest minivan, seafoam green with a Florida Tag.

CHAPTER 2
DETECTIVES FIGHT AGAINST TIME

Early Tuesday, June 30, 1998: Detectives Jorge Fernandez and R. Nolan parked their vehicle in front of Whispel's house. The sun was coming up in the east, lighting the large palm trees behind the property. While they waited for the large crew of deputies to gather, they put on the green utility jump suits over their clothes.

"No one could miss we're from the Sheriff's department with the big yellow letters—even without the eight uniformed guys," Nolan said pulling on his green cover-up.

"On the far side past the canal, where the high school is, there used to be a shooting range. The yellow might have helped then. A bunch of guys walking around near people's property dressed in green might scare some one," Fernandez said. He turned to the uniformed deputies. "You all know what we're looking for. If we find a path or paths, we'll spread out two by two."

They walked single file along the high chain link fence surrounding Swift Mud's preserve, moving in the direction of Woodlake Park, a small tamed area that bordered the preserve. They found an opening and walked the narrow path between the palmetto, heavy vines, and scrub pine, trying to imagine how far a body could be carried. They looked under the heavy brush, and sniffed the air to catch a whiff of decaying flesh. One man with a sensitive nose discovered a dead armadillo three feet off the trail.

Nolan said, "I'm glad it was only an animal."

The deputy laughed and then said, "Don't let any one from an animal rights group hear you say that." He joined the group and they pushed forward holding palm fronds back to keep them from slapping the men behind them.

The path split into several narrower trails that led into one path that appeared to go straight toward the canal. Jorge Fernandez signaled Nolan to follow him on that path. He turned toward the deputies and directed, "Separate and follow the paths, but keep in mind the distance from the house where we entered. A dead body can only be carried so far." He glanced at his wrist watch. "We'll meet back there in two hours. If you find a way to go west different from the path we came on, take it."

As Detective Fernandez suspected, the north path ended at the canal, where he and Nolan found an old battered boat they turned over. The canal water was murky and didn't reveal anything. They found nothing but old beer cans and cigarette butts. The Florida summer sun beat down, and the clothes they wore under their green jump suits were wet with sweat. Their coverups and shoes were covered with pollen, dust, and thorns.

"There's no way the ten of us can examine this big area on foot," Fernandez said. "When we get back, if the deputies haven't found a body, I'll ask for the helicopter. Caimano and I learned from an employee at Papa John's Pizza last night that Jon Whispel walked off his job early on Friday with Adam Davis and Vicki's daughter, Valessa. The girl thought he was fired for deserting his position, but that has to be confirmed by a manager."

"Today's Tuesday. If the mother is alive, she has to be tied up somewhere," Nolan said.

"Let's hope, but I've worked too many homicide cases. If her boyfriend hadn't described her as responsible, I wouldn't be out here beating bushes. Where could they hide her?"

"A hotel?"

"Yeah, three teens are going to carry in a struggling woman and not be observed."

The two detectives shared possibilities as they made their way back to Whispel's house, where the sweating deputies gathered. They all took off, while some neighbors watched from their front yards.

Back at the Criminal Investigations Bureau, Detective Fernandez peeled off his utility suit before entering. The air conditioned room made his damp clothes feel even cooler. He welcomed it after sweltering in the hot morning sun. He was putting in an order for the helicopter, when Detective John King returned.

"You need to go through a wringer," King observed.

"I should have gone home to change, but didn't want to take the time. Nolan and I were searching for the woman's body and didn't find it. If she's alive, none of us have much time."

"I've been examining Vicki Robinson's credit cards and checking account with Sun Coast Schools Credit Union. Her ATM was used at several locations in Hillsborough County since Saturday, June 27," King informed Fernandez.

"Do you think she could be using her card?"

"Not that lady," John King said with a positive sound in his voice.

Detective Fernandez stared at him. "How could you know that?"

"None of the other detectives told you? She was the realtor who found our house three years ago. My wife chose her. She met Vicki Robinson at some function she attended for one of my daughters. We have girls the same ages as hers."

"So that makes you positive?"

"I remember her as friendly, but businesslike. She wouldn't be sneaking around spending her money in Ybor City, Home Depot, or any of the other six locations her credit cards were used."

Detective Iverson got up from his desk and assigned each of the detectives to investigate one location King's research provided: The Circle K Store on Handy Road in North Hillsborough on the twenty-seventh at 9:04 A.M., a Super Seven Store on Bears Avenue on the Northern Border of Hillsborough twenty minutes later, and Wesley Chapel in Pasco County on Route 54.

Detectives knew the suspects were traveling north until an attempt to use the ATM had been made at the Sun Coast branch in Town 'n' Country, Sunday morning at 7:23 A.M., where Whispel and Davis had lived. The teens had made a circle that perplexed detectives.

Detective Iverson had given the warrant information to the Public Information Office to be passed out to the media early in the morning. He withheld that detectives were investigating businesses in Ybor City near the ATM where Vicki Robinson's account had first been accessed.

The detectives interviewed Valessa's boss at the Carrollwood McDonald's. He said, "Valessa called on Thursday the twenty-sixth to say she and her mother were going to take a trip." Bob Cunningham, Valessa's boss and the spokesperson for McDonald's, told deputies, "Valessa and Adam picked up her check near midnight on Friday."

Michael Moyce, an assistant manager at Denny's and Davis's boss, told Hillsborough Sheriff's deputies, "I last saw Adam Davis who worked as a dishwasher on Friday the twenty-sixth at about 3 P.M. when he came in to ask for his check. I told him he couldn't have it until he provided proof of citizenship. He was hired on June 21, 1998 and had only worked about three days at that time. The next day, Saturday June 27, he called J.R. Heacox, the night manager, and said he would not be in until 1 A.M. He was scheduled for 11. Adam claimed he needed to visit a friend who was hurt in a car crash. Between 9:30 and 10, he got a call saying Adam would not be in at all. Heacox told him he needed him at 1 A.M, but he didn't show."

"What else can you tell us about him?" Detective Nolan asked.

Mike Moyce shrugged, "Only that he talked about his girlfriend all the time. He was impressed that Valessa's family had money. She visited him when he was on breaks. There was always another guy with her. I don't know his name. She seemed happy-go-lucky. Jeff Brantly, the cook, had become friends with Adam."

Jeff Brantly confirmed that although he only knew Adam a few days, they had become friends. He saw Adam last on Friday, June 26, around 10:30 P.M.

The detectives were about to leave when Brantly said, "Earlier in the evening, Vicki Robinson came to Denny's looking for Valessa. Vicki said there was a large sum of money was missing from her bank account and she needed to talk to Valessa right away about it. Vicki asked me to tell Valessa to come right home if I saw her. She told me Valessa had been out all night on Thursday and hadn't returned yet. I knew Vicki Robinson from a real estate transaction we did together."

Brantly lifted his white apron and wiped his hands. "I went to Vicki's house Friday morning to drop off Adam's CD tote bag that he left at work, but did not see Adam or Valessa until they came into the restaurant after 11 P.M. with Jon Whispel and another guy. Adam claimed he had about fifteen hundred dollars on him and wanted to party when I got off work. He asked me to drive him to buy six cases of beer and a pound of weed. I told him I didn't know where to buy a pound of weed and that I had to drive some of the boys from work home. Jon Whispel said he had several hits of acid and they would wait. When I returned, they were gone."

"So you didn't see them again?" Nolan asked.

Jeff Brantly hesitated before he replied, "Adam saw my car parked at a friend's house and came in. He asked me to drive him where Valessa was staying. We ended up at Richard Cunningham's house at on Railford Court. Valessa was really high at 10 o'clock in the morning. I told her she needed to call her mom and she said she wasn't going to."

"Was Whispel there?" both detectives asked simultaneously.

"I didn't see Jon Whispel at Cunningham's house. Adam told me they were going to rent a car and go to Trenton, New Jersey to visit a relative, and then drive to California to live. I thought the relative was Adam's mother."

The detectives stood silently contemplating another question when Brantly said, "Adam bought a gun on June 16 from a friend. I thought it was Richard Cunningham. It was a .357 automatic. I saw the gun on one occasion, but don't know where it is now."

Back at the Criminal Investigations Bureau, Detective Iverson took accounts from detectives who had investigated the locations Vicki Robinson's ATM card had been used in Hillsborough County, as reported to them by Linda Fales of the Suncoast Schools Credit Union security department.

He and Detective John King responded to the Ybor City location on Fourteenth Avenue East in an attempt to recover any video recording available, but found the tapes replayed automatically after they were filled. The

June 27 tape was destroyed and could provide no visual information.

Undaunted, King and Iverson proceeded to Pete Gracio's Amoco Station on North Dale Mabry, where they learned the tapes were changed daily. They left with a tape that coincided with Vicki's ATM withdrawal. The service station was in front of the Home Depot on North Dale Mabry where they retrieved a videotape from the previous twenty-four hours. Both detectives returned to Criminal Investigations to view the tapes. The Amoco Station tape clearly showed two figures with tattoos. They were barely discernible in the grainy pictures.

After examining the tape from the ATM surveillance camera, Detective Jorge Fernandez determined it was the Jester on Davis's forearm. He called the tattoo parlors in Ybor and described the tattoo, as well as the two men and the young girl he was looking for. One artist responded back, and Fernandez met with the tattoo artists that had made the new tattoos on Adam Davis and Jon Whispel. One identified a skull on Whispel and a Jester on Davis, and he gave the detective copies. "They paid $600 and came in on Saturday and again on Sunday."

"Were they alone?" Detective Fernandez asked.

The second man with "Murder" tattooed across the front of his shaved head answered, "a girl was with them, but she just watched and complained about not being well. She said something about having a baby."

When the detective showed Valessa's picture, the man identified her.

Iverson learned a photo had been made at the Sun Coast Schools Credit Union at their branch in Town 'n' Country on Sunday, June 28, at 7:23 A.M. and he proceeded to pick it up, while the other detectives studied the Amoco and Home Depot videos. Iverson could clearly see a white male in a FSU (Florida State University) peaked cap wearing dark glasses in front of a van, with a cross dangling from his left ear. Detective Iverson obtained the copy of the transaction and photo that identified Adam Davis.

Detectives were stunned the fugitives headed north before doubling back. The picture of Davis and Whispel in the Circle K store on Gandy Boulevard registered later than the cluster of stores north of Tampa.

Detectives realized the mounting information created a bleak outlook for Vicki Robinson. James Iverson and Jorge Fernandez met Assistant State Attorney Shirley Williams at the State Attorney's Office. She determined they had probable cause to charge Adam Davis and Jon Whispel with grand theft for taking money from Vicki Robinson's ATM and grand theft auto for taking her van. Judge Ralph Stoddard signed the warrants and Detective Iverson entered them in the FCIC/NCIC System and notified the Public Information Officer, Lieutenant Greg Brown. Valessa and Vicki Robinson were already listed as Missing Persons in the system.

Lt. Brown spoke for the Hillsborough Sheriff's Department. He told the press they received Jim Englert's Missing Persons report on Vicki Robinson along with the name of Valessa's boyfriend, Adam Davis. They discovered a long list of crimes Davis committed including convictions for burglary, armed trespassing, and grand theft, and he was currently awaiting a trial on child abuse charges.

CHAPTER 3
THE MEDIA

June 30th, 1998, the headline "Search on for Missing Mother and Daughter" appeared in the *St. Petersburg Times*. There was a picture of Vicki Robinson and her daughter, Valessa, printed on the front page. The article announced that the forty-nine-year-old divorced mother of two had a solid relationship with a boyfriend, a good job selling real estate, and close involvement with the church.

The story quoted Lt. Greg Brown of the Hillsborough Sheriff's Department, "She (Vicki Robinson) had a history of being responsible. We have not ruled out foul play."

Vicki's boyfriend, Jim Englert, gave his account of the last day he saw Vicki before he reported her missing. He told the reporter that Valessa had been in counseling and Vicki decided recently to seek additional help. The article reported that Englert was forty-five, lived in Safety Harbor and had dated Vicki Robinson for two years. After describing Valessa as stubborn and willful, Jim Englert said, "She thinks she can do anything she wants and her mother can't do anything about it."

Becky Eckley, Vicki Robinson's broker from RE/MAX Realty of Carrollwood, told reporters that Vicki wasn't comfortable with Adam Davis and had confided to coworkers that her daughter's problems included truancy, drugs and running away. "Vicki gave Valessa tough love, good love, but nothing worked."

The report included the arrest records of Adam Davis and Jon Whispel. Vicki's van was described as a blue-green 1994 Nissan Quest with a Florida tag. Sheriff's officials asked that anyone with information call them or Crime Stoppers.

Television news on all the local stations carried the story along with the picture of the missing mother and daughter.

July 1, 1998, the *St. Petersburg Times* again published the beautiful picture of a smiling mother and daughter with the headline, "Mom and Daughter Remain Missing." The article reported that warrants had been issued for two Tampa men last seen with a missing Carrollwood mother and her teenage daughter. According to Hillsborough Sheriff Department spokesman Lieutenant Greg Brown, Adam Davis, nineteen, and Jon Whispel, nineteen, were charged with stealing Vicki Robinson's minivan and her money.

The article, written by Amy Herdy, repeated the information provided the day before, but after listing Adam Davis and Jon Whispel's crimes she added, "Whispel was charged with armed trespassing, criminal mischief and petty theft. The judge withheld a finding of guilt and ordered probation.

The *Tampa Tribune* headline, "Missing Girl's Boyfriend Sought" appeared on July 1 also. The story was far from a carbon copy of the *Times*. The paper had missed the big exposé on Tuesday, but their Wednesday edition flew out of the newspaper dispensers and all the convenience stores. It contained the shocking news that Adam Davis was sporting a new tattoo of a Jester on his arm, possessed a stack of credit cards, and was showing off the keys to a minivan he drove. The author, Paulo Lima, credited the information to a friend of Adam's named Robert Anderson.

According to the article, Davis told Anderson he put a down payment on the van. He also said he was going to kill someone with heroin and make it look like an accident—but Anderson dismissed it as an empty drunken boast.

The article then related information given by Richard Cunningham, seventeen. He said he was with a group of teens on Friday night, and they dropped off Valessa before 11:30 P.M. Vicki Robinson's boyfriend left the house, and they all hung out on the porch smoking cigarettes, while Robinson made macaroni and cheese for them. Nothing seemed strange to him that night.

CHAPTER 4

CRIMINAL INVESTIGATIONS BUREAU

An off-duty Tampa police officer spotted Jon Whispel and Adam Davis buying cement at Home Depot early Sunday, June 28th. He noticed their new tattoos and engaged them in a conversation. After he saw the six o'clock news on Tuesday, Officer William Rosenblume called the sheriff's office and informed them the two men had paid with a credit card.

The Dispatch Officer immediately alerted Detective Iverson, while he and Fernandez researched tapes to produce more pictures. After reading the Dispatch Officer's report, he slid it over the desk top to Fernandez.

The report said that Rosenblume spotted the two suspects at the Home Depot on North Dale Mabry at 1:45 P.M. They were loading Sakrete into a van similar to the one that had been described in the news. He looked for signs that the steering column had been popped, but he did not run the license tag.

"They must have appeared suspicious for the police officer to check to see if the van was stolen. He didn't mention there was anyone in the van," Fernandez said, and passed the report on for the other detectives to read. "Valessa's been seen with them. She has to be somewhere."

"This case is frustrating. The publicity should help, but read the story about Richard Cunningham. It says Vicki made food for the teens Friday night. That's not what her boyfriend told us," Detective Caimano said slapping the folded newspaper down next to his empty coffee cup. "I interviewed a guy named Robert Anders."

The detectives passed the newspapers among them. They reviewed the report on Robert Anders after they read Anderson's quote in the newspaper. Anders statement that he let Adam Davis share his home and gave him a job hanging drywall when he got out of jail didn't appear in the newspaper, but everything else matched.

"Davis showed up at a party on early Saturday morning acting weird looking to buy heroin. He said he was going to kill somebody with it and make it look like an accident. I dismissed the threats as drunken nonsense," Detective Iverson read aloud. "It's Anders's report, but I need to interview Richard Cunningham. His account refutes Jim Englert's description of the last night he saw Vicki."

Detective Fernandez met with Detective Dan McGill the pilot of the Hillsborough sheriffs' helicopter. They studied maps of vast empty areas in and around Hillsborough County. The area behind Whispel's house got most of their attention. The pilot swooped down over the canal while Fernandez scanned every open area for signs of digging. There were wide trails made by vehicles, but the land didn't appear disturbed. The detectives knew it would be difficult to penetrate the ground in thick brush.

Before giving up, they flew behind Valessa's house and the lake at the end of her street. The water was shallow and a body might be visible even if it was weighted down. Again Fernandez didn't find one.

On July 1, an anonymous caller contacted the telephone receptionist at the Hillsborough Sheriff's Department. The receptionist recorded for deputies out chasing down other leads what she described as a young female. She called Detective Hurley and told him, "A female voice said, 'I've been told that Vicki Robinson was knocked unconscious, killed, and dumped outside Tampa, and that Valessa Robinson witnessed the crime.'"

Hurley and Iverson rushed back to their CIB office to listen to the voice to hear if they could determine an age, accent, manner of speech, or anything unique to identify the voice.

Detective Iverson contacted AT&T Wireless services and had them check if Vicki Robinson's cell phone had been used within the hour, but was informed that there had been no activity for several days.

The consensus of the detectives who studied the voice of the female intensified questioning of teens who knew the trio. Detective Nolan and Detective Walter finished their paperwork and returned to the areas where teens hung out, hoping to interview someone that sounded like the anonymous voice. Many congregated in and around Joffrey's Coffee House, talking excitedly about the news to reporters.

The detectives followed leads, checked details, and questioned people in an orderly manner, but they were surrounded by an army of reporters who took stories from teens hanging out near Joffrey's in Carrollwood. They talked to teachers at Valessa's Presbyterian grammar school, students at Sickles High, Christian friends who knew Vicki and almost any one willing to give their name.

Jose Castillo, an eighteen-year-old, described himself as a friend who hung out with the couple and Jon Whispel. He told detectives, "Rattlesnake Davis's prime income came from dealing LSD called Jack-in-the-Box." He added that during a party at his house, Valessa overdosed on alcohol, opium, and marijuana, and they had to call paramedics. He claimed that Valessa planned to run away with Adam, but that Jon Whispel was not included in the plan.

Josh Moon, fifteen, told sheriff's deputies and reporters interviewing teens near Joffrey's, "I was paged by Jon Whispel on Saturday, June 27, and called him back. Jon confided that Valessa and Adam told her mother that Valessa was pregnant, and she flipped out." Moon related, "Before Jon hung up, he told me he was concerned about his mother and asked me to check on her." He added, "Valessa's relationship with Adam Davis was positive. Me and my friends thought Adam loved Valessa and was protective of her. Adam would do anything for the people he cares about."

Seventeen-year-old Richard Cunningham stopped one of the detectives after talking to news reporters and told that he lived close to Jon Whispel, and saw his friends several times over the weekend. "Adam flashed credit cards and said he put a down payment on the minivan he was driving. I met them at 3:00 P.M. at the home of a mutual friend in Town 'n' Country. Adam and Jon showed off their new tattoos. Valessa said she wasn't feeling well while resting on the couch. She asked Adam, 'When are we going to have a baby?' He answered 'When you support me.' Jon and Adam were like Siamese twins. They were pretty tight. They did everything together." The deputy and reporters took down his new information.

A photograph of Vicki Robinson with Valessa flashed on all the television stations. Reporters and the Hillsborough Sheriff's Department were deluged with reports from people who wanted to remain anonymous claiming they saw Jon Whispel, Adam Davis, and Valessa in their usual hangouts; Joffrey's Coffee House in Carrollwood and Papa John's Pizza in Town 'n' Country Saturday

afternoon, where Jon had worked. A call placed the teens
in Ybor late Saturday and again on Sunday in a tattoo
parlor, Valhalla. The male voice included information
that the teens had paid six hundred dollars in cash for
two tattoos; a Jester on Davis and a skull on Whispel. "They
both had their eyebrows pierced," the voice added.

Detectives Iverson and Hurley went to Cunningham's home on Railford Court to interview him. It was
almost 9:00 P.M., but Detective Iverson gave him an affa-
ble smile. "You're friends with Valessa?"

The boy appeared relieved and said, "I'm a student
at Sickles High and have known Adam Davis five years,
Valessa four, and Jon . . ." He stopped to think. "Maybe
three. I've been at Valessa's house with Adam and Jon
on several occasions."

"How about Friday, June 26?" Detective Hurley asked.

"Mrs. Robinson came home about 6:30 Friday. We
were out by the pool. She was cool about us being there
and didn't appear angry. She changed into a blue and
white dress and went into the kitchen to cook for
Valessa. She made macaroni and sausages, and we all
ate."

"Did you go there every Friday?" Detective Iverson
asked.

"No," Richard said, then swallowed and glanced down.

"But you went last Friday." Detective Hurley's voice
sounded serious. "You're sure about that?"

The teen's face flushed. "It was another night," he virtually whispered. "I did see Adam at Robert Anders'
house Monday afternoon. Adam, Valessa, and Jon drove
up in Vicki's minivan." The boy looked directly at the
detectives. His voice grew stronger. "Robert's mother
asked where he got the van. He told her he put $100
down on it and was planning to buy it."

"How long did they stay?" Detective Iverson asked in
his soft pleasant voice.

"About thirty minutes. Long enough to show off their new tattoos. They had their tongues pierced and Adam was wearing a cross earring in his left ear."

"Could you describe what they were wearing?" Detective Hurley asked.

"Adam wore black pants and shirt. Jon, a white T-shirt and black jeans. But I can't remember what Valessa had on." Cunningham then volunteered. "Later, I saw on the Monday night news that Vicki and Valessa are missing persons. I called Valessa's pager, but she didn't call me back. I lost my pager, so if they tried, I didn't get their message."

The detectives thanked him and were leaving when Richard Cunningham stated, "I was just mistaken when I told the news media that I was at the house Friday night."

Both detectives looked at one another knowingly before they got in their vehicle and drove away. "Some people will say anything to get their name in the papers," Hurley said.

They were returning to the office when Hurley was paged. A deputy advised that a Matthew Mielke had been arrested for possession of drugs and was acquainted with Adam, Jon and Valessa. He informed police that they had been staying at local La Quinta Motel over the past weekend. The detectives asked to have Mielke brought to CIB instead of Central Booking, then they rushed to the La Quinta.

The motel on Melborne Avenue was within the city limits of Tampa. The register revealed that Jon Whispel signed in on Sunday, June 28, 1998. The detectives had the desk clerk make a copy. Whispel was assigned Room 207, next to the office of a Tampa police officer in charge of security. The hotel Dumpster had been emptied, so it was too late to gather any other information.

The detectives returned to their CIB office and waited for the deputies to bring Matthew Mielke in. It was late, past midnight, when they watched him shuffle into the interrogation room with his head down.

James Iverson conducted the interview. He learned the man was twenty-four and worked at Carrabbas Restaurant in South Tampa. He dated the form July 2, 1998, approximately 12:15 A.M. "You knew Adam Davis, Jon Whispel, and Valessa Robinson."

"I met Valessa five or six months ago through a mutual friend James Scott*. I met Adam and Jon through her. I've been at her house a couple of times. My girlfriend knew Vicki."

"You mean Valessa?"

"No, her mother, but they were driving Vicki's van when they came to my apartment late Saturday or early Sunday a little after midnight. Adam parked around the corner, so I asked him to move it in front of my door."

"Why?"

"I didn't want them to draw attention to me by parking in someone else's spot. The cops are always watching, trying to catch me selling drugs. I walked to the van with Adam and got in while Jon moved it. It had a lot of trash inside, like they were living in it, but they said they were staying at a motel in Brandon. They came into my apartment and chilled for a while and played Nintendo for about half an hour."

"Did they say anything about Vicki or why they were driving her van?"

"No, and I didn't ask. Adam paid me the $70 he owed me and they left," Mielke said, shifting in his chair.

"Is that the last you saw of them?"

"Adam and Jon came back late Sunday night, could have been early Monday, and bought a quarter bag of marijuana and ten hits of acid. They said Valessa was back at the motel. Adam had three to four hundred dollars on him."

"What were they wearing?"

"Black pants and shirts. They each had a new tattoo. On Monday night I saw the news about Vicki and Valessa's disappearance. I called her pager. Adam called back. My caller ID registered the La Quinta Motel. I asked Adam about the news and he said there was nothing to the report and he and the others were heading to Arizona."

Detective Iverson showed him a copy of a video taken at the Circle K Store on Gandy Boulevard. "Can you identify those men?"

"Sure, that's Adam and Jon. They're wearing the same clothes they had on Sunday night. Probably it was early Monday." He shook his head. "I don't know what may have happened to Vicki."

The Gandy Circle K Store tape was dated June 29, 1998 at 3:00 A.M. Detective Iverson thanked Mr. Mielke and concluded the interview, and the two detectives left the room.

"He identified Jon and Adam and claimed they were wearing the same clothes at his house. He didn't see or talk to Valessa on that day," Hurley observed.

"That could be ominous, but I've got to get home and get to bed. It's a good thing I've been married twenty-five years and my wife understands detectives have to work late during emergencies."

"A lot of our guys have problems with that."

James Iverson smiled. "I did pretty well. I met my wife in Sunday School, when we were both nine years old."

Hurley stopped and held the front door open. "Nine! I guess you understand teenage love."

Iverson frowned and walked into the night.

CHAPTER 5
FOLLOW THE MONEY

From the day Captain Rocky Rodriguez called Sgt. John Marsicano and James Iverson received the assignment to find Vicki Robinson, Detective John King chased every hit Vicki's credit cards registered on June 26, 1998. The detectives learned where Davis and Whispel had been.

The news media never learned that James Iverson had contacted the Sun Coast Schools Credit Union and that the supervisor agreed to cooperate and put Linda Fales in charge. After reviewing the debits from Vicki's account, she had new video tapes installed in the ATM machines in Ybor City, and she went over the old ones with Detective Iverson. He recognized Adam Davis and Jon Whispel and asked if they could be tracked through the bank's records.

The Sun Coast Schools Credit Union's biggest concern was that Vicki's account only contained $1,800, which was almost depleted. Detective Iverson arranged with the Sheriff's Department to supply money to track the fugitives who now had warrants for grand theft of the Nissan Quest and stealing from Vicki's account. In order to follow the fugitives' movements, the bank put a hundred-dollar restriction on each withdrawal.

Suddenly, the leads dried up—until July 1, 1998. The first hit registered in northern Florida, and two that followed in Alabama were denied. In Gulfport, Mississippi, on Route 10, the card spit out one hundred dollars. Detective King determined they were traveling on Route 10, and Detective Iverson released an APB to police departments along the route.

The Hillsborough Sheriff's Department received a call from Ms. Linda Fales that a bank employee who had carried his lap top home to follow the progress of the fugitives notified her Vicki Robinson's card was used in Luling, Texas at 2:45 A.M. Thursday, July 2. Detective Iverson was awakened minutes later and called the Luling Sheriff's Department to send police to pick up anyone in a green Nissan Quest near the ATM. They arrived too late. The bank employee informed him the withdrawal was just an attempt and they received no cash.

Detective Iverson again contacted the Sheriff's Office in Luling, Texas and asked them to add the information to the bulletins, as well as send it west to all law enforcement agencies along Route 10. A Luling sheriff informed him a clerk in the store remembered the trio driving in the green van; two guys and a girl.

Detective Iverson stayed in contact with the credit union through Linda Fales during the day on July 2, waiting for Vicki Robinson's ATM card to be used again. Due to the anonymous call to the Sheriff's Department received the previous day, he was preparing another search warrant for Robinson's home approved by Assistant State Attorney Shirley Williams.

Linda Fales reported Vicki's card had been used in Ozona, Texas at 12:35 A.M. Tampa time—about thirty minutes earlier. He immediately phoned authorities in

Ozona and then called the Pecos County Sheriff's Department in Fort Stockton, Texas. It was the next large town to the west, and he alerted them to the fact that the subjects in his alert were heading their way from Ozona, Texas.

An hour and fifteen minutes later, Shirley Young from the Pecos County Sheriff's Office called him and said, "Detective Iverson, the vehicle was stopped. Shots were fired. Two males and a female are in custody."

"Were there any injuries?"

"That's all the information I have. I'll call back when I hear more," she said.

"Thank you," Detective Iverson said. He hung up and shared the information with Detective John King. Then he called Sgt. Marsicano and left the message on his voice mail.

King shrugged and continued to fill out his forms, but he looked up when Iverson's phone rang.

Shirley again announced she was calling from the Pecos County Sheriff's Office. "Valessa Robinson, Adam Davis, and Jon Whispel are in custody. There were no injuries," she said.

"Good," Iverson said. "Maybe we'll learn something."

When Sgt. John Marsicano got back, he immediately made plans to fly to Texas with James Iverson. Continental Airlines flew into the closest airport, Midland/Odessa, one hundred miles east of Stockton. The five hour flight was leaving Tampa at 5:50 P.M., so they had to hustle to catch it. Their wives helped by packing the few items they needed into carry-on bags.

The setting sun turned the shining waters of Tampa Bay and the Gulf of Mexico into gold as the plane took off. They flew west toward the sun, which prolonged daylight. They used the time to review what they knew about the two nineteen-year-old guys, in order to better interrogate them.

Adam's long list of burglaries began after his father

was killed on a motorcycle when he was fourteen. He stole a car from relatives and had lived in South Dakota, Oregon, and Arizona. After seventeen, he had been arrested six times in Tampa. He got extra time for fighting in jail. Jon Whispel's record was shorter. He was only arrested once with Adam.

"I talked to Jon's mother. She was concerned with her son's drug use and blamed Adam for his arrest," Iverson added.

The detectives chose coffee instead of the stronger drinks offered by the stewardess. "I need coffee to keep me awake," James Iverson said.

"After we go over the detectives' reports, we should catch some shuteye. It's going to be a long night," Sgt. Marsicano responded.

They reviewed John King's copious reports on every debit from Vicki Robinson's ATM account and the photos Jorge Fernandez and Iverson tracked down. The reports from the teens' friends detailed the days after Vicki's disappearance. Valessa was mentioned, but she didn't appear in any of the pictures captured by the ATM machines. Valessa didn't appear in any of the store videos at Home Depot, Amoco, or Circle K. Tampa Police Officer William Rosenblume talked to Adam and Jon and investigated the van, but didn't report seeing Valessa.

Detectives John Marsicano and James Iverson put their reports away when the stewardess passed out sandwiches.

The drone of the engines lulled them to sleep. From the time they received the responsibility to find the missing mother and daughter, sleep had become a luxury. The bump when the landing gear dropped down awakened them.

They made their way off the plane to the rental car agency and managed to get on the road by eleven-thirty P.M. Tampa time. The moonlight illuminated oil rigs pumping on the large ranches in the small town, and announced that they were in oil country. It took almost an hour to find the Ector Youth Center in Odessa, where Valessa Robinson was detained.

The two Tampa sheriffs talked to the intake officer Cory Williamson, and showed their credentials before he picked up the phone. "I'm calling the nurse, Janet Johnson," he explained.

The nurse arrived and smiled at the detectives. She explained, "I was assigned to check on Valessa when she was brought to the facility. I talked to her and then examined her. It took about thirty minutes."

"Did she tell you about her mother?" Sgt. Marsicano asked.

The nurse furrowed her brow. "No, she said her parents didn't love her or care about her."

"Anything else?" Detective Iverson asked.

The nurse cleared her throat before she said, "Only that she was sexually active with her boyfriend and did acid as recent as the day she arrived."

"What did she say about her boyfriend?" Detective Iverson queried.

"Her words were, 'They really screwed up this time.' I thought she meant the two guys arrested with her."

"It's about time we spoke to Valessa," Sgt. Marsicano said.

Janet Johnson looked at the intake officer. He led the two Tampa sheriffs into the conference room to wait.

Detective Iverson had imagined Valessa to be similar to his own fifteen-year-old daughter and hadn't expected her to appear so small or young. The bright lights made her skin appear whiter than parchment paper. Her long dark hair accentuated her pasty color. He asked her in a voice he would use with his daughter, "Where is your mother?"

Valessa looked down and said, "I don't know."

"We've been looking for her." James Iverson used a soft, thoughtful tone. The girl's appearance touched him.

"I have no idea where she is."

"You came all the way here to Texas in her van with Adam and Jon. Help us find her. If she's alive, we need to know where she is. If she's dead, she needs a decent burial."

Valessa's eyes widened and her mouth flew open. "We were going back to bury her, but we didn't have time."

"Where did you leave the body?" Iverson asked carefully.

"On a trail near Whispel's house."

"If I gave you paper and pen, could you draw where you mean?"

She nodded and drew a crude map. Valessa's tiny chubby hands shook as she looked up at the detectives and said, "I stabbed my mom."

"What happened?" Iverson asked carefully, not wanting to show the surprise he felt.

"I had an argument with my mom in the kitchen after taking LSD with Adam and Jon at Denny's Restaurant."

Detective Iverson glanced a John Marsicano, realizing they were on dangerous territory. "Can we tape your confession?"

Sgt. Marsicano brought a Miranda form and Iverson read her rights. She signed the form on July 3, 1998.

Iverson asked her about what happened with her mom late Friday and early Saturday morning, particularly an argument in the kitchen. Valessa said the best she could recall, due to the fact that she was on acid at the time, was that she had stabbed her mother in the throat and "it released a lot of blood." She then said she had stabbed her mother twice in the back, because she wasn't yet dead—then Jon and Adam helped her clean up the blood, and they put the body in the trash can down past Jon's house. She said they were going to bury the body, but when they found out that there were Missing Persons reports, they decided to leave Florida.

Iverson asked Valessa a series of questions about what credit cards they used, to which Valessa said, "We tried 'em all at different times." Then he asked about the knife, and she said it was about a foot long. Though the altercation with her mother was in the kitchen, it was not a kitchen knife—she had gotten it from her friend Danny. Valessa described the direction her mother was facing during the stabbing, and she admitted to pinning her mother down in order to stab her. The detective asked what Vicki Robinson was wearing at the time, and Valessa described a peach-colored nightgown. At 1:30 P.M., Valessa said she couldn't talk anymore, because her stomach hurt.

Detective Iverson turned off the recorder and put the hand drawn map and consent form into a brief case.

Valessa stood up and grabbed her stomach. She had tears. "I'm not feeling well and have a lot of pain."

Sgt. Marsicano made arrangements with the Ector Youth Center to have her transported to a local hospital to be examined and treated. The detectives followed the Intake Officer Cory Williams to the hospital, where Sgt. Marsicano signed the chart authorizing Valessa's treatment.

Their footsteps echoed along the hallway as they left. Once outside Detective Iverson said, "Kids talk about being cool and chilling out, but Valessa was cold."

"Her deposition rendered me speechless."

Before entering the car, they studied the map and directions to the Pecos County Sheriff's Office in Fort Stockton. "What did people do before MapQuest?" Iverson asked.

"Computers have made our jobs easier. Without them the dead woman's van would be in Arizona by now,"

Sgt. Marsicano said as he started the car. "The trip to the hospital took almost two hours. Forget about getting any sleep tonight."

"I'm so hungry that's the last thing on my mind. We've arrived at the jail. Look beyond the sheriff's sign at the green minivan under the sallyport," Detective Iverson said. He parked close to the vehicle.

The detectives walked around the van and noted the four shredded tires hanging off the rims. They examined a bullet hole in the left fender, above the wheel well. Detective Iverson stopped and stared at the Florida tag. It was not the one registered to the van that he put in his bulletins. It explained why the Texas sheriff's notification of the capture didn't contain the correct tag number for Vicki Robinson's van. He shared his observation with Sgt. Marsicano.

"That tells us the guys we're going to interview are experienced, even if we hadn't reviewed their records. You're familiar with the case. Which one would be more likely to tell the truth?"

Jon Whispel entered the brightly lit interview room at 4:30 A.M., Tampa time. He yawned and rubbed his red eyes, before he put on his glasses. The action brought the detectives' attention to a cut in his eyebrow. Since there was nothing dangling, they had to assume that he had lost his new piercing in the scuffle with Texas sheriffs. His sandy hair was tousled and unkempt.

He suddenly appeared alert when Detective Iverson stated, "We're here to question you about the disappearance of Vicki Robinson. We talked to Valessa, so she's no longer missing. She told us what happened the night of June 26 and the early morning of the twenty-seventh."

Jon Whispel ran his fingers through his hair, giving him time to think. "What do you want to know? I'll tell you what happened."

Sgt. Marsicano offered, "She drew us a map describing where her mother's body is, near your house."

"I didn't kill her mother. I can draw a map too," Jon exclaimed.

"Would you sign a statement? Have you heard of Miranda? It's the right to remain silent, but anything you say can be used against you once you sign that right away," the detective explained.

"I'll sign it. I'll sign it," Whispel begged.

"Can Detective Iverson record your statement?"

"Yes, sir."

"Draw us the map while we set the recorder," Sgt. Marsicano said.

Jon Whispel drew a more detailed map than Valessa's. His showed two gates west of Sheldon Road just south of Walters. He included driving paths made by two wheeled vehicles.

Detective Iverson recorded that it was fifteen minutes before five A.M. He had Jon Whispel respond in many different ways that he was given his rights, understood them, and was speaking voluntarily.

IVERSON: Okay. What I want you to do is go back to Friday night. Just tell us what happened. Starting when y'all were at Denny's earlier in the evening . . . or later in the evening, I guess.

WHISPEL: I remember I was sitting in Denny's with Adam and Valessa and I heard something about killing her mother and I was like, there's no way we could actually do something like that. And we were tripping and I was like (inaudible) you can't do it. We went back to the house, got the van, and tried to go down and get some heroin for an overdose.

Detective Iverson then asked many questions, before Jon Whispel clearly stated the overdose was for Vicki Robinson.

Sgt. Marsicano asked another barrage of questions

about where and with whom they went to buy heroin before Whispel provided a vague answer. "It was somewhere off Walters. I don't remember whose house it was."

When the sergeant asked who located the house, Whispel responded, "Adam," in a loud, clear voice. "We went down there and couldn't get it, so he bought a needle to put in an air bubble."

Detective Marsicano quizzed Whispel about where the needle came from and finally had to accept his answer, "The same location. I don't know the dude's name. So then we went back to the house and Adam said, 'Wait a minute, we can put some bleach in it.'"

Detective Iverson asked, "Valessa's room?"

"Yeah. Then he was saying we could put bleach in the needle. So they get some bleach and put some bleach in. So they go to her mom's room, but she wakes up. They came back and told me that she woke up."

Detective Marsicano asked, "Where were you at?"

"In Valessa's room."

Iverson stated, "Apparently they didn't stick her with the needle."

"No. When they came back, they told me she woke up. Two or three minutes later, she knocked on the door and said Jim should have taken us home last night. Then she told Valessa to grab her sleeping bag. Valessa didn't grab it quickly and she was like, 'Valessa, now!' So she grabbed it and then turned around and started walking away and then Adam went out there with her."

"You're talking about Vicki?" Iverson said.

"Yeah. I heard 'em talking. Then I heard choking. I went out to see the commotion. She was on the ground."

"You looked out from the bedroom?"

"I walked out from the bedroom."

"Okay. Where were Adam and Vicki at the time?"

"In between where the refrigerator and the bar is."

"In the kitchen?" Marsicano asked.

"In the kitchen area. Vicki was on the ground with Adam behind her like this. He put his arm across his throat bent his head and closed his eyes. He was trying to put her to sleep."

"He had his arm around her throat like a sleeper hold?"

"Yeah."

Marsicano tried to get a clear picture of what Whispel was saying. Vicki was on the ground. Adam was behind her. He had his arm around her throat.

Whispel looked across the table at the brown-eyed detective and responded after each statement, "Yes sir."

"Choking her with his arm?"

"No sir. He was trying to put her to sleep."

Sgt. Marsicano said, "In a choking manner."

"Not really in a choking manner. I wouldn't say that."

Detective Iverson offered, "Like a carotid restraint hold."

That sounded better to Whispel and he said, "Yeah, yeah."

"Sleeper hold," Iverson ventured.

"Yeah, like a sleeper hold. And then I went back to the room and he was like 'Get the syringe. Get the syringe.' We couldn't find the syringe. So Adam came in and got the syringe and went back out there and he's like 'Fuck that doesn't work.' He's like 'I need a knife.' I seen him go like this." Whispel reached in his pocket. "He had a knife. He st. . . . He killed her like that. We all were—"

"You saw him do it?" Iverson said.

"I didn't see him do it, 'cause where he was the bar covers it."

"Was Valessa over there with him?"

"Yeah. Valessa said she seen it. And then from what I remember is that they both came in and then we were all just sitting there and like I was scared myself. I was scared for my life."

"Did you think Adam was gonna harm you?"

"I don't know. I really don't know if he would. But after that, we cleaned it up."

Sgt. Marsicano asked, "Who cleaned it up? Was the blood in the kitchen on the ceramic tile?" Sgt. Marsicano asked.

"Yes, then we cleaned it up. Me and Adam did with towels and mops."

"Where are the mops?"

"We threw them away in the Dumpster behind Denny's."

"What about the towels?" Detective Iverson asked.

"The towels were thrown out where the body was."

"So they're near the can?"

"Yeah, 'cause there's a site where we were gonna dig a grave for her."

Sgt. Marsicano took over again. "Is that on the path on the way down?" He pointed to Jon's map.

"Yeah. It's actually farther where there are big openings. You'll see it because the ground's disturbed."

"And you have drawn a map to show that?"

"Yes sir, I did."

"You signed it?"

Detective Iverson asked, "You go through two gates to get to the body? Do they have locks?"

"Yes, sir. The first gate we used wire cutters. After that we went back to the house to get some of Valessa's stuff."

"That's when the neighbors saw the van, at seven A.M?"

"I guess. Then we went to Dade City to see Adam's father's grave. Came back went to a hotel room out near Brandon off of Columbus." He closed his eyes briefly as if he was thinking. "Let's see where did we go after that? We chilled there for a little bit. I guess I got some sleep. Then we went to Target to get me some pants. Couldn't find any. Then we went to Ross I think. Got pants and socks there and went to Ybor. There we got some rolls and Ecstacy and had some tattoo work done. I got my eyebrow pierced. Adam got a tattoo and got another re-done. We left there to go down to Cream."

"Down on Franklin?" Iverson asked, trying to place it.

Jon Whispel tapped the side of his head. "Where did we go? Fuck, from there we went back to the motel room. We stayed in the room that day. The whole day."

"That's Saturday so that's the La Quinta?" Sgt. Marsicano asked.

"No, that was—"

"Motel 8," the sergeant said when Whispel hesitated.

"Yeah."

Detective Iverson asked, "You registered in your name all three times?"

"Yes."

"You're the only one who had an I.D.?"

"Yeah. We went to the La Quinta and got some trips that night. We chilled there for a while and then went out to get some medicine for Valessa."

Sgt. Marsicano inquired, "what kind of medicine did she need?"

"Vicks 44."

"Vicks 44. Okay," the sergeant repeated.

"And then we went back down to Ybor City."

"The same night?"

"I think that was when I got my tattoo, but I'm not sure. Chilled out in Ybor for a bit. Adam got another tattoo. Huh. Then we went back to the La Quinta. Huh. Went to get some trips that night. Me and Adam went to Apollo Beach, then back to the motel to get Valessa." Jon made a few stuttering "huh, huh" sounds, searching for words.

"Then we went to my house. Actually, no, we stopped at Wal-Mart to get some glasses for me and then went to

Best Buy for some CDs. We went back to Wal-Mart to pick up my glasses and then went to my house. Chilled around my house for a little bit. Adam went on some errands with somebody, came back, picked us up, and then we went to the Budget Inn motel."

Detective Iverson waited for Jon to stop talking. "What errands did Adam do?"

"I don't know who it was. He picked up some drugs." He corrected himself nervously and answered the detective's question. "I don't know what it was."

"That's when he bought the stuff from Matt."

"For Matt," Whispel corrected.

"They brought two guys over to the house that day, Monday," Sgt. Marsicano stated.

Jon Whispel was caught off-guard. "Monday, that was . . . one of them was Robert. I don't know who the other guy was. I guess it was Richard. From my house we went to the Budget Inn."

"So that would have been Monday night," Sgt. Marsicano announced.

"Yeah. Monday night I got an hour-and-a-half worth of sleep, and then Adam woke me up. We found a Home Depot to get some concrete and everything. And then——"

"Where was Valessa at that time?" Marsicano interjected.

"At the motel room. And then this dude Matt paged him and said we was all over the eight o'clock news and all that, so we went back to the hotel room to get Valessa. We left and have been on the road ever since."

Detective Iverson asked, "What did you get the garbage can for . . . the metal one?"

"Metal one?" Jon Whispel thought a minute. "To mix concrete."

Sgt. Marsicano inquired, "Where did you end up dumping the concrete?"

"Behind some warehouse type of building off Columbus."

"Near 40th Street?"

"Yeah, it was off 40th Street," Whispel answered, and looked at the sergeant, whose eyebrows were raised above his glasses.

"Do you remember the name of the warehouse or what side of the street it's on?"

"The left-hand side. Like when you get off the Interstate and go past the Budget Inn motel. You go past the first light and before the second light, that building right there on the left-hand side. We dumped the bags of concrete behind it."

Sgt. Marsicano changed his focus. "Who put the body in the garbage can?"

"Adam did."

"Where was it done? In what room?"

Whispel didn't hesitate or mumble his words. "In the house where she was in the kitchen area."

"Who carted it out to the van?"

"Adam did."

"Where was it loaded in the van, and in what part of the van was the garbage can transported?"

"Huh, in between the two front seats and the very, very back seat."

"Where . . . Aren't there two seats behind the two front seats?"

"Yeah, we took those out. And he laid it with plastic bags."

Sgt. Marsicano pounced. "Was there leakage from that garbage can?"

Whispel made his guttural uncontrollable noise, "Huh-uh."

"Was there blood on the sides of the garbage can or anything?"

"Huh-uh," Whispel groaned louder that usual.

"I'm sorry, the clothes that y'all were wearing." The experienced sergeant apologized to the young man who appeared to be suffering. Sgt. Marsicano continued. "Was there blood on the clothes y'all were wearing?"

"Not that I remember."

"What did y'all do with the clothes you were wearing when this occurred Friday night?"

"Huh, I still had mine in the car . . . in the van."

Iverson interjected, "What were they?"

"Tommy Hilfiger jeans and a plain white T-shirt."

Marsicano's voice elevated. "No blood on 'em at all?"

"No."

"What about Adam's clothes?"

"He was wearing black jeans. I can't remember what shirt. The jeans had blood on 'em, but they were thrown in the washer."

Detective Iverson asked, "Were they, are they, in the washer?

"No we got 'em out. They're in the van."

Sgt. Marsicano asked. "Did Valessa's clothes get blood on them?"

Both detectives stared at Jon Whispel.

"No."

Sgt. Marsicano exclaimed, "None?"

"None that I know of," Jon Whispel responded.

"The three of ya transported the garbage can where?"

"To the spot behind . . . not right behind my house, but it's like behind it. That's it."

"Who actually pulled the garbage can out of the vehicle and toted it down the trail?"

Whispel hesitated. "Adam needed some help getting it out, so I helped him get it out but he then toted it down the trail."

Iverson said, "Dragging it as he went?" His voice suggested a question.

"Yeah."

Sgt. Marsicano asked, "Where is the hypodermic needle?"

"He broke it and threw it."

"Where?"

"In the woods. I don't know where. I don't think y'all would be able to find it 'cause he threw it as far away as he could."

The sergeant concentrated. "In what direction from the garbage can, do you recall? Farther down the trail, to the left of the trail, the right of the trail?"

Jon slumped in his seat. "There's, like, a little open spot."

"In the trail?"

"Right where the garbage can is on . . . the body . . . like almost directly across from it [is a] nice wide open spot. I seen him standing there and he just threw it."

Again Sgt. Marsicano said, "Okay. And the towels, where are they in relation to the garbage can?

"When you go down the corner to where that big open area is—"

"On the walking trail?"

"No, on the driving trail."

Sgt. Marsicano indicated he was satisfied. "Okay."

"You're gonna see a little grave on the right-hand side . . . there's gonna be . . . You'll see the big bag of towels."

"You carried a bag?"

"Yeah."

"What kind of bag?"

"Garbage bag . . . brownish with red handles."

Detective Iverson changed the direction when he asked, "When it was all over and y'all took off to town, obviously you had a chance to get away. Why—"

Jon Whispel quickly responded talking over the detective. "Okay, actually, no."

"Why didn't you take off and leave?"

"Because I was scared that if he was ever to come back down here and find me that he would hurt me and whomever I was with, and I didn't want that to happen."

"Anything we haven't asked you that you think's important?"

"Huh-uh."

Sgt. Marsicano had one. "Have y'all discussed this amongst the three of you at any point in time since it occurred—what was gonna be said, what we're gonna say, if anything?"

"No."

"There's never one word said about this murder?"

"Huh?"

"Between the three of you?"

"I remember between them two, Adam said, 'I'll take the blame because I did it.' I remember Adam saying that."

Detective Iverson asked, "Do you believe he did it?"

"Huh?"

"Do you believe he did it?"

"Did it, yeah."

"As opposed to Valessa doing it?"

"Yeah."

"Could you see Valessa, where she was when the knife was being used?"

"Huh-uh."

Sgt. Marsicano said, "Okay."

Detective Iverson stated, "This concludes the tape. It's now five o'clock Tampa time."

The detectives were exhausted by that time, and stopped to get some coffee in the employee's lounge. The snack machine was a welcome sight. Even the sound of the little plastic bags being dropped in the bottom made them salivate. "The coffee's hot, don't gulp it," Detective Iverson said, blowing into his little plastic cup.

"I'm still eating my muffin and I'm going to get another." He jumped up from the table. "You want one too?" Sgt. Marsicano asked, plunking more change in the machine.

"Sure. That looked better than my cereal and nut bar."

Both detectives were anxious to hear what Adam Davis had to say so they hurried. The night was almost over and they had to collect and label all the evidence in Vicki Robinson's van.

Sgt. Marsicano signed the Pecos County Sheriff's paperwork requesting to interview Adam Davis. He was brought into the same room where they interrogated Whispel.

The thin young man with olive skin and dark hair stared into the eyes of one detective flashed to the other and back again. The pictures of him recovered from the ATMs and store videos didn't display his apparent arrogance. He smiled revealing white, even teeth when Sgt. Marsicano indicated where he should sit.

"Mr. Davis, we're here to ask you about your involvement in the death of Vicki Robinson," Detective Iverson explained. He watched the young man nod affirmatively. He glanced toward the sergeant.

Davis shrugged. "What do you want me to do?"

"Draw a map to help us find her body."

"I can do that."

Iverson explained to Davis his Miranda rights, and Davis signed the form waiving them. The detective told Davis to draw a map of where Vicki Robinson's body lay, which he did, indicating the area off Sheldon Road near Jon Whispel's house. Iverson then reiterated the time of the interview, 5:35 A.M, gave Davis instructions on how to speak into the tape recorder, and asked him to begin his version of the facts, starting with the night of Friday, June 26.

Davis stated that he, Valessa, and Jon were tripping on acid in Denny's. They were discussing how they could be together, despite the fact that Valessa's mother was trying to break them up. He said they decided to try to get heroin, so they could give her a lethal overdose. They weren't able to find any, but they did get a syringe and he filled it with bleach. Davis said that as they entered Robinson's room, she woke up and asked what was going on.

Valessa said the guys needed a place to stay, so they all went into her room, but Robinson followed them, yelling at them. When Robinson turned around, Davis said he put her in a "sleeper hold." Once she "went to sleep," he said he injected bleach into her neck. Valessa was holding down her legs, and Jon brought out the knife, saying, "Here, use this." Davis said he couldn't remember where he sliced her, "probably in her throat," and then he turned her over and stabbed her twice in the lower back. He said that after panicking and then collecting his senses, he and the others got towels started to clean up the scene, and they got a trashcan and put the body inside. They planned to bury the body, he said, but the ground was too hard, so they just put the can down the trail and covered it with dried palm trees.

Next, Iverson asked about the concrete. Davis said that they planned to put it in the bottom of the trashcan and put it in the dam at Pinhurst, but they just ended up dumping it off the side of the Interstate. Iverson asked if Davis had anything more to say. He said that he didn't realize what he was doing until it was too late, and that he regretted it, and he thought Valessa felt the same way.

The interview concluded at 5:45 A.M.

Sgt. Marsicano went to the Pecos County Sheriff's office to contact the Hillsborough Sheriff's homicide department in Tampa to direct Lt. Craig Latimer to Vicki Robinson's body. He called the hospital to inquire about Valessa and learned she had been returned to the Ector Youth Center. He made arrangements with Detective Iverson to bring the missing runaway back to Tampa in late afternoon.

Detective Iverson proceeded out to the sallyport to photograph Vicki Robinson's van and its contents. The front seat contained a large road atlas, Vicki Robinson's purse, transaction receipts for her ATM card, and credit cards. He took the picture and then inventoried them.

The van inside had an obvious lived-in look made worse by the upheaval the van had suffered. There were three pairs of black pants and a sleeveless shirt similar to the type Adam wore in the video taken at the Circle K Store on Gandy Boulevard in Tampa. He set them apart to photograph them separately. The bolt cutters and the garden hoe also got individual attention. Everything pertaining to the crime needed to be detailed to be used as evidence. Confessions could be challenged in court. *It's enough to make an honest detective sick.*

The detective stared at the keyboard and guitar. They weren't connected to the crime, but suggested the murderers' future plans. He took a close-up photo of the Tampa newspaper headlines that announced that Vicki and Valessa were missing.

He boxed up the evidence and gave the boxes to Deputy Jackson to be overnighted to Tampa. He learned Jackson was responsible for stopping the van without incurring any casualties, and complimented him.

Before Jim Iverson and John Marsicano finished a late breakfast, they learned the homicide detectives in Tampa had recovered Vicki Robinson's body.

The county paid fifty-seven dollars for a hotel room for the two detectives. They used it to shower before picking up Valessa and returning to the airport.

CHAPTER 6
SO NEAR YET SO FAR

Lt. Latimer alerted the homicide detectives working on Vicki's case to the information Sgt. Marsicano and Detective Iverson had learned in Texas. Detectives Jorge Fernandez and John King drove directly to the gate the sergeant described on the phone. They passed two gates, and the car bumped along the two ruts made by vehicles. Fernandez said, "The helicopter flew directly over this area and some of the uniformed guys walked close."

"The garbage can is supposed to be under the trees covered with palm fronds. I sure never expected to be searching for Mrs. Robinson this way, but I suspected she was dead," John King said.

"It must be tough since you knew her even if it was as a realtor."

"A body is a body, but I was ill after Hank Earl Carr killed three of our own. I was there when the bodies were retrieved," John King said.

"Whispel claimed they started to dig a grave in the open area. I don't know how I could have missed a big hole even from the air," Fernandez complained and then stopped the car. "Look at that. There's the garbage bag under that bush. It must be full of towels. Good God, no wonder I couldn't see a hole. Those lazy bums must have taken two shovels of earth before they gave up."

"She must be around here somewhere. I can smell the rotting flesh," Detective King said.

"It's under the trees covered by the fronds." Detective Fernandez pointed. "I can see the green garbage can underneath. We'll go back to the gate and wait for the coroner now that we know where the body is."

Deputy Lewis was busy setting up the perimeters of the crime scene with yellow tape at the fence line gate west of Sheldon Road and south of Waters to maintain security before the right away entrance to the canal. Detective Fernandez checked his watch. It was 7:55 A.M. Friday, July 3, 1998 five days after homicide began their investigation. He couldn't see Whispel's house, but he knew it was close.

Deputy Kenneth Minton, the crime scene technician, arrived at 8:05—the same time as Detective Baker. King and Fernandez showed them to Vicki's body, and the detectives remained on the dirt road until the tech examined the bag of towels, two shovels, and the pitchfork. He labeled them for exhibits after taking pictures of their location. The detectives then searched through the surrounding brush for a hypodermic needle, and possibly a knife.

The Assistant State Attorney Investigators Shirley Williams and Doug Bieniek came and checked out the area. They all waited for Dr. Miller to open the garbage can, but no one doubted what it contained. The odor had attracted flies. Captain Rocky Rodriguez arrived at nine, followed by crime scene tech, detective Carolyn Service.

The big white van from American Ambulance Response dispatched to pick up the body appeared amidst a cloud of dust.

Dr. Miller briefly lifted the lid while pictures of the corpse were taken. The freelance photojournalist groaned and said, "Those things covered with maggots are her feet. She's upside-down."

The seasoned professionals were horrified by the gruesome image and putrid smell.

Vicki Robinson's body was solemnly loaded into the big white van.

CHAPTER 7

VALESSA

Valessa remained silent on the airplane ride back to Tampa with Detectives Iverson and Marsicano. If her life flashed before her eyes, only she could know. Did she reflect on her mother's death or escape into memories of a more exciting time?

Gasparilla 1997 attracted the usual huge crowds to the streets of Ybor. It was up to the club owners to entice, entertain, and keep the clientele coming back. The clubs catering to teens hired bands that encouraged slamdancing and created a mosh pit. Since the floors were flat, teens were encouraged to launch themselves over the crowd before the elevated stage, called the mosh pit. The bands hired an entourage of strong males to keep the action going and save teens who landed on the floor.

Valessa Robinson jumped to the music along with her girlfriends at Ybor's popular rave club. The heavy metal band behind the mosh pit sounded similar to some of her favorites: Korn, Garbage, and Nine Inch Nails. The loud sound that reverberated inside her

head was very different than that of her and old favorite
group, Boyz II Men. She had even liked Michael Jackson
last year, when she was a seventh grader, she thought to
herself. Could she have ever been that young? The boy
next to her slammed into her and she bumped him back
feeling angry.

He laughed and slammed into her friend, Grace*,
who appeared startled. Valessa looked around and saw
others doing it. "Grace, slam him harder."

The girls reeled toward the stage bumping and
laughing. The crowd was very dense, making it almost
impossible to slam any one. A tall girl squeezed between them and put a pill in their hands. Valessa swallowed the pill and tapped her feet along with the crowd
moving toward the mosh pit. They could see the kids
ahead of them go up on the stage and dive over the
crowd, which passed the divers back to where they had
started. Grace tried to turn away. "It's too late now,"
Valessa shouted to be heard over the blasting music
wishing she could escape too. She climbed the steps behind Grace who appeared fearful and vowed to launch
herself like she was diving into her own pool.

Valessa giggled with glee as she felt the hands pass
her baggy-clothed body over the mosh pit. She was
thrilled to be so close to the band and a part of the exciting experience. The jitters in her stomach were as
great as any she felt on the big rides at Busch Gardens.
She was on top of the world. As the hands let her down
into the crush of dancers, she stumbled before she
could recover her balance. A tall, handsome guy caught
her and helped her to her feet. She watched his black
cap disappear in the crowd before she could thank him.
Oh well, all the guys in her life had disappeared sooner
or later, she thought briefly.

She found Grace with her new girlfriends from Ben
Hill Junior High and shared her wonderful mosh expe-

rience. "That was great. Let's try it again," she shouted over the loud music. Grace hung back, but Jean*, Dorothy*, and Ruth* smiled and shook their heads in agreement and started to wind their way into the crowd. The beginning of the mosh pit was filled with strong guys protecting the band. Getting close to the band appeared to be the best game in town.

Valessa recognized the tall girl wearing a belly necklace and a tattoo over her breast who had handed her a bottle of water. She was the girl who had given her the pill. "I'm Glenda*. You'd better drink some. Ecstasy creates a thirst." She hugged Valessa. "You kids who started at that Christian school impress easily."

Valessa blinked when she realized the little pill was Ecstacy. No wonder she felt sky high. She appreciated Glenda's hug, but resented that she considered Valessa and her old friends from Seminole Presbyterian naïve. Besides, she was in public school now. "Some of them go to rave clubs," Valessa said. "I admit we don't wear cool outfits like you. I like your tattoo."

Glenda laughed and then bent closer to confide, "It's fake. I can wash it off. My belly necklace just clamps on. I cover my bra top with a big T-shirt before my mom can see me. I'll be a junior at Sickles High."

"Oh," Valessa said, but wondered if all the girls at Sickles High School would be as friendly as Glenda. The pill did make her thirsty and Glenda shared her water. Valessa began to slam her way toward the stage again.

When Valessa returned from the Gasparilla, she reveled in the thrill of the mosh pit and could hardly wait to tell her diary. She had finally found acceptance. Glenda even shared her secret. Her own mother wasn't home so she entered her bedroom and retrieved her diary, just like her mother would. She wondered what her mother wrote in hers, but realized diaries were private.

She flicked through the pages to make a new entry, but stopped to read her complaints about the band with the stupid name, Dead End. "Gepeto" would be her choice. If only her mother would let her leave a band called Dead End. She found the fresh page and wrote: Glenda is a people person.

She was lonely and complained that her relationships with boys only lasted a few months. The teen noted her several short romances that appeared on previous pages with frustration. In juvenile terms, she described to her diary what she imagined sex would be like.

Days before her fourteenth birthday, she sat making out on the couch with Bobby*. Her mother was out with her boyfriend, but her sister and boyfriend were in the house so Valessa invited Bobby* into her bedroom. She flipped her shoes off and reclined on the bed. He kissed her and fumbled with her clothes and got on top before he removed his pants. She felt grateful he was experienced at fucking. It felt good. They both smoked a cigarette afterwards. Bobby had to leave since it was after his curfew.

Her mother was home for Valessa's birthday celebration on the eve of March thirty-first. Fifty kids came. Valessa felt elated but resented that her mother threw most of them out and locked the door. Most had to spend the night by the lake. Three girls and two boys stayed and got into Valessa's bed and took their pants off. It was a real bash that Valessa felt delighted her mother had slept through.

On her birthday, her mother took her to the mall

and bought her a gold necklace, two pairs of Unicorn jeans, a beeper and passes to Busch Gardens and Adventure Island. When her mother dropped her at home, she was so delighted with her presents she called her favorite friend who still attended her old Christian school. "Hi Jennifer, it's me, Valessa. I wish you could have come to my birthday party." She picked up one of the pink heart pillows from the end of the couch, but quickly replaced it. As she listened to her friend, she brushed her fingerprints off the pillow. "Yes, I know your parents won't let you come my house. I forgive them, because they're so kind to me when I'm there. I'm sure my mother will let me go to Busch Gardens with your family. She gave me a pass along with jeans and a gold necklace. I'd love to stay the weekend. See you on Friday. Good-bye," she said, hanging up.

The girls giggled and talked about old times. "Remember when we used to play Pogs," Jennifer said as they got ready for bed.

"Yes, and sing in the choir. After you told me Tommy* liked me, I was afraid to look at him," Valessa said, and laughed until Jennifer's dad came into the bedroom and reminded them that they had to get up early to visit Busch Gardens. Valessa closed her eyes and remembered those carefree days and wished it had been her father who had come in to say goodnight. She brushed the thought away and planned to enjoy the day ahead on the big rides and seeing the animals. Jennifer was so lucky to have a family, she thought going off to sleep.

Valessa tried LSD in June at Cream, the best teen hangout, and liked the sensation it gave her, but was more impressed with the guys who sold it. Some carried guns. They were so macho compared to the boys from her high school.

Two weeks later, her mother informed Valessa that she had planned another trip to Michigan to see her family. Valessa stamped her foot. "I'm not going. Last year, when that boy I was with on the fourth of July threw a firecracker that burned down the shed, I was blamed. I won't go there again. I'll run away."

"You'll have to come with us, but it will be fun. We'll stop at a lot of attractions and be away two weeks," Vicki said.

Valessa ran to a neighbors after standing up to her mother and Vicki came to get her. The night before the trip, she set her alarm for 1:30 A.M., escaped on her bicycle, and rode to Glenda's. She returned her mother's page in the morning. "I'm not going to Michigan again. I told you why."

"You'll lose your two best friends, Michelle and me," Vicki said.

"I can take care of myself," Valessa responded, and hung up.

After spending hours at Joffrey's, Valessa rode her bicycle toward home in the late afternoon. She crossed busy Dale Mabry and entered South Village Drive, passing the condos near the highway. She turned left onto Palmwood Lane, where the houses were larger, and then right on Carroll Village Drive. As she got closer to the golf course and the lake near her house, her anxiety rose. She pumped past the manicured lawns and huge trees surrounding the big houses. The silence was broken only by the sound of her bicycle tires and occasional laughter from neighbors. The aroma coming from outdoor barbecues made her hungry, but she hoped her mother wasn't home waiting for her. She stopped pumping hard and coasted into her driveway. The van wasn't there, but Jim's car was.

She opened the front door and patted Lady on the head. The dog welcomed her by jumping up to lick her hand. The Sheltie went wild. Her mother, sister Michelle, and mom's boyfriend Jim Englert had left for Michigan without her. She breathed a sigh of relief. It was the seventeenth of July, and Valessa knew it was a special day for her mother to celebrate her nine-month anniversary dating Jim.

Valessa felt delighted to have the house to herself for two weeks. She was used to being in the house alone. She fed her mother's dog and took Slick, her pet ferret, out of his cage and fed him.

As the days passed, she was even more pleased that her mother didn't bother her with phone calls. She had no one to answer to, just like a grown-up. She walked the dog and fed the animals daily before she went to her job.

Valessa enjoyed working at McDonald's and took a bus every day she could get hours. Afterward, she was free to hang out in the mall without getting a page to come home. She stalked the mall even on the days McDonald's didn't schedule her.

One day in the Smoke Shop, she heard a friend was threatened with a gun. When she saw the gun toter in the Food Court, she told him to lay off and smacked him on the face, leaving red marks. The guy just walked away. It made her feel almost as powerful as defying her mother. She wrote Mall Madness on the margin of her diary as a sort of keepsake. Valessa noticed the calendar on the kitchen wall. She had circled July 31, 1997, and realized two weeks had passed, so she scoured the house to pass her mother's inspection. Before going to the mall, she even cleaned her room.

When Vicki returned, she paged Valessa. "I'm glad you left the house clean. Where are you?" She picked Valessa up at the mall. "You missed a wonderful trip to Michigan. I recorded every detail, including all the wonderful restaurants and the great food we ate. I will miss Jim terribly after being with him for two weeks."

"Did Michelle have a good time?" Valessa asked.

"I think she did. You'll have to ask her."

In August, Valessa suffered through trips in the new van with her mother, sister, and Jim's three children, and resented every moment. Her mother fawned over Jim's two young boys and his daughter, who was sixteen; two years older than her and a year younger than Michelle. Jim did too. She couldn't wait for September to enter Sickles High School and end the cozy mutual gatherings that included Jim's parents. They seemed to love their grandchildren, she thought resentfully.

Valessa couldn't imagine what happened to Jim's wife. No one talked about her or Valessa's father. She got to visit him for weeks at a time. He had a new wife, Vanessa. Strange how close her name was to hers. She liked Vanessa, but she had her own children. If her mother married Jim, his children would become her stepsister and brothers too. It was too confusing. Her religious school and church taught that marriage was sacred.

On Sunday, October 5, 1997, while her sister and mother went to church, Valessa entered Joffrey's Coffee where she met her friends from Sickles High. A tall, handsome guy talking to boys at another table got her attention. He smiled at her, revealing white, even teeth. She glanced down at the round, green, marbleized tabletop, listening to her friends giggle because they saw him too. "It's Rattlesnake," Jean* said.

"Rattlesnake?" Valessa asked. "I've seen him before."

"Of course you have. He sells Jack-in-the-Box LSD. All the girls like him," Glenda said.

"You mean that stuff soaked in the purple paper?"

"Yeah, as if you didn't know. Sometimes I wonder about you, Valessa," Glenda said.

Valessa gathered courage and got up to talk him. "Rattlesnake, I'm Valessa. I've seen you around at the rave clubs."

"Don't call me that. I used to wear a rattler around my neck that my dad gave me, when I was fourteen. Unfortunately, the name stuck. I'm Adam Davis." He pulled the guy next to him forward. "This is my friend Jon Whispel."

Valessa glanced at the sandy-haired guy smiled and said, "What's up, Jon?" If he said anything she wasn't aware, because being near Adam made her blood rush to her face and her knees knock together. She liked his voice as much as his dark hair and tanned skin and his name, Adam Davis.

"I live in Carrollwood right near here. Do you think you and Jon can come to my house someday. I get out of school at three o'clock." She felt ecstatic that Adam and his friend Jon agreed to visit the next day.

When she heard the door chime, she ran to open the door. Adam and Jon swaggered into the living room. Their timing was bad, since Valessa had to see a counselor her mother had arranged. "I'm so happy to see you both, but when my mother arrives I have to leave for about an hour. I forgot she made an appointment for me."

Adam shrugged, "We can wait."

"You will?" Valessa could hardly keep from jumping up and down. "I'm so glad. Would you and Jon like a Coke?"

"Okay," Adam said.

Valessa ran into the kitchen to get the Cokes and returned just as her mother came through the front door. "Valessa we're in a hurry, but introduce me to your friends."

"Mom, this is Adam Davis and Jon Whispel. They're going to wait for me until I get back."

Vicki shook hands and smiled at Valessa's friends. "She'll be home soon."

"I'm pleased to meet you, Mrs. Robinson," Adam said, taking off his black cap. He bowed his head.

Valessa watched with admiration. She thought her mother was impressed too.

"Me too," Jon said, leaving his hat on.

"Wait for Valessa out by the pool," Vicki said, glancing at her cherished living room furniture before she closed the front door.

On their return, Valessa sprang out of her mother's van. She could see Jon's car in the driveway. They waited. They really waited for her. Her mother's words explaining where she was going were muffled after she slammed the van's door. Valessa didn't care. Happiness filled her as she anticipated talking to Adam Davis. Butterflies in her stomach made her body tremble, thinking he was in her house. She imagined he was the guy who helped her after her stumble from traveling over the mosh pit in the spring.

She ran through the living room and headed for the pool area. She could see Adam and Jon playing with her mother's prize Sheltie dog through the glass doors. She stopped to control her emotions. It wouldn't be cool to appear too anxious. She watched Jon pass a joint to Adam and felt sophisticated that she had been smoking marijuana since the eighth grade. She slid the glass door aside, stepped onto the deck surrounding the pool, and stroked Lady. "You're such a good dog to entertain my friends."

Adam smiled, palmed the joint, and hid it behind his back.

"It's okay, my mother isn't with me," she said. "I saw you smoking."

"Do you want a drag?" Adam said, offering the small remnants smoldering in the roach clip.

She stepped toward him and inhaled deeply as he held it to her lips. She didn't feel the acrid smoke enter her lungs, but his fingertips on her lips sent thrills through her body.

As if coming from a distant planet, Jon Whispel's voice entered her consciousness. "You live like the swells in this great house."

Valessa coughed and expelled the smoke from her lungs. "It was my grandfather's until my mother divorced my father. I guess it's a nice house. I liked staying here this summer, when my mother and sister went to visit him in Michigan."

"My parents are getting a divorce. Our house is a doghouse compared to this. I only hope my mother can keep it," Jon said.

"Hey Jon, get over it. That's why we're going to Phoenix," Adam said.

"You're leaving here. I was hoping to get to know you, Adam."

"Come with us," he said.

"I can't. I don't have any money," Valessa answered, feeling desolate.

"How can you say that when you live in a mansion?" Jon asked.

"It's my mom's," Valessa answered. "In time, I can gather enough money to leave. I have a job at McDonald's."

Adam smacked Jon's arm, as if to quiet him. "Can I see you tomorrow?"

Valessa agreed immediately.

Adam arrived with six red roses. "You should come with us," he encouraged. Jon nodded.

Valessa smelled the roses with her eyes closed.

"I love the fragrance. October 10 will always be special. I'd like to go, but I'm afraid to leave my job. It's hard to get one at fourteen." She kissed him good-bye.

Adam and Jon needed money so they decided to sell the car Jon's parents gave him. After they left Valessa they crossed Dale Mabry and entered the new area of Carrollwood. Adam jumped from Jon's car and sneaked toward a van parked on a broad driveway in front of an elegant house. The doors weren't locked, so all he had to do was connect the wires under the dash. He followed Jon to a used car lot on Dale Mabry, where they sold Jon's car.

They left Tampa and headed toward Arizona. Their trip ended abruptly after a Tallahassee police chase damaged the van. Adam and Jon managed to get away, using a stolen check to buy bus passage back to Tampa. The eighteen-year-olds escaped detection and headed toward Valessa's house.

Valessa was thrilled to see Adam again only two days after she kissed him good-bye. Adam rekindled the sparks of their romance with words of praise and intimate kisses she had never experienced with boys her age.

She felt proud to enter Joffrey's with Adam and Jon. Adam nudged her toward a table. "This is where you were sitting when I met you," he said. "It's our table." He took out a pocket knife and engraved their initials on the tabletop while he waited to order.

Valessa felt special. The initials would be there forever. *He loved her. He really loved her,* she thought.

Six days later the fourteen-year-old—intoxicated with the attention of a handsome older guy who made her feel loved—planned to run away with him and decided to have his baby after a passionate kiss. She liked Jon too, and they would become her family.

Valessa and Adam's plans were crushed when he and Jon were arrested days later for staying in an abandoned house, and charged with stealing a taser gun. Valessa felt outraged at the injustice when they went to jail.

The cause of people Valessa thought had been wrongly imprisoned interested her after Adam went to jail. The highly publicized trial of Bernice Bowen ended, and she was sentenced for concealing her boyfriend's real name from investigators after he shot her two-year-old. Hank Earl Carr, a man with a record, killed three police officers while he was trying to escape for the murder of Bernice's young son. The blond mother of two ignited sympathy in the community. Some people who were trying to raise money to free Bernice Bowen claimed she lied to police because she knew that Carr had a gun.

Helping those who were trying to free Bowen gave Valessa something to think about besides Adam's jail time. The issue divided the public. Many believed Bernice had tried to protect the criminal.

Laughter in the kitchen attracted Valessa to leave her room. She spoke about her concerns with her mother's Christian friends. "I'm trying to raise money for Bernice Bowen's defense fund," she said. Deborah, her mother's best friend, appeared shocked and covered her mouth after she gasped. Carlton Huff and Jim, her mother's fiancé, frowned. Theresa Goscinski and Bonnie Smith were equally displeased. They seemed more horrified than her own mother, who gave her a look of disapproval.

"Don't you realize Bernice Bowen has a seven-year-old daughter at home? The kid didn't kill anyone," Valessa said, retreating back to her room and avoiding Carlton's efforts to restrain her.

In November 1997, the whole world crashed down. Her sister's fiancé was killed in a terrible automobile accident. Vicki, Valessa, and Michelle united to share her terrible grief. Valessa didn't have to be told to wear an appropriate dark dress instead of baggy jeans to church, and resented her mother for thinking she would. Now that she knew what love felt like, her heart bled for her sister's loss. Michelle was only sixteen.

Days after the funeral Valessa received an especially poignant three-page letter from Adam, requesting that he be given the opportunity to prove to her mother that he wasn't a bad person. Valessa savored his words "I want her to know how much I love you." She felt proud to show her mother the letter.

When Jon Whispel's parents managed to have him released before Christmas, her sympathy went out to Adam, who would spent his nineteenth birthday alone and in jail.

Before Christmas, Valessa learned Adam was moved to another facility for fighting, and gave up hope of ever seeing him again. She expected he'd be sentenced to prison, possibly for life.

Valessa took his letters to Joffrey's, and cried while reading them at her table. She passed her fingers over the initials he had carved on the plastic tabletop to relive their special day. Some of her girlfriends cried along with her. A few boys from her class stepped forward to pat her shoulder and offer her comfort. They realized that she was experiencing a terrible tragedy. James Hardee, a twenty-year-old college student who hung out with her friends, sympathized too. He needed a place to stay until the new semester started. Valessa felt surprised her mother welcomed him to stay with them for three weeks. Valessa enjoyed long intellectual conversations with James, and thought he liked hanging out with her because he didn't make her feel fourteen.

Even her mother liked him, and returned from work early to watch television with them. She made her special cookies, laughed, and shared her impressions of the programs. A part of Valessa resented her mother's attention to James. After all, he was Valessa's guest. Valessa didn't share Adam's daily letters with anyone. James moved out in January 1998.

In February, she went to a tattoo parlor and had an 'A'—for Adam and Aries, her astrological sign—emblazoned on her right hand between her thumb and forefinger. With every prick, she thought of how much she enjoyed talking to James, but how he was too busy at college to write to her. She should break up with Adam, who will probably go to prison and ruin her life, she thought, frustrated.

In March, three weeks before her fifteenth birthday, Valessa planned to see Adam in court to finally decide whether or not they could have a future together. It was too much to hope he'd be released after his brawls in jail.

When the judge announced Adam would be released on April fifteenth, Valessa almost jumped out of the seat. Adam, her Adam, would be coming home. She bought a silver ring with a stone to represent their relationship, and even showed it to her mother's friends at a Christian singles party.

Valessa felt so happy that Adam would return that she didn't mind her mother refusing to have another big party to celebrate Valessa turning fifteen. Having dinner at a restaurant was so much more grown up. She celebrated becoming fifteen with the knowledge her wonderful lover would be home in two weeks.

* * *

On April 15, 1998, Adam was released and brought Valessa six red roses. Jon stood aside while she kissed Adam in her living room. She invited them both into her bedroom to listen to music and celebrate. They set up her video camera to record the occasion. Adam danced with her while Jon reclined on her bed and watched. It was a special day to be remembered forever. Adam held her pet ferret, Slick, as gently as she did, and posed for a picture.

On May 10, Valessa and Adam celebrated their seven-month anniversary by making a baby. He entered and left the house via Valessa's window. Early one morning two weeks later, Vicki discovered Adam in Valessa's room, and after the sun came up she drove him to a friend's house in the Town 'n' Country area.

Valessa joined him the next day, but came home. She skipped school on Wednesday, May 27. How could she have known her mother would send the police after her? "No, I'm not Valessa," she lied to the policeman and gave him another name, but he saw Adam's name and hers on her bookbag. She regretted writing "Valessa Loves Adam" and "Adam Loves Valessa" all over her bookbag. She tried to fight the police officer, but couldn't stop him from arresting Adam.

"Child abuse!" Valessa screamed at her mother when a police officer brought her home. "You charged Adam with child abuse. I'm not a child."

"You ran away and skipped school. It proves you're a child," Vicki explained.

"Adults wouldn't try to kick windows of a police car, young lady," the officer said.

Valessa ran into the house, threw herself face down on her bed, and beat the pillow with her fists.

During the time Adam spent in jail charged with abusing Valessa, she managed to convince Vicki to help her visit Adam. Vicki drove Valessa to meet Colleen Macklem, whose boyfriend shared Adam's cell. Colleen was older, but seemed to understand Valessa's frustration with her mother. One minute she was having Adam arrested, and then she would be kind to him and even help Valessa to see him.

Valessa felt thrilled he was released before his trial. When he got a job at Denny's on June 21, she began to believe they could start a life together. His job pleased her mother. She stopped being such an ass when he came to visit, and had even made up the guest room for him.

Valessa felt alarmed when she opened her diary to confide her happiness, and found five pages missing. They contained her hopes of having a baby with Adam. She wanted to confront her mother and demand to know how she could interfere with her privacy and remove pages from her diary. It was time to run away again. Adam had worked at Denny's only a few days, and Jon changed jobs all the time. She asked her boss for her pay on Thursday, June 25.

Valessa gave Adam the code to her mother's ATM card, and expected to feel happy when he and Jon came back to the van with money to buy drugs. It took quite a few calls on her mother's cell phone to find a connection. Yes, she needed to dull the pain in the pit of her stomach and between her legs. Being high would cure it.

At the rave clubs, Ecstasy made her feel good. It cost twenty bucks so she didn't use it often. LSD cost seven. Just being with Adam made her happy. They scored three beans so she would put all the bad stuff out of her mind.

As she walked with Adam and Jon trying to find an empty tattoo parlor, she said, "I'm glad Mom's dead. Now I can do anything I want." Saying it didn't change the hollow feeling inside.

The drugs didn't relieve her pain. Nothing did. Not even lying on the couch watching Jon and her handsome lover get tattooed. "Adam I want a baby. When are we going to have a baby?" Hearing him say "When you can support me again" made her pain worse. She wondered why he seemed to think it was a joke.

Valessa tried to remember when the pain started. Did she have it before Adam took her with Jon to his father's grave on Saturday? He even purchased a plastic rose in the convenience store and asked her to pray. Jon prayed too. She should be happy he wanted to share that. Instead it made her think of her mother who was in heaven with his father.

That night, in a Motel 6 close to Valessa's home, Adam got very passionate in bed. It hurt. She would have cried out if Jon wasn't in the next bed.

Even in Best Buy, when she collapsed into the wheelchair in the lobby waiting for old people, they tried to make her laugh by pushing her into the store. It didn't help her discomfort, but she enjoyed their efforts trying to please her.

Dear sensitive Adam realized her unhappiness and bought her a beautiful ring at Wal-Mart while she waited in the van. "What does it mean?" she asked. He flashed his beautiful smile and shyly said, "What do you think?" He bent down and kissed her, making her heart beat wildly. "We're married!" she exclaimed. He made her feel warm and happy all over. The pain almost disappeared.

As the days passed, and they partied with friends her discomfort grew. Changing motels for safety was an extra annoyance, because Jon Whispel was the only one who had a driver's license. Without him, Adam couldn't rent anything even with her mother's credit cards. As much as she liked Jon, she realized he was indispensable to Adam, so she couldn't be alone with her lover.

Bodily pain consumed her waking hours. But she

knew that it would be too dangerous to go to a doctor in Tampa. Waiting for Adam and Jon to return to the Budget Inn, she drifted off to sleep.

Adam burst through the door waking her exclaiming it was time to go. "A friend paged me. When I called him back, he said 'You guys were on the news.'"

Jon added, "It's about time."

Valessa felt their excitement as she packed, while Adam made quick plans to head for Phoenix, where Adam knew a guy who sold crystal meth. Adam and Jon decided to sell Vicki's van there, using the profits to flee to Canada.

"It's June 30. We should be in Arizona by July 4 and have a lot to celebrate," Adam said.

Adam turned south into a residential area. She glanced back at Jon, who gave her a vacant stare and shrugged as if he didn't know where they were going either. South was the opposite direction. Adam screeched to a halt, when he saw a green Nissan Quest and removed the license plate.

"This will buy time," he explained when he stopped at a convenience store near the Howard Frankland Bridge to change plates. "We can't risk using I-75, so we'll take the slow route north on U.S. 19."

While Adam and Jon were in the store buying cold cuts and snacks, she realized how smart Adam was. Her estimation of Adam's resourcefulness grew. He was not only tall and handsome, but his actions proved how much he loved her. He was worth all the remorse she felt in the pit of her stomach. It was worth everything, even her life. Love between a man and a woman was more important than anything. Both her parents confirmed that. So did the church and all her mother's friends.

Adam's efforts to hide their identity made her realize they were in danger. Crossing the Howard Frankland, Valessa feared every police car, siren, and helicopter until they entered Pinellas County and turned north onto U.S. 19. It was dark, but the traffic was increasing. The van blended in. Every mile brought them closer to a new life. The sun came up, giving all the buildings a rosy glow. Valessa knew she loved Adam enough to love his children. If the three friends could escape, they would stay together forever, unlike their parents.

The farms in north Florida seemed endless. It was late afternoon when they reached Perry—short of their goal, Route 10, but Adam needed to sleep. They checked into a motel and resumed their journey after dark. It was ink black once they left the small town. Adam passed the lights of Tallahassee and headed toward Alabama. Valessa enjoyed making him sandwiches. In time she'd make all his meals. Until she and Adam had a baby to unite them, she, Adam, and Jon would be her family.

Adam stopped to fill the gas tank in Mossy Head, Florida, but the ATM didn't work. Their cash was getting low so Adam tried ATMs in a few towns in the panhandle. The card didn't produce any results. Valessa felt anxious as she noted Adam's growing disappointment. At 1 A.M. in Alabama, the card popped out of the slot. It was such a mystery that the ATMs only worked once in a while. Adam was always pleased when they spit out cash, and that made Valessa happy. Adam didn't like having to stop all the time.

In Gulfport, Mississippi, the signs along I-10 were almost as big as the parking lots filled with truckers filling up with gas and $9.95 steaks. It was 4 A.M., Wednesday, July 1, when Adam put the plastic card in the ATM at The Flying J truck stop. It returned along with $100. They all felt rich. After filling up the van and eating, they bought fireworks to celebrate the Fourth of July in Arizona.

They stopped at Oasis Travel and took showers costing five dollars apiece. Before getting back on the highway, they shared a joint and dropped some acid into their soft drinks. Valessa's pain didn't disappear, but she felt safer as the distance from Tampa grew. She could tell Adam and Jon did too. After the van rumbled across the long bridge over the Mississippi River and entered Louisiana, Adam put the cruise control on 75 mph. He tapped the steering wheel in time with the music coming from the tape player. Valessa relaxed too as the van wove through the darkness. She could hear Jon snore and periodically glanced back at him. She rested her head against Adam's shoulder and closed her eyes.

Valessa yawned and stretched. "It's nice to see the countryside in the daytime. The big farms and little towns look different from Florida, but the oil pumps ruin the scenery."

"You're awake," Adam said. "We're going to pass Houston in an hour. Then I'll pull into a rest stop to catch a few winks."

Jon climbed out of the back when Adam stopped and let him take his place. While Adam slept, Valessa wrote a poem called "Tear Drops" that expressed her desire to be with him "forever."

Near dinner time she made more sandwiches. Jon wolfed his down and paced, watching the traffic. He cringed when a police car entered the rest area. Valessa breathed a sigh of relief when the cop entered the men's room and then drove off. Adam roused and ate at twilight, then joined the traffic on Route 10.

He stopped at Luling, Texas to fill up the van around 2:20 A.M. on Thursday morning, July 2, halfway to Arizona. Valessa felt thrilled her mother's credit card worked. Adam jumped back in the van with a smile on his face.

The van traveled fast but Texas seemed to go on forever. It was 10:00 A.M. when they rolled into a little town called Ozona to fill the gas tank and use the restrooms.

Valessa pointed to the sign and noted that there was also an Ozona in Florida.

Adam and Jon frowned disapprovingly. Her spirits improved when Adam waved five twenty-dollar bills he had retrieved from the ATM. They stocked up on soda, snacks, ice, and cold cuts.

Sheriff Bruce Wilson at Fort Stockton checked the bulletins like he did every morning when he arrived at his office. Luling was 400 miles east. He determined an approximate time the green Nissan would enter Pecos County, his territory, and alerted his deputy to be ready. The sheriff savored the idea of catching another criminal on Route 10 to add to his collection of triumphs. His deputy was equally proud of the captures. Larry Jackson had become an expert at shooting out tires.

The sheriff reminded the Texas Highway Patrol to watch out for a green Nissan Quest with a Florida tag, and then to use spike strips. He pushed away from his desk and put his white straw Stetson back on his head. "I'm going to lunch, Shirley. Call me at home if you hear anything."

His secretary Shirley Young had just begun to eat her sandwich when a new teletype registered that an ATM had been hit in Ozona 100 miles east an hour before. She immediately called the sheriff and the deputy.

The lawmen headed for the overpass and parked on the median, next to the Texas Highway Patrol trooper. Larry Jackson got in the sheriff's cruiser as they had done in previous chases. It gave him the ability to concentrate on shooting out the tires.

The sheriff's cruiser traveled east toward a curve in the road that hid the vehicle from the vast long straight road, but it gave the sheriff and his deputy a long view of oncoming traffic. They barely rolled to a stop when they sighted a green Nissan Quest. The sheriff's gut instincts made him drive off the medium and follow. As they drew nearer, the sheriff could see a Florida plate. The numbers didn't match the bulletin, but he turned on his lights. The driver of the green van increased the speed. The sheriff turned on the siren, hoping the van would stop or have its tires punctured by the trooper's spikes.

Near Fort Stockton, Texas, Valessa heard a siren and saw the dreaded red and blue flashing lights behind her. Jon, laying on the back seat, sat up and put on the safety belt. Adam kept focused on the rear view mirror and floored the gas pedal. The van swayed through traffic. Valessa noticed the muscles in his arms swell as he held the steering wheel tight. He maneuvered around the cars on the highway almost clipping one.

The police were gaining on them. A loud popping sound made Jon cry out, "Those are bullets!"

"They're shooting at us!" Valessa screamed. "Stop, I'll take the blame!"

"If they catch us, I will! Get rid of that," Adam said, using his head to indicate the Jack-in-the-Box LSD lying on the front seat.

Valessa swallowed six times the usual dose of LSD and threw the rest at Jon. The sheriff pulled alongside the van and shot out one of the tires. The next blast hit another tire, and the van spun out of control. It sent the van down an embankment. Valessa tried to stop her body from being thrown around but the momentum was too strong. Slam! They hit the road and her head flew forward and jerked back. Her guitar, keyboard, and other possessions became flying missiles.

The van swayed but stayed upright, and Adam continued to keep his foot jammed on the gas. The slapping of the deflated tires was deafening. Valessa and Jon screamed as they realized Adam was turned around and heading directly for the sheriff's car. One of the front tires exploded under Valessa.

Adam saw the troopers aiming guns at him and swerved away. Three flat tires slowed him down as he headed toward the highway overpass. The cops shot the final tire out. For a few minutes the van rode more steadily on the two-lane road service road, and the bumping lessened. Four flat tires also let him increase the speed again. Valessa could see chunks of tire rubber fly by as they shredded. The van went under the overpass, where a bullet hit the metal near Adam's head. He stopped.

Two men wearing white cowboy hats, jeans, and boots got out of a Chevy Blazer marked Sheriff of Pecos County. They came forward with their guns drawn. A Texas State trooper in his green uniform jumped out of his vehicle and ran toward Valessa's side of the car. He pointed his gun too. Another sheriff's car appeared.

Terror engulfed her seeing all the guns pointed at them. What would happen to Adam? The door next to him jerked open and Adam tried to push the man in the cowboy hat away. Valessa screamed, seeing Adam get smashed on the side of his head with a gun and thrown to the ground. She loved him more than her life.

"Get out of the car," the trooper on her side commanded, but she couldn't move. He released her seat belt, pulled her out, and pointed to the ground. He forced Jon and her to lay on their stomachs, and cuffed them too. She stayed still, because when Jon moved he got kicked. The gravel on the road stuck to her arms.

"Where is Mrs. Robinson?" the old sheriff shouted, searching the van. Valessa heard Adam answer, "The last time we saw her, she was at the house."

The sheriff backed out of the van rear first, "No sign of her there. Deputy Jackson, take that little lady in the big britches to Juvenile." He removed his hat and put his fingers through his red hair darkened by sweat. "She doesn't even look old enough to be fifteen."

Valessa wished she could shout at the sheriff that she had been fifteen for a full three months. Worse than death the mean bastards forced her into a separate car. Would she ever see Adam again? She struggled to look back, but the hand cuffs restrained movement. The sheriff's car with Adam and Jon followed for a few moments and then turned in another direction.

"Why are we being arrested?" she managed to ask as the minutes separated her from Adam.

"You were caught in a stolen vehicle wanted by the state of Florida," deputy Larry Jackson said.

"It's not stolen. It belongs to my mom. Are the cops in Florida going to take me home?"

"They might," the deputy said.

"Adam and Jon too?" Valessa questioned cautiously.

"They might," he again answered. He looked at the girl in the back seat through his rear view mirror. Her pale face with long dark hair spiraling in every direction wasn't remarkable. She was just like the sheriff said when he saw her, "just a little lady in big britches." I'm taking you to the Fort Stockton courthouse to turn you over to juvenile authorities."

Valessa sat in numbed silence during the court's procedure of providing an attorney and a guardian due all minors under Texas law. The adult's words didn't reach through her drug-induced haze. The LSD she ingested during the harrowing car chase incapacitated her.

It wasn't until she entered her cell at the Juvenile Detention Center that she remembered her pain and her separation from Adam. She screamed for medical attention. She cried and curled up in a fetal position. She fondled her navel, wondering if a new life was growing in her. Adam was going to give her a new beginning: a new little Valessa she could love.

CHAPTER 8

VICKI

Vicki recorded her romance with Jim in her diary. She knew that Valessa too kept a journal, and decided to read it after finding a naked Adam hovering in her daughter's closet one day. It confirmed the fifteen-year-old's desire to have a baby with the criminal, Adam. Vicki ripped five pages out of Valessa's diary to show the counselor. She called Jim and Valessa's father to make plans to save Valessa.

June 26, 1998

The Roadhouse Grill on Fletcher Avenue and Dale Mabry Highway served such good food that Bonnie Smith anticipated a wonderful lunch with Vicki Robinson. In the four years since they met at the church ministry, Single Purpose, she valued every minute they spent together and realized it had been a few weeks since their gathering at the First Baptist Church meeting with the Sun Coast Singles. It had been such fun to see Deborah and Theresa too.

Bonnie looked around the country and western bar until she found Vicki, who waved and smiled. While she walked carefully through the peanut shell-covered floor, she thought of how gracious Vicki was to share her precious time. Bonnie leaned her crutches down and sat at a table. Vicki must have arrived at exactly at 2 P.M. Bonnie apologized for being five minutes late. Vicki got up and gave her a hug in response.

Vicki looked beautiful as usual with her blond halo around her smiling face. Her hair, clothes, and jewelry were perfect, but Bonnie felt they didn't reflect her inner warmth. The woman gave more than anyone she knew, and treated all with utmost respect.

Before even looking at the menu, Vicki said, "I'm so excited about Deborah and Ralph's wedding. When I marry Jim, we'll be sisters-in-law."

"Of course, I never thought of that. It will be a happy time. You and Deborah are so close, even though she's only a few years older than Michelle."

"We're like sisters. Tomorrow I'm getting fitted for my maid-of-honor dress. I can't wait to dance with Jim at the ceremony. He becomes even more sentimental at weddings."

"Our singles club gets smaller all the time with so many marriages. I'm going to have the sirloin steak, baked potato, and iced tea," Bonnie said to the waitress.

"So will I," Vicki said. She put the menu aside.

"If you marry Jim at the same time, you could have a double wedding," Bonnie laughed, adding. "Two brothers and two brides for the same price. Think about it."

"Oh, if it were only that simple. I love Jim so much. He's the perfect man for me and more romantic than I ever dreamed of. We've been going to pre-marriage counseling and worked at uniting our families by taking trips together," Vicki said.

"That sounds wonderful," Bonnie said, patting Vicki's hand to emphasize her delight. "So what's stopping you?"

"You know Valessa has given me some problems. I told you the day I took her to the counselor. As we were leaving his office, she ran up the stairs ahead of me, leaned over the railing, spit on me, then claimed it was an accident. That was nothing," Vicki said.

"What? You thought she did it on purpose."

"Bonnie, she thinks she's in love. She wants to marry Adam Davis, the guy with the criminal record. That's not exactly what she said. She wants to have his baby!"

"You can't be serious. She's fifteen," Bonnie stated as the food arrived. Hunger distracted her and she began to eat.

"I caught them together. I suggested I'd take her for an after injection. She refused." Vicki made no effort to eat.

Bonnie had stabbed her meat with a fork and held the tender morsel in midair. "You mean you caught them having sex? Do those injections doctors give really prevent pregnancy?"

Vicki nodded. "My doctor claims they do."

"You mean like an abortion?" Bonnie asked.

"No, but it could prevent one," Vicki said.

Bonnie relaxed and continued eating her steak. "You're so good to your girls, Vicki. Throw the guy out and never let him in the house again," she suggested. "Girls without fathers are so needy."

"Chuck, Valessa's father used to take the girls for short periods. I never told them that he was cutting their visits short. I know how much girls need daddies. Now he takes them one at a time. Michelle is visiting him now. She's getting over being rebellious, even after the death of her fiancé. It gives me hope."

"You never talk about their dad. I didn't know," Bonnie said. "Michelle is seventeen and over the volatile early teens."

"I made a decision I'm hiding from Valessa. I'm going to send her to Steppin' Stone Farm. Jim and I researched and found it near Valrico. Chuck has agreed. It's a place with Christian values to help teens." Vicki pushed her salad around.

"That sounds sensible. You've tried counseling, but nothing that intensive. Good for you," Bonnie said, smashing her baked potato into the gravy. She added the sour cream and enjoyed the savory result.

"Adam's taking her down the wrong path. My efforts at Christian love aren't working," Vicki said, looking at her plate.

"You're doing the right thing. Be happy," Bonnie offered.

"When I suggested it to Valessa, she said she wouldn't go, and had friends who'd 'take care of me.'" Vicki announced, appearing serious.

"I can't believe she'd threaten you like that. Not the shy girl you brought to our meetings. She was quiet and withdrawn. I was surprised she sang for us when you asked her. More than one song too. She has a beautiful, sweet voice," Bonnie said.

"She's good, isn't she? She wants to sing with a band some day." Vicki smiled, appearing to enjoy the positive praise. "She's crazy in love. I'm going to promise her that if she sticks it out at Steppin' Stone Farm until she turns sixteen and feels the same way, I'll give them my blessings. At least she'll be drug free."

"When I suspected my son was in drug trouble at her age, I'd creep into his room after he fell asleep and pray over him. It was all I could do," Bonnie said.

"Maybe I should reconsider sending her away right now. The idea upsets her so." Vicki appeared close to tears. "I've always wanted my girls to love me. The mere suggestion of being separated from Adam makes her angry with me."

"You made a plan. Stick to it. Some day she'll know you had her best interests at heart," Bonnie encouraged. "We should pray about it."

Vicki looked at her watch. "I've got some work to prepare for a real estate client I need to see tomorrow. Then I'm going to ask Valessa to run some errands with me so we can talk." She got up. "Thanks for offering to pray and listening to my problems. We'll pray together some evening at my house." Vicki left her money for the check and rushed away.

Bonnie looked at Vicki's barely-eaten meal and could hardly swallow. She recalled watching Michelle and Valessa scoop up Vicki's wonderful pumpkin-chocolate-chip Halloween cookies. Michelle had rinsed her hair red for her costume that year. She and Valessa wore black and went trick or treating together. Vicki had held a Halloween party that year. Had Adam been there? Bonnie felt pleased Vicki was going to send Valessa to Steppin' Stone.

Bonnie tried to remember how she knew about Adam's record. He had called Valessa from jail during Vicki's lovely Christmas party, hadn't he? Bonnie held up her hand and counted on her fingers eight months. Valessa only met Adam in early October, didn't she? Some how she lost her appetite too and asked the waitress to bring her a box to go. She didn't dare to include Vicki's leftovers, too.

Sunday morning June 28, 1998, Deborah Sartor-Englert called Bonnie and announced "Vicki's missing!"

Deborah's voice held a tremor like she was about to cry.

Bonnie tried to console her, but instinctively felt dread. "Maybe she had car trouble."

"The van isn't at the house. Vicki had some real estate appointments in the morning and didn't appear. Her broker, Becky Eckley, is worried, and so am I. She told Jim and me Vicki never missed a business appointment. I know she was looking forward to participating in my wedding to Ralph and wouldn't miss trying on the dress she was to wear. If Vicki could, she would have called. Jim had a date with her to go to the beach Saturday afternoon. Jim reported her missing late yesterday. He told the Hillsborough Sheriff's Department that Valessa had refused to send her friends away before he left Vicki's house around 11:30 P.M. Friday night."

"Where is Valessa and Vicki's dog?" Bonnie asked.

"The neighbors found Lady in the yard and brought her into their house," Deborah said. "Vicki's house is empty. Valessa's missing too. Michelle is with her father in Missouri."

Bonnie thought about Vicki's conversation at lunch on Friday and felt sick remembering her own advice. After placing the telephone receiver down, she prayed for her friend before attending her Lutheran service.

CHAPTER 9

AGONIZING REALITY

Vicki's fiancé Jim Englert reconstructed the last evening he saw Vicki over and over with most of his friends, as they made plans for a prayer vigil Friday evening. "I left soon after Vicki told Valessa's two friends to leave but Valessa refused to let them go home. I kissed Vicki good-bye in the garage, and made a date for the beach on Saturday afternoon. If only I had realized Vicki was in danger and had stayed to protect her."

Jim and his friends talked extensively about Vicki's possible whereabouts. Valessa's escapades with two male pals splashed through the papers everyday, informing the public about the case.

Vicki shared confidentially that Valessa wanted to have Adam's baby. All the adults talked about it with Vicki, but seeing it in print shocked all who read it. Learning Valessa broadcast that information in a tattoo parlor assaulted their senses. The little girl in a school uniform who had sung in the choir had gotten a tattoo, and had watched two friends get their eyebrows pierced. God! Vicki's complaints about Valessa were gentle compared to what news writers exposed.

Adam had so many charges against him, he had even turned Jon Whispel into a criminal. Vicki never complained about Jon. Is it possible she thought, that when he was present, Valessa and Adam couldn't be intimate? His association with the couple was bizarre, impossible to fathom. Vicki's friends didn't want to examine that relationship carefully.

There were no answers. What were the three teens doing Saturday night and Sunday at an Ybor City tattoo parlor? Each bit of information created a bleaker picture of Vicki's whereabouts. Her traumatized friends arranged for a prayer vigil at Vicki's gracious Carrollwood home, a place where they had often enjoyed her hospitality.

One hundred and fifty people gathered on Vicki's lawn the night of July 3. Telephone communications spread the bad news before the meeting. Most of the gathering had learned the terrible news via a friend or family member who had been contacted by authorities.

The discovery of Vicki's body, dumped at the end of a dirt road five miles away, shocked everyone and destroyed all hope. Bonnie Smith remembered telling a friend at her church on Sunday, after hearing from Deborah that Vicki was missing, of fears that her friend's daughter was going to kill her. Valessa's first-degree murder charge added complicated sorrow mingled with anger. Tom Klug, Vicki's brother, reminded everyone, "Vicki lived her life for her daughters. She loves them both very much. We found a body today. Vicki is in heaven." Kirt, the younger brother, opened his mouth to say something but his voice cracked holding back tears.

Vicki's fiancé, Jim Englert, dropped to his knees and

cried. The meeting of friends united to pray for Vicki's safety turned into a ceremony dedicated to a farewell forever. Each felt their loss in a personal way but they hugged and cried together after singing Christian hymns planned for the occasion.

Ed Philips told the group he was going to put up a banner dedicated to Vicki's memory on the gate leading to the spot where Vicki's body was found. Shock and disgust ran through the crowd when they learned that the path leading to her body was near Jon Whispel's house.

The meeting ended and people broke up into little groups all sharing memories. Valessa's involvement became the main topic. Tom and Kirt Klug talked to a reporter about Vicki's intentions to send Valessa to a Christian boarding school in Valrico. Neither was sure if Valessa knew, but both agreed if their niece knew she would be angry. Kirt said, "If you didn't like Adam, she didn't like you. She had said she would not let anyone keep them apart. Her seventeen-year-old sister, Michelle, is especially grief-stricken. She's lost a mother and a sister."

Tom Klug said, "Valessa was closer to Chuck, her father, than she was to her mom. So even if the divorce wasn't particularly bitter, the divorce was hard on her. It changed her whole life. She moved and left her Christian school. Chuck moved to St. Louis and she and Michelle stayed with Vicki in Tampa. She fell in with the wrong crowd. Adolescence is one of the roughest periods of life. The choices you make and direction you take can end up affecting you for the rest of your life."

Kirt remembered, "The family thought that Valessa would lose interest when Adam went to jail for breaking into an abandoned house. It only deepened. Vicki worried constantly about her relationship with Davis even after she charged him with child abuse for running away with her in May."

Laura Klug holding treasured family pictures of her cousins stepped forward. "Valessa was a fun-loving, active tomboy." Laura showed a picture. "This is Valessa at ten. Both of her arms are in casts from a fall off a swing. She was a sweet, innocent little girl. I look in her eyes and at that face and can't understand how she could have killed her mother. I can't see it. I can't see what went wrong."

Friends of Vicki held back from confiding their anger to the press. Out of mutual respect for their beloved friend, they didn't talk openly about her daughter. After all, she had been charged mere hours before the prayer meeting.

Vicki Robinson's friends shared experiences to help each other understand how and why this happened. They talked about Mother's Day when she and her first daughter, Michelle, had attended the morning service together at Idlewild Baptist Church. At the mother and daughter lunch afterward, Vicki's friends remember she couldn't stop talking about it. Valessa had gone off with friends. "Valessa is not a throwaway child," she told Michelle and friends.

Gibbs Wilson reminisced, "I saw Vicki's familiar happy face entering the Idlewild Baptist Church early in June. I reached out and Vicki gave me her usual friendly hug. I told her it was great to see her. 'You haven't used my title company for a while. I thought you were mad at me.' She apologized and explained how distracted she was and hadn't been selling houses the way she used to. Vicki's smile disappeared when she said, 'It helped me so much to talk to you about it when you provided that nice lunch for my open house. The many people around us prevented me from asking what was going on with Valessa.' Vicki's expression gave me the feeling that things hadn't changed. She was kind enough to ask about my dad, who died on Mother's Day. We talked about how difficult death was, even when it was expected."

Theresa's eyes filled with tears. "I remember the day Valessa proudly showed me a little ring with a stone in it that Adam had given her. She said he was a good guy even though he was in jail. Who could have expected this?

"If only I had been able to help the day Vicki confided her problems to me at the 'open house'. Fifteen years of counseling possible suicides on the Christian telephone helpline hadn't prepared me to hear that someone like Vicki would find drugs in her daughter's room or that the girl was in love with a young man just out of jail. This whole affair shakes my belief that a Christian education and loving parents invested in prayer can protect children from drugs. Vicki was aware of her daughter's problems and reached out for advice. But we let the matter drop."

Everyone of the crowd had a personal experience to share, and they all felt remorse for not realizing she was in danger. Charles Klug, her cousin, said, "We haven't had any signs of her at all. If she is still alive, this is the time to find her. We hoped, in spite of no signs of her, they stashed her in an empty home or trailer. We asked the landlords to check their property." Their words echoed hollow when the paper hit the newsstands hours before the prayer meeting.

Michelle returned to Tampa with her father and step-mother Vanessa the Monday before the funeral. They were Valessa's first visitors at the W.T. Davis Juvenile Detention Center. Chuck held Valessa while she sobbed. Michelle asked, "Did you kill mom?" Valessa answered "No."

* * *

In the Tampa Bay area on July 2, the *Tampa Tribune* headline reported, "Three Teens Spotted, But Not Mother." The *St. Petersburg Times* announced, "Missing Daughter Hangs Out With Pals."

The Hillsborough Sheriff's Department investigated Jon Whispel and reviewed his records at Jefferson High School. They learned that Jon Michael Whispel, whose photograph appeared in the 1997 yearbook, quit school two months before graduation. He never joined any clubs, played sports, or engaged in any other other school activities like the high school band.

Adam Davis's extensive records contained his nickname, 'Rattlesnake.' He and Jon Whispel were arrested for breaking into a home in Hillsborough County and stealing a knife and a 120,000-volt tazer gun in October 1997. Adam spent time in jail for child abuse for running away with Valessa in May after Vicki Robinson pressed charges.

Keith Morelli and Paulo Lima of the *Tampa Tribune* scooped all the local news with their story, "Runaway Teens Arrested In Texas" on July 3, 1998. Their vivid description of the teens capture included Jim Englert's statement, "I'm very excited that this is coming to an end. If we can just get those teens to talk."

On July 4, the *St. Petersburg Times* headline screamed "Missing Mother Found Dead." By July 5, reporters pieced together bits and pieces of Valessa's life in an article with the headline "Divorce Changed Teen's Life." Angela Moore's article contained the statements made by Vicki's family at the prayer meeting.

The article said that Valessa was was charged Friday night with first degree murder in the death of her mother. It reported that friends and relatives saw the violence as the culmination of months of conflict over Valessa's relationship with Adam Davis, and that Davis and Jon Whispel will also be charged with first degree murder. Friends were quoted as saying Valessa got "darker and a lot deeper" the year after her parents' divorce, and that the divorce affected her more than her sister, Michelle.

The *Tampa Tribune* and the *St. Petersburg Times* carried Vicki Robinson's obituary—it acknowledged one daughter, Michelle.

CHAPTER 10
FUNERAL BECOMES A MEDIA EVENT

Tuesday, July 7, 1998

Cars and reporters surrounded the gray stucco, red-tiled roof house on Cartnal Avenue, and filled the cul-de-sac when Chuck and Vanessa arrived. They avoided the press, and were grateful when Michelle opened the door. Chuck hugged his daughter and Vanessa sat on the sofa next to a blonde who appeared to be in her twenties. She offered her hand and said, "I'm Vicki's best friend, Deborah Sartor-Englert. You're Chuck's wife?"

"Yes, Vanessa." Michelle's uncle and grandfather took her into the kitchen. They announced they were going to reenact the crime committed against Vicki.

"I'm going to be on TV, along with Michelle," Deborah said.

Chuck Robinson ignored the family's cheers of approval and said, "I don't want my daughter in front of a camera. She might say something she'll regret later."

The television crew in the kitchen had cameras

rolling when Michelle said, "How can a human being, first of all, kill another human being?"

Chuck heard his daughter's voice and turned to stop her, but was too late. He stood out of camera range at the entrance to the kitchen and watched Michelle continue. "How can a daughter kill her mother? How could she do this to me? How could she do this to herself? We had just said good-bye for the summer. The next thing I knew, it was all over. Everything was gone. I want to see these guys punished." Tears ran down her face when she said, "My sister should be held accountable for her actions. My mother was so innocent, so beautiful. She wouldn't hurt a fly. She was scared to kill cockroaches."

When the television cameras were turned off, Chuck Robinson entered the kitchen to hug Michelle and remind her that he loved her, too. She clung to him, grateful for not being blamed for deserting her sister. He stroked her hair in a wordless communication between father and daughter before he released her.

Michelle's body trembled, but she smiled bravely and accepted congratulations from family members for her televised comments. Before leaving for the funeral, her grandfather and uncles discussed the sale of Vicki's house and the disposal of her effects. Michelle knew her statement about losing everything was true, but she still had a loving father.

She left the place called home with her father and stepmother, Vanessa, who embraced her before they entered the car. Vanessa squeezed her hand as Chuck maneuvered the rented vehicle into the long procession headed for her mother's funeral ceremony at the Idlewild Baptist Church. "Your dad served as a deacon at Idlewild, and I met him there after we were both divorced. I never expected to return under such terrible circumstances. I hope the church will give you comfort, because it was your mother's church too," Vanessa said, as they arrived at the familiar imposing building dignified by a tall steeple. Lightning flashed and mourners poured somberly into the church.

The massive news coverage attracted crowds of people. Some knew the victim, but there were also curious interlopers and writers and reporters from every medium. In the parking lot, big trucks from every TV station in the Tampa area hummed with activity. The thunder clouds matched the mood of Vicki's distraught friends, but just as clouds hide sunshine, Vicki's bright spirit provided solace.

Inside, mourners gathered to bid farewell to a daughter, sister, mother, fiancé, friend, fellow church member, good neighbor, and business associate. The huge, opulent, 1,800-seat church was more than half full. It overflowed with grief for Vicki Lyn Robinson, who had died ten days earlier at the hands of her fifteen-year-old daughter and her two male friends.

Photographs from throughout Vicki's life—from early childhood through a glamor shot she had given her fiancé—stood on a table. There was no coffin because of the time the body had spent in the hot Florida sun. An ocean of flowers flooded the area and created a heavenly scent. Soft organ music echoed on the walls and ceilings of the huge church and provided a soothing message to the bereaved. The stained glass windows sent rainbow colors down for the brief periods when sun peeked out from behind the clouds. The magnitude of the building testified that Southern Baptists took their religion seriously.

The television crews respectfully remained outside, but scattered among the grieving mass of people were some reporters who scribbled notes and whispered into tape recorders. The well-dressed beautiful people who noticed nudged one another. Some smiled, as if it made Vicki's funeral more important. Hushed murmurs, oc-

casional coughs, and the sounds of shuffling feet stopped
when a choral group began to sing Vicki's favorite song,
"The Great Divide."

Pastor Ken Whitten opened the service by saying,
"We are not here of our own choosing. We are here by
divine appointment. Vicki Robinson has something to
say to us about our faith. She has something to say about
our family and our friends. Jesus forgave his killers.
Vicki Robinson would want Valessa to receive forgiveness."

His words caused a ripple of movement as people
squirmed in the pews. The obituary hadn't mentioned
that Vicki was the mother of two girls, but Pastor
Whitten noted a second daughter. He read passages
that Vicki had highlighted in her gold-trimmed bible.
He noted her prayer card had Valessa's name on the
top. "Any mother would lay down her life for her children. You can say that at least Vicki Robinson did not
suffer the horror of burying a child."

Vicki's mother cried openly and her father put his
arm around her. Jim Englert stepped forward and took
the pastor's place. He described Vicki as his fiancée,
and told how wonderful and special their love was.

Tom Klug, Vicki's older brother, remembered a
cheery girl growing up in Michigan. "She was a cheer-
leader. An active girl with a lot of friends. She enjoyed
life."

Deborah Sartor-Englert told how she met Vicki three
years before at a Christian singles group. "She was quick
to smile, eager to please. Vicki loved people and
reached out to people around her."

The lurid newspaper details of Vicki Robinson's
murder were lost in the beauty of the words describing
Vicki by her oldest brother, fiancé, closest friend, sister-
in-law, and seventeen-year-old daughter, Michelle, who
read an original poem that brought strangers to tears.

Outside, Vicki's beautiful blond friend Deborah

Sartor-Englert talked to reporters about Valessa. "We know her personally, and as much as we feel hurt and anger over what she's done, there is a part of us that loves her."

Many friends and relatives spoke of how Vicki continued to love her daughter, even as Vanessa's rebellion deepened. They echoed these sentiments like a mantra.

Vicki's brother said, "Valessa got involved with a bad crowd. I can't believe she would commit murder but for that fact. Vicki's last wish was that Valessa would come to know the Lord Jesus Christ."

CHAPTER 11
THE PRODIGAL

Tuesday, July 7: Valessa sat alone with her thoughts in the Hillsborough County W. T. Davis Juvenile Detention Center during her mother's funeral. Friends, relatives, law professionals, reporters, and strangers debated what she had been thinking during her mother's murder. The time and money squandered in the days following the heinous crime left more questions.

It was the day Valessa's mother planned to turn her over to Steppin' Stone Farm, an eighty-five-acre Christian-based retreat for troubled girls in rural Lithia, near Plant City. The nonprofit organization, funded by donations and help from the United Way, catered to girls thirteen to seventeen. The farm used a 4-H program that assigned each girl a farm animal to care for. They lived in trailers and cabins in groups of eight and were responsible for doing personal laundry. They had limited television viewing and were provided Christian music for entertainment. If Valessa knew the program she rejected it.

Vicki's communications to the facility described her

daughter as a defiant runaway who used drugs and wanted to have a baby with her criminal boyfriend. "I have no control over her," Vicki wrote.

Detective Iverson learned that Vicki Robinson planned to send her daughter to Steppin' Stone Farm after he brought Valessa back to Florida. It was a coincidence that it was his pastor's wife who had created the retreat for wayward girls.

CHAPTER 12

THE GRAND JURY

Wednesday, July 8: State Prosecutors held a Grand Jury to seek first-degree murder indictments against Valessa Robinson, fifteen, her boyfriend, Adam Davis, nineteen, and Jon Whispel, nineteen, for using a syringe full of bleach and a knife to kill Vicki Robinson in her home on Cartnal Avenue on June 27, 1998.

Slim, petite Shirley Williams, an Assistant State Prosecutor, paced and told the Grand Jury that "The motive likely to emerge in the trial is that Valessa didn't want to be separated from her felon boyfriend, Adam Davis. They were pretty much determined not to be separated and said as much to a Tampa police officer who investigated her mother's complaint after they ran away together on May 28th." She threw her head back, twirled on her heel, and continued, "He and his friend Jon Whispel sported new tattoos and pierced eyebrows provided by $600 of her mother's money. Valessa had her initials inscribed on her right ankle and an 'A' for Adam on her right hand. They deserve to be charged with first-degree murder."

Assistant Public Defender Dee Ann Athan told the Grand Jury, "At fifteen, Valessa is a minor, and should have been accompanied by a guardian and attorney before she was questioned." She asked Hillsborough Detective Lt. Jim Iverson, who had gone to Texas to interview Valessa, if he thought Valessa's rights had been violated when she made her confession.

The detective answered, "No, I interviewed her as a missing person." He held up a form for the jury to see. "She signed this consent form once she understood that I knew of her involvement in the crime spree."

Susan Black, a secretary and bookkeeper in the Texas juvenile facility, had observed Valessa in a fetal position playing with her navel. "She was asking about the two gentlemen that were with her. If they were okay and if we knew what was going on with them," she said.

Sandra King, a juvenile probation officer, described Valessa as calm.

Corey Simone, the tattoo artist, testified for the defense, "Valessa wasn't well when she watched Adam Davis and Jon Whispel get tattooed."

The Grand Jury indicted Valessa Robinson, Adam Davis, and Jon Whispel on charges of first-degree murder, armed robbery, and grand theft of a motor vehicle without being eligible for bail.

Charles Robinson, Valessa's father, reminded reporters after the hearing that Texas law provided his daughter with a lawyer and guardian. Neither had been contacted when Detective Iverson questioned his fifteen-year-old daughter.

Valessa emerged from the Hillsborough County W. T. Davis Juvenile Detention Center hours after being indicted for murder. Her long dark hair, parted in the middle, made her appear even younger than fifteen. Clear white skin with no makeup gave her a just-scrubbed look that many mothers wanted for their own daughters. Her gray prison uniform replaced the wide-leg skateboard jeans she had worn when she returned to Tampa. The uniform hung loosely on her slim body. Unlike so many young teen girls, she didn't show off her sexuality. She liked to wear big T-shirts that hid her developing breasts.

She appeared small, handcuffed between two deputies. Her head hung down and she avoided looking at the reporters waiting for a story. "Did you stab your mother?" they shouted. "Why was her body dumped in a garbage can?"

Valessa raised her head and told reporters, "You'll find out later. I'm glad to be charged as an adult. It gets me out of the juvenile detention center."

Reporters shot more questions at her. "How are you involved in your mother's death?"

"I'm not answering questions like that," she stated flatly.

"What about Adam Davis?" a female reporter called.

"I love Adam!" she yelled angrily, and turned away from the clamoring mob of reporters. Settling back in the sheriff's van, Valessa waited silently to go to her new home: Orient Point County Jail.

The scene had been filmed and was broadcast on every station, solidifying the opinion among Vicki's friends and family that Valessa was unrepentant.

A few of Valessa's friends viewed her actions as bravado.

"I Love Adam!" greeted *Tampa Tribune* readers on Thursday, July 9. Ladale Lloyd didn't write about a romance but reiterated Valessa's arrest in Texas, where she tried to divert the blame for her mother's murder from Adam Davis and Jon Whispel to herself.

That same day, Valessa sat before Hillsborough Circuit Court Judge Walter Heinrich. She had graduated from the juvenile gray prison suit to adult orange. The judge ordered her held without bail in the adult jail on the charge of first-degree murder.

The judge looked down at her. "You are to have no contact with Adam Davis, Jon Whispel, or any other witnesses. If you had relationships with any of these people, that relationship is now over."

Valessa put her cuffed fists over her ears.

On Friday July 10, Tampa television station WFTS-28 managed to scoop all the other stations and secure an interview with Adam Davis from his Texas jail cell. Promotions featured brief flashes of his capture while he lay in the dust next to Valessa and Jon Whispel. The voiceover announced that Linda Hurtado would conduct a forty-minute interview for the special.

The young, attractive brunette with brown eyes looked into the camera and told the audience, "Vicki Robinson's body was found with multiple stab wounds in a garbage can covered with palmetto brush near Waters Avenue and Sheldon Road, close to Jon Whispel's home. It is alleged that she was also injected with bleach. Her daughter Valessa, Jon Whispel, and Adam Davis are all charged with her death. Adam Davis is on the telephone from the Pecos County Jail."

Adam's voice sounded loud and clear. "I had nothing to do with the slaying of my girlfriend's mother. Neither did Valessa or Jon Whispel. Me and her mom got along great. We never had problems."

"The Grand Jury had enough evidence to charge you with murder."

"Me and Mrs. Robinson got along fine," Adam repeated, laughing. "We used to swim in the pool together. Or she'd invite me over and we'd watch movies."

Linda Hurtado shot a surprised look at the camera but her professionalism took over and she asked, "Did you do that the night of her murder?"

"No, she asked us to leave after her boyfriend left. We went to Denny's, where I washed dishes."

"If you got along so well with Valessa's mother, why was Vicki planning to send her away to a boarding school?"

"I don't know anything about that. Any problems were between them. Actually, she had no problem with me dating her daughter, because I made her daughter happy. Vicki liked the little gifts I gave her, too."

"What about the incriminating statements you made to Hillsborough County Sheriff's detectives?"

"I haven't talked to an attorney. I plan to plead not guilty and spend the rest of my life with Valessa. I used to have a real bad problem with drugs. Heavy use of crack cocaine and heroin. I met Valessa and she helped me realize that I don't need drugs. She helped me be a better person."

"Why were you driving Vicki Robinson's Nissan Quest and using her credit cards?" the reporter asked.

Adam didn't answer directly but said, "My fondest wish is to wed Valessa and raise a family. I'd like to be just like my dad. He died in a motorcycle accident when I was fourteen."

"What about your buddy Jon?"

"Jon and I are each other's family now. He's like a brother to me. He didn't have a lot of friends. I would never do anything to hurt Valessa's mother or family. I hope to have children and build a normal life with Valessa."

"You're facing a death sentence, or at least life in prison."

"I just want people to know I'm not what they think I am. I'm not a crazy murderer. I'm a good person and I get along with everybody."

"You still think that's possible?"

"I think anything is possible. I hope and pray it will be," Adam said before a recap of recent case footage played.

Florida media outlets remained fixated on the sensational murder case. Valessa, Adam Davis, and Jon Whispel were receiving some national coverage, too.

On Sunday, July 12, during a telephone interview from Orient Point County Jail, Valessa told Linda Hurtado, "I miss my mom terribly. I mean it's hard to believe, but I really do miss her and wish she wasn't dead. And if I could see her, I'd really want to tell her I love her and now though she's dead, I know she's in a better place. What happened that night wasn't supposed to happen. It wasn't planned at all. I hope people wait for the 'whole truth' before judging me."

The reporter stated, "Jon Whispel and Adam Davis didn't fight extradition and are on their way to Tampa."

"Adam's my 'soul mate'. We've pretty much given each other a reason to live, and we're going to spend the rest of our lives together," Valessa said.

Linda Hurtado's eyebrows shot up, creating a look of surprise. "You face life in prison and Jon and Adam face possible death sentences," she said loudly, then shook her head in disbelief.

"Anything is possible in the eyes of God," Valessa said, childlike.

The television coverage included visuals of their wild capture in Texas, ending with the three teens lying in the road and being handcuffed.

In response to questions about their actions after killing her mother, Valessa paused and then said, "I was on acid that night. All three of us were. I really didn't know what was going on until after the fact. In the past, I used marijuana and Ecstasy, but did acid a lot because I could get it really easy."

The reporter reminded her about visiting friends, getting tattooed, and using her mother's credit card for three days before leaving. "We were trying not to think of the events of June 27."

Before the reporter could pursue her original question, Valessa said, "My mother's family haven't visited me. I hope someday they'll forgive me. I hope they find it in their hearts to love me again. My father has visited me and forgives me. He told me he loves me. I know my mother does too. I cry every day, when I think of her."

Sunday's show ended with a cliffhanger when the TV reporter asked, "You told everyone you wanted to have Adam's baby. What were the results of the pregnancy test you were given?"

On Monday, after seeing the WFTS-28 Sunday Report, Chief Assistant Public Defender Joe Registrato spent an hour talking to Valessa at the jail. He then openly criticized the interview for taking advantage of a fifteen-year-old. The television crew from WFTS preparing a segment of Valessa in jail noted his observations.

On Monday's Five O'Clock News, viewers were informed by a tearful Valessa that the pregnancy test proved to be negative. Valessa's Sunday telephone interview encouraged reporters to contact family members out of the area who never saw the Tampa television show. Her grandparents were informed by telephone in Michigan that Valessa asked for forgiveness.

"Ridiculous! There is no excuse for what she's done. We love her, but this is awful, awful hard to take," Arthur Klug, her grandfather, responded.

"It is so hard, so unbelievable, so heartbreaking to lose a daughter because of a granddaughter. There is nothing so horrible," Donna Klug managed to say. "I saw Valessa a year ago. She was the way she's always been most of her life—moody and hard to get close to. I did coax a hug and the last words we said to each other were, 'I love you.'"

Charles Robinson, her father, added that he loved Valessa and was behind her 100 percent. "You can't abandon your child in any type of need or crisis." His interview from St. Louis came in the "Valessa Jail" segment on Tuesday night.

After Linda Hurtado's report, WFTS-28 TV anchor Brendan McLaughlin commented that it could do potential damage to Valessa's defense.

CHAPTER 13
RATTLESNAKE ROMEO

Shortly after Adam's interview on television, he and Jon Whispel began their journey back to Tampa in a prison van. The van rumbled back through Texas, Louisiana, Mississippi, and Alabama. In all the hours Adam and Jon managed to communicate from a distance. Jon spread out on the back seat, the position he took in Mrs. Robinson's minivan, but this time Adam was separated from the driver by two transportation officers.

When Whispel shared his knowledge that Valessa had taken the blame for the murder, Adam shrugged, "I don't care."

The Florida signs on the border signaled they were closing in on their destination. The sound of wind and the roar of the motor that had lulled them quieted. The van stopped to let on another prisoner.

For Adam the trip got more interesting. An attractive young woman in a prison jumpsuit struggled up the step. She stumbled on the van due to her chains. She managed to get in the seat next to him, while transportation officers exchanged her paperwork. "This is Leanna Hayes. She broke parole from Tampa, Florida. Got caught in Knoxville," the transportation deputy from Tennessee said.

The prison van got underway again and merged into traffic. As the driver gained speed, the wind bounced off the van creating a whirring sound that usually put the passengers to sleep.

Adam smiled at the prisoner next to him. She didn't appear any happier to return to Tampa than he was. While the van rumbled onto the last leg of the journey, Adam asked his seatmate, "What have they got you for?"

Leanna looked down. "Cocaine."

"Your first arrest?" Adam asked.

"No, my second," Leanna answered looking at the handsome man.

"Do you know you're sitting next to a dangerous person?"

"No."

"I've been in all the headlines in Tampa and all the television news. I was even interviewed when I was in jail in Texas," Adam bragged.

"Why? What did you do?"

"I'm charged with first-degree murder for killing my girlfriend's mother. She was tryin' to break up my girlfriend and me."

"Did you kill her?"

"Sure. I sliced her up with a knife. I injected . . ." Adam stopped and looked back at his friend, Jon Whispel, who was laughing and putting his hand up to his mouth. He stopped when Adam looked at him and frowned.

"That's my friend. He handed me the knife. We're both charged with the first-degree murder." Adam said, frowning back at Whispel. He knew Jon well enough to realize his laugh was to get his attention.

"Didn't you see the headline, 'I Love Adam!' in the paper a couple of days ago?"

"A couple of days ago, I wasn't in Tampa."

"Well my girlfriend and I have been in the headlines since the beginning of July. You can call us 'the Romeo and Juliet of the 90s.' I killed her mother so we could be together."

Leanna Hayes listened to Adam Davis relate his claim to fame for an hour before she was dropped off at the Orient Point Jail.

A half hour later on, Thursday, July 16, Adam Davis and Jon Whispel arrived in Ybor City greeted by a gaggle of reporters and photographers that followed them to record the handcuffed pair from the Hillsborough Sheriff's Office in Ybor City. They took Jon Whispel to the Hillsborough jail on Orient Point Road, where Valessa was in solitary. Adam Davis had a shorter trip to the Morgan Street Jail.

Lieutenant Greg Brown announced to reporters, "They were very cooperative. They did what was asked of them. They wanted to get out of Texas. I don't think they had a fun time there."

Davis and Whispel were put into separate cars for the short journey. Lt. Brown explained, "Because of their notoriety, they will be kept apart and away from other inmates."

The two young men in chains and prison garb said nothing. Jon Whispel's eyebrow appeared to be healing, after having had his new piercing ripped out during his scuffle with the Texas sheriffs.

Friday, July 17, after a court hearing before Judge Walter Heinrich, Jon Whispel's attorney Stephen Crawford—a former state and federal prosecutor—described Adam Davis as "very charismatic" and his client as "a scared little kid" who may have slept through the killing. "It's too early to speculate about a plea deal in exchange for his testimony against Davis and Valessa. He simply helped dispose of the body."

"He wasn't asleep when it happened," Shirley Williams, the young brunette prosecutor, countered. "It's unlikely the State will need a plea bargain. Since his arrest, he has described how Robinson was killed."

Whispel and Davis appeared on video monitors. "Obviously you're in a lot of trouble," Judge Heinrich said, grimacing at the two accused.

The judge heard testimony from Assistant State Attorney Dean Tsourakis who stated that jail officials confiscated several letters. Adam Davis and Valessa were trying to communicate, despite his order they were to have no contact.

Judge Heinrich ordered that Whispel and Davis have no communication and threatened to put them in isolation and revoke telephone privileges if they didn't comply. He scheduled the arraignment of the three teens before Circuit Judge Cynthia Holloway for Monday, July 20, 1998.

Monday morning Judge Cynthia Holloway entered the court room at 8:30 A.M. Orange clad prisoners lined the walls on either side of the bench. There were few spectators in attendance today. The judge disposed of the petty thieves and parole violaters by setting future court dates.

At 9:15, the docket was cleared for the arraignment. Valessa entered with her Assistant Public Defender, Joseph Registrato. Mike Benito, the dynamic ex-prosecutor who had gained a reputation for being an even better defense attorney, represented Adam Davis. Jon Whispel appeared with an equally prominant defense attorney, Stephen Crawford.

As each of defendants took their place before the

judge to plead innocent, Adam Davis kept a silent communication going with Valessa. She mouthed, "I love you," before she left with her attorney.

Ten days later on Thursday, July 30, Jon Whispel appeared in court with a shaved head, along with his codefendant Adam Davis. Attorney Stephen Crawford, who had been Whispel's attorney until his family couldn't raise funds to retain him, asked that his previous client not be considered notorious and misinterpret his haircut. He explained, "Jon Whispel suffered hair loss from an iron deficiency and a nervous disorder."

Circuit Judge Cynthia Holloway appointed Brian Gonzalez to represent him. Whispel wiped away tears during the exchange. Apparently he didn't want to lose Stephen Crawford, who had described Whispel's involvement in the murder as "minor" during an earlier hearing. If he was crying for his mother who was newly divorced, suffering from breast cancer, and had just lost her house to foreclosure, only he would know. The last time he was at the family home, immediately after Vicki Robinson's murder, he left his mother nine dollars for phone calls he made and never told her good-bye.

Adam Davis's attorney Mike Bonito too left, as Davis's family could not afford him. The judge appointed Charles Traina.

Because Valessa had public defenders, Gonzalez and Traina would be paid through a government fund for defendants who couldn't afford attorneys. Public defenders couldn't represent all three due to conflict of interest for their client.

After Davis heard that Bonito had quit the case, he signed a request to retain him, and asked for more money from a family friend.

CHAPTER 14

VICKI'S LIGHT BURNS BRIGHT

Vicki Robinson's friends gathered on a sunny morning—October 11, 1998—to memorialize her existence with something positive for the future. The New Port Richey Stadium Golf League that Jim Englert, her fiancé, and Frank Seger belonged to organized the event as memorial to the woman who inspired their admiration. Before the eulogy, Frank Seger said, "As members of the golfing community, we wanted to do something immediately in memory of Vicki."

Only four months after Vicki Robinson's untimely death, fifty-six of her golf friends teed off at 8 A.M. at the Lansbrook Golf Club in Palm Harbor to establish the Vicki Robinson Foundation. "Our short-range goal is to provide an education fund for Vicki's other daughter, Michelle. Long-range, we hope money from this foundation will help other parents of troubled children," Frank Seger told reporters gathered for the event.

The game cost $100 per person, with the opportunity to win a car if a hole-in-one was scored. Raffles and auctions brought the total contribution up to $7,000.

The group cheered. There would be money to help mothers like Vicki. The happy occasion allowed her friends to share how much they missed her. She was the star even after death.

Whispers about Valessa's preoccupation with contacting Adam in jail passed from ear to ear. "The girl is pure evil," one woman said. A few who heard her nodded in agreement.

Vicki Robinson's friends and family united to keep Vicki Robinson's memory alive and not let her be forgotten in the lengthy court process. By the time most perpetrators arrive at sentencing, the reason they are in court is overshadowed by battles between attorneys. Even before any trial, hundreds of words reach the public about the disadvantages of the criminals.

Unlike other cases where the murder victim vanishes into oblivion and is replaced by the alleged murderers, Vicki Robinson took center stage in many reports of the crime due to her friends' willingness to talk about the situation publicly. The community refused to put her to rest and consumed every detail of her life like they would a celebrity. They had been jolted from a "it-can-never-happen-to-me" state of mind common to tragic events.

Golfers waiting to play answered eager reporters questions that enabled them to create a picture of Vicki's life for television and the print media.

Vicki was born October 17, 1948, the second of four children: two girls and two boys. She graduated from Eastern Michigan University and earned Master's credits at Michigan State University. A pretty blonde wearing white shorts and an Izod golf shirt added, "Vicki planned to become a teacher because she loved children. She married a Grand Rapids attorney like her father when she was young. The marriage ended with no children in the mid-1970s."

The woman next to her with bright red hair leaned

on her golf club pushed her dark glasses up and said, "Vicki relocated in Tampa, got a divorce, and met Charles Robinson, a veteran of Vietnam. They opened a real estate office together."

A tall gray-haired man stepped forward and wiped the sweat off his brow before he added, "They married in April 1980. I attended the wedding. Vicki was his third wife and almost immediately became his fourth. They had problems and separated after two months. They reconciled and their first daughter, Michelle, was born on December 20, 1981. Chuck was my friend and the kid was born on my birthday."

Reporters fled the pastoral scene of the golf course and examined public records to feed the hungry populace waiting for information. January 1982 contained a record of a divorce between Vicki and Charles Robinson. He kept their two-year-old Toyota Supra and the home in Town 'n' Country and agreed to $100 a month child support. She retained the 1977 Audi Fox and their home in Hastings, Michigan, as well as custody of Michelle.

In less than a year, the Robinsons reunited and married a second time on December 27, 1981. Valessa Lyn (her mother's middle name) was born March 31, 1983.

When Michelle was thirteen and Valessa eleven, the Robinsons divorced for a second time on September 13, 1994. Vicki kept the twelve-year-old Cadillac DeVille and Charles the old Audi, a Datsun truck, and a utility trailer. He assumed the responsibility for the $51,000 mortgage on their house in North Tampa and paid $800 a month in child support.

When Vicki and Chuck Robinson divorced, she was working in her daughter's Christian school, Seminole Presbyterian, and even drove the school bus to be near her children and get a tuition discount. Perhaps expecting to be hired as a teacher, she waited two years before leaving. Some parents of children attending

Seminole Presbyterian confided that Vicki had complained that she believed the school didn't want divorced women to teach.

Vicki's single admirers held her up to the community as the epitome of perfection. Most saw Valessa as the ring leader who had manipulated both her mother and the two men who murdered her. The special golf tournament organized to polish Vicki's image, which had been tarnished by news reports, only gave the media another chance to reveal her private life.

CHAPTER 15
REVELATIONS

The religious school on Habana Avenue serves students from kindergarten through twelfth grade where the students wear uniforms and attend chapel daily. Valessa's attendance until the seventh grade created her resurrection and her sister's too.

Valessa's teachers at Seminole Presbyterian School remember a solitary, friendless girl. Aura Jordan, her seventh grade science teacher, recalled that Valessa would sit in a corner by herself if teams were chosen by other students. Other teachers described a girl who shuffled along with her head down. Before she left the school, teachers and parents said that Valessa rebelled by embracing a "Goth" image and wearing black lipstick and nail polish.

John Dipple, her Bible teacher, recalled that she came to the vehement defense of anyone she perceived as being criticized, and defended them like their attorney. When he encountered her as a substitute at Sickles High School, they had a long talk about her reactions in Bible study. Valessa told him she felt badly about her experiences at Seminole Presbyterian. He thought things were going better for her at Sickles.

At Seminole Presbyterian, during a parent-teacher conference, he reflected that although Vicki was interested in Valessa's progress, she glazed over problems as if they didn't exist. She hoped they would go away on their own.

Teachers observed that Michelle was popular, played sports, and joined clubs. They saw Valessa as a loner with a beautiful voice who traded singing in the choir for heavy metal in a garage band. She gave up going to church, and started dating boys in the public school. They regarded her black nail polish and black lipstick as unmistakable signs of rebellion.

At fifteen Michelle was arrested and charged with burglary after she and a group of boys broke into a townhouse in northern Tampa. This fact gave some a reason to want to blame the victim, Vicki Robinson.

The press discovered that, upon learning his daughter was a struggling single mother making only $1,500 per month at the school, Vicki's father gave her an exquisite four-bedroom house in Carrollwood as part of her inheritance. The gray stucco Mediterranean-style home with a red-tile roof, pool, and lanai was valued at $186,000 and contributed to Vicki's image of being a wealthy, successful businesswoman.

CHAPTER 16

A MOTHER'S WISH

On Friday, October 16, 1998, during a hearing dedicated to Adam's desire to send Valessa letters in jail, Mike Benito asked Judge Cynthia Holloway to withdraw Judge Heinrich's order forbidding contact between the two.

"None of their communications could be private," the attractive judge responded while reviewing some handwritten notes before her.

"He knows they'll be monitored, but he still wants to write and talk to her," Mike Benito said.

Valessa, on one end of the jury box, gazed at her former lover. Instead of mouthing "I love you" like she had done on previous occasions, she cried. He smiled and then hung his head.

Judge Holloway glanced from one prisoner to the other, and said, "I'll rescind the order."

Adam appeared triumphant, sat up and grinned at his attorney.

Attorney Rick Escobar, Valessa's court appointed guardian frowned. "There would be no benefit for

Valessa. I know her family feels as I do. That means no letters or phone calls to people on the outside who could hook them up together."

"He wants to tell her he loves her," Mike Benito pleaded.

"I think Valessa's listening for the first time," Escobar said. "She has agreed with my recommendation that there be no contact."

No one reminded Valessa that she met Adam a year before, or that it was the eve of her mother's fiftieth birthday. If Vicki's spirit was in the courtroom, only Valessa could feel it. Public Defender Joe Registrato, Rick Escobar, and Deputy Robert Emery separated her from Adam Davis, who talked seriously to Mike Benito before leaving the courtroom.

Adam "Rattlesnake" Davis was criticized in many articles for his relationship to Jon Whispel. Jon's aunt Cheryl Van Nuil said, "He (Jon) was a fun lovin' kid who loved his family. Things changed when he quit school and fell in with Davis. He's a follower, not a leader. He's gone downhill in the year since he's known Adam. Jon got mixed up with the wrong people and changed 180 degrees." Whispel's friends and family refused to believe Whispel could murder. Indirectly, they exposed a different picture of Adam than the romantic guy his attorney portrayed in the hearing.

Shana Clark, Adam's old girlfriend, said of Whispel, "I could not believe he would ever do this. He would do anything for Adam, but not to this extent," she said when questioned about Vicki Robinson's murder.

Friends of Valessa described the couple's relationship as one of leader and follower. Jon Whispel said in a deposition, "If Adam asked her to jump, she'd say how high. She wouldn't talk back to him, but when she said, 'I love you,' she meant it."

CHAPTER 17
THE SKULL

Jon Whispel spilled his guts again at the Hillsborough county jail with his lawyers present on October 24th. The cell crammed to capacity afforded privacy, but the prisoner's voice echoed beyond its four walls. "It should never have happened." He pulled his orange prison sleeve over the skull tattoo self-consciously. "Someday I want it erased."

If it reminded him that it was bought with the murdered woman's ATM card, he didn't say so. His attorneys didn't ask why he chose a skull.

"If I get a chance, I'm going to have it removed," Jon Whispel said. "I don't want the memories of it." The tattooed skull was the evident reminder of what Vicki Robinson's beautiful face had become in the days after June 27, and Whispel lived with the image.

He went on to admit that although he came from what he described as a middle class family, who took him to Disney World as a child, he started to smoke pot as a junior in Jefferson High School. His father, an accountant, and his mother, a clerical worker, split up when he was seventeen—leaving him shattered and angry. He graduated to drugs like crank, crack, and Ecstasy, and used cocaine regularly. Even their dog, Polly, didn't mean anything. He attended "trip parties" and skipped school, until he ultimately quit for good. "It was that or getting kicked out," he added. He met Davis and thought he was tough since some called him "Rattlesnake," and he bounced from one house to another. He had an arrest record. They stole a van and tried to get to Arizona, where Adam had friends, and were able to escape prosecution by abandoning the vehicle in Tallahassee. The owner didn't press charges when police caught them. Valessa became Adam's girlfriend soon there after. When Davis and Whispel were caught in an abandoned house with a stun gun and a knife, it was his first arrest.

Whispel began relating that he tagged along with Valessa and Adam as Mrs. Robinson ran errands in the minivan in the afternoon and she bought them an early dinner at Burger King. He digressed to add Mrs. Robinson never swore, wore a gold crucifix around her neck, and always treated him with respect. She even dropped him off at his job sometimes so he wouldn't be late.

After spending a some time at Valessa's "big expensive home," he and Adam headed for Denny's on bicycles. Valessa rode her bicycle to meet them after Adam called her and asked Vicki if Valessa could join them.

Whispel's description of events at Denny's when the three shared a booth focused on taking LSD. They ordered orange juice to peak up the effects of the LSD they had divided among them. "We were tripping and everything. I got hungry and concentrated on the sample platter I ordered." He explained they were talking about enhancing their high in Valessa's bedroom under her black lights when he heard Valessa say out of nowhere, "Let's kill my mom." Adam agreed immediately. Whispel said, "'You're kidding, right?' The drugs we were taking were nothing new. Part of my mind knew it might be true. Davis talked about getting heroin to "'do it that way.'"

They rode their bikes back to Valessa's house and pushed her mother's van out of the garage quietly so the motor wouldn't wake her. Then Adam used the van to look for heroin. He had no luck finding any, but did buy a syringe that cost two dollars. Despite the talk of murder, Whispel convinced himself that the syringe would be used to shoot up cocaine.

He claimed, to those listening, that there was no conversation on the way back to Valessa's house. They entered Valessa's bedroom, where he became fascinated with the glow of his white shirt under the black light.

Davis talked about putting bleach into the syringe and told Valessa to get some. He filled the syringe from a drinking glass she provided. "That's when I knew he was serious," Whispel said. Adam filled the syringe and pumped it until the tip squirted. "At this point, I was scared to do anything. If me and Valessa would have run, done anything, he would have killed us. Emotionally, I was torn apart. Like, what do I do?"

Jon Whispel's voice was raspy and cracked with tension. "Davis and Valessa left the room and returned in less than two minutes and hid the syringe in the closet. They left again and entered Valessa's mother's bedroom and ran back to Valessa's when her mother woke up. In minutes, Mrs. Robinson tapped on Valessa's bedroom door and entered wearing her peach nightgown and ordered Valessa to grab her sleeping bag and come with her. 'Now!,' she yelled when Valessa ignored her."

Whispel claimed that he never left Valessa's bedroom. He professed to seeing what was happening to Vicki Robinson in her kitchen from his vantage point on Valessa's bed. Davis held her in a chokehold and sent Valessa to get the injection of bleach. She retrieved the syringe from the closet and held her mother's legs down while Davis used it. They both returned to the bedroom when they heard her mother moan. Adam said, "The bitch won't die." Whispel provided a knife and Adam and Valessa returned to finish her off. Valessa left Adam and her mother in the kitchen and sat next to Jon. They heard Vicki again gasp for breath. When Adam joined Jon and Valessa, she suggested he wash her mother's blood off his hands, literally.

He remembered talking to Adam after he returned from Texas and telling him that Valessa said she was going to take the blame. Adam said, "I don't care."

Mike Benito, Adam's attorney, said, "I think the entire truth as to what exactly happened that night and who participated and to what extent will eventually come out. Anything that a person in Whispel's position would say at this time would be viewed as self-serving."

Valessa's attorney, Joe Registrato, wasn't impressed either. "I'm not surprised that young Mr. Whispel is pointing the finger at anybody he can. He's facing a death penalty."

CHAPTER 18
THE JESTER

Adam Davis didn't apologize for spending his share of Vicki Robinson's $600 on a Jester tattoo for his arm. But he was deadly serious when he wrote a letter responding to a demand for payment notice from his attorney, Mike Benito. He dated the letter November 16, 1998, and signed it Adam William Davis.

Davis argued that Benito should have taken "all necessary precautions" to ensure payment before filing a notice of appearance in Davis's case. Because the charges were so serious—the most serious possible—and because the defendant's very life was at stake, Davis asserted that Benito's filing to withdraw the case over money was irresponsible and selfish. Davis also claimed that his case had attracted enormous publicity, and that his case didn't need any more "bad press."

November 20, 1998: Adam Davis addressed a legal form to Honorable Judge Cynthia Holloway at the courthouse in Tampa. In his request to keep Mike Benito as his attorney, he claimed that a family friend had paid 60 percent of Mike Benito's fee. "I hope one or two of my

out-of-town family members will contribute to the re-
mainder. I ask Honorable Judge Holloway to postpone
Mr. Benito's motion to withdraw from my case. We're
extremely close on the fee. If I lose Mike Benito as my
attorney, it will jeopardize my case. The defense council
has known personally the third party providing funding
for six years."

Day after day, he paced the length of his tiny cell,
until he realized his letters to the judge weren't helping
and he had to accept Rick Terrawa an attorney the state
would provide.

He sat bent forward on his cot and held his head,
wishing the newspapers didn't make him look so bad.
Davis's skirmishes with the law were obvious, but what
rat fink confided that he inhaled freon from air condi-
tioners when drugs were unavailable? Surely not Jon.

On Monday, November 24, Jon Whispel appeared in
Hillsborough County Courthouse to complain that his
attorney, Brian Gonzalez, an ex-local football hero, hadn't
been helpful in obtaining documents. Whispel asked
for another attorney.

Judge Cynthia Holloway informed him he would have
to represent himself if Gonzalez was removed. Whispel's
mouth dropped open in surprise. "I'll keep him," he
said.

CHAPTER 19
THE INTOXICATION DEFENSE

Only weeks before St. Patrick's Day, 1999, a day when alcohol is consumed in dedication to the Irish, the murder of Vicki Robinson brought legislators together in Tallahassee to review the Voluntary Intoxication Defense. It became evident from the numerous news stories that the three teens who were involved in the murder of Vicki Robinson all claimed to be so high on LSD that they weren't aware of what they were doing.

Intoxication can be used as a defense in crimes that require prosecutors prove intent, such as murder, burglary, and assault. To prove first-degree murder and send someone to the electric chair, prosecutors must prove that the defendant planned and intended to murder. Jurors can choose to convict on a lesser charge if alcohol or drugs played a part in the accused's actions. A defendant can be considered too drunk or stoned to prove intent.

Two local legislators, Republican Representatives Chris Hart and Tom Lee, reacted to the horrified community's fear that the teens could get light sentences at trial. "When I first heard about the issue, frankly, I was appalled," Hart said.

Many in the legislature agreed, and the House Crime and Punishment Committee and the Senate Criminal Justice Committee signed off. The Senate version would make penalties for crimes against family members more serious.

Charlie Bronson, from Indian Harbor Beach, reminded his fellow legislators, "It could be used for drunk drivers who killed someone." It was in honor of Vicki Robinson or in reaction to Buddy Jacobs, the lobbyist for the Florida Prosecuting Attorneys' Association who bellowed, "It's nonsensical. What happens is that everybody knows he or she is guilty and you've got them dead to rights and then they say, 'Gosh, I was drunk so I shouldn't pay the same consequences or do the time.'"

Paul Fermani, the Senior Assistant Public Defender of Pasco County, didn't get a chance to present his position. He reminded reporters that the law was there to make a distinction between "someone that shoots in a cold calculating manner or one who drinks two six-packs, gets mad, and shoots his wife."

Mike Benito, who no longer represented Adam Davis at this time, noted that there was a big distinction between first- and second-degree murder. He attributed it to what was going on in the mind of the defendant at the time of the crime. "How can intoxication not play a part in it?"

Benito and Bernie McCabe, Pinellas County's State Attorney, stated that intoxication was necessary as a defense but that juries knew it was a flimsy one.

Also in the sunny state of Florida, fifteen-year-old Ronny Zamora and his lawyer Ellis Rubin used Twinkies and television-induced catatonia as defenses in Zamora's 1977 trial for the murder of his neighbor. The jury convicted Zamora of murder, burglary, and unlawful posession of a firearm. That didn't stop Rubin from using the

Voluntary Intoxification Defense later in his career for clients who commited crimes under the influence of Prozac.

On April 20, 1999, two students killed a teacher and twelve students at Columbine High School in Littleton, Colorado. Ellis Rubin's eighteen-year-old Florida client, Michael Ian Campbell, had threatened "to finish what they began." Soon thereafter, Campbell's school had to close for two days, and he faced five years in jail and a $250,000 fine if convicted of transmitting threatening information over the Internet, a felony. Rubin claimed he was intoxicated by the Internet only a month after the Tallahassee gathering before legislators.

Legislators cannot deny attorneys the right to use this dubious defense. In the Bible, Lot's daughters used his intoxication as a reason for Lot's having committed incest, impregnating them. The only state that currently doesn't have a Voluntary Intoxification Defense is Montana, which dropped the law in 1996.

CHAPTER 20

THE SHADOW PAL

On June 29, 1999, Jon Whispel's attorneys managed to help him get a plea agreement with prosecutors. The attorneys he had tried to dismiss saved his life by cutting a deal whereby Whispel would testify against his friends Adam Davis and Valessa Robinson.

"He didn't minimize his role in Vicki Robinson's death in the slightest bit," Brian Gonzalez said. "He's certainly not thrilled to be getting out of jail at forty years old at best."

Brian Donerly, Whispel's second court-appointed attorney added, "He's realistic enough to realize it's the best alternative."

Rick Terrana, Adam's court-appointed attorney, said, "He doesn't expect the jury will consider Whispel's testimony any differently than they would that of any other jailhouse snitch who sold his soul to save his life. Desperate people do desperate things. The guy just talked his way out of the electric chair."

* * *

A week later, on Thursday, July 8, 1999, Davis requested to be in the courtroom to observe Whispel's deposition before Judge Holloway.

Whispel's attorney Brian Gonzalez fought for his client. "They have to get an order from the 2nd District Court of Appeals, before my client would sit in a court with him. It's an attempt to intimidate."

Davis would not be allowed to observe the proceedings, as per the order of Judge Holloway. Rick Terrana, Davis's attorney, complained, "My client's got no effect on this guy. He's a monster in his own right."

Terrana tried to convince the court that local publicity would prejudice the community against his client, and researched the number of stories each local TV station had done on the case. Channel 9 responded that they had done 147 news stories on Valessa Robinson, 235 on Vicki Robinson, and 150 on Adam Davis. WFLA had broadcast 100 stories on the case, only a quarter of what WTVT had aired. He added that Texas stations had provided the car chase footage and interviews to several national talk shows.

Bubba the Love Sponge, a favorite disk jockey on Tampa station WXTB, had talked to Adam on the air while he was cruising Ybor City just after the murder, and kept replaying the tape. Terrana criticized, "Bubba never misses a chance to tell about it. The references are uncountable."

Rick Terrana, the attorney whom Davis fought against, filed fifty-two motions on his behalf before the motion to change venue was denied.

CHAPTER 21

TRIAL FOR ADAM DAVIS

November 3, 1999

The wooden benches set into the walls outside the Hillsborough courtroom on the third floor were filled with little groups talking quietly. Three women huddled together whispering, appearing wary of strangers. After a few minutes a blond woman who was standing near the group got shut out of the conversation. A female news reporter pounced and asked, "Are you related to Adam Davis?"

"Yes," the blond woman said. "I'm his father's sister, Carol Elliot. My brother Kenny died January 6, 1994. The kid's life has been hell since then." She pointed at a tired looking woman with long, dark, wavy hair. "This is Adam's natural mother." Another woman didn't wait to be introduced. "I'm Donna Davis, his adopted mother, but I'm the one who took care of him," she said loudly. Adam's mother looked down.

Adam's two mothers looked similar in age and appearance, with long dark hair, and pinched desperation on their faces. Their casual sweaters and slacks set them apart from the formal dress of Vicki's friends and relatives and members of the press and legal profession. His father's sister, an older woman with bleached blond hair, stood above them and explained that she had lived in Tampa and, like Valessa's family, had attended the Idlewild Baptist Church.

"The records described Adam as homeless," said the reporter, jotting notes in her legal pad.

"That's not true. He was eighteen before he was on the streets!" his stepmother, Donna Davis, said.

"He didn't have any problems until the State of Florida interfered," his birth mother offered. "He got in a little trouble and . . ."

The stepmother frowned. Adam's mother stopped talking.

The reporter looked up at the tall blonde, who appeared to be in her late fifties, and said, "I'd be interested in how that happened."

Carol Elliot said, "He didn't have a chance after his father was killed. My second brother, Niel, died in Tampa, too, in February of '82. We're originally from Iowa and should have stayed there."

Donna Davis refused to say any more about her stepson's past. After an awkward pause, the group of observers who had been silently listening returned to their seats and prepared for the trial to resume.

Judge Cynthia Holloway was a brunette like both of Adam's mothers, but with fuller hair. The sides were tied in a knot on the top. Her makeup and pleasant face made her appear younger than one would expect a judge to be. Her efforts to keep jury selection private, had failed. The *St. Petersburg Times* got a court order to keep them public. It took only two days to interview one hundred possible jurors and choose six men and six women, as well as one alternate, a younger male.

The prosecutors began the trial with Vicki's neighbors as witnesses. One saw her van before dawn, but couldn't see who was driving. The couple who took her dog, Lady, into their garage described the angst the discovery of Vicki's body had caused. They filled in the time before the state's main event.

After the break, the prosecution's star witness, Jon Whispel, was sworn in. The sandy-haired friend of Adam Davis looked toward him through stylish, small, wire-rimmed glasses that were the last vestige of his private life. He opted to wear orange prison garb. On June 29, 1999, a year and two days after Vicki's death and five months before the trial, Whispel agreed to a plea bargain. For his testimony against Davis and Robinson, he would receive a twenty-five year sentence. Now, Whispel focused on Assistant Prosecutor Pam Bondi.

Adam stared at his friend over his darker rims dressed in a black suit and tie like a seminary student. Both had their eyebrow piercings removed. They both sported short prison haircuts. Jon avoided eye contact.

Bondi stood at the lectern, wearing a dark suit and her hair tied up in a bun. To her right, facing the jury, was a big screen that would be used to present exhibits pertinent to the case. "Did you draw police a map to find Mrs. Robinson's body?"

"Yes."

"Did you ever drive the van?"

"Yes."

"Did you use Mrs. Robinson's credit cards?"

"No."

"Do you recognize the State's exhibit six?"

Jon Whispel twisted to his left and looked at the screen.

"It's Mrs. Robinson's body."

Under a mass of palmetto brush, a garbage can was barely visible. The sight elicited groaning sounds from the courtroom.

"And that?" Pam Bondi asked immediately.

"The hole we started to dig."

"We'll come back to this. Describe what we're seeing now."

"It's the laundry room in Mrs. Robinson's house."

The state's clear pictures of Vicki Robinson's house flashed one after another. Exhibit ten, the sliding glass doors to the pool. Exhibit eleven, the modern kitchen with white tile like the laundry room appeared. Exhibit fourteen focused on that floor.

"That's where Adam had Mrs. Robinson by the neck," Jon Whispel said.

The state's exhibit twenty, the living room, didn't elicit any comment. The jury and everyone in the courtroom could witness the opulence of the arched windows and a grand entrance. The mauve and white color scheme and lavish furnishings also included heart-shaped pillows. The same colors continued in every room. It looked like a builder-decorated model home.

Views of exhibits thirty-six through forty-two in the garage displayed the State's evidence of the tools and a garbage can. The prosecutor used a laser pointer as she submitted exhibits. She pointed to an empty space.

"The space held an identical can we used for the body," Whispel said.

Exhibit forty-three showed inside the back of Vicki Robinson's van. "The suitcase on the right?"

"Valessa's bag. My bag. Fireworks . . ." Jon Whispel responded.

"Exhibit forty-four. The back seat," Miss Bondi announced.

"The cooler," Whispel responded when the red light landed on that item in the photo.

"Exhibit forty-five."

"A hoe and shovel," Whispel answered.

"What is that?" Attorney Bondi asked.

"Crystal Light or Meth," Jon Whispel said as the bright red light landed on a plastic baggy.

Exhibit forty-seven focused on a newspaper described by Jon Whispel as coming from a vending machine they bought to read about Vicki Robinson's disappearance.

Jon Whispel identified exhibit fifty-three, a metal gate. "It's before a path leading to the area where we left Mrs. Robinson's body."

"Does it have a lock?" the prosecutor asked.

"We snapped it," Jon Whispel answered.

The prosecution then returned to pictures of Vicki Robinson's beautiful bedroom, containing a high poster bed and expensive antique furniture.

"Valessa's mother was asleep in her bedroom when we returned without finding heroin," Jon Whispel said. "Adam, Valessa, and me sat at Denny's Restaurant in Carrollwood drinking orange juice, doing LSD. We talked about Mrs. Robinson's intention to separate Adam and Valessa. She giggled and suggested we kill her mother. Adam came up with the idea that injecting an air bubble would kill Valessa's mother without being discovered. Heroin would make her sleep during the process."

"Do you see the person who killed Vicki Robinson in this courtroom?" the tall, pretty blond prosecutor asked.

"Yes, right there, Adam." Jon Whispel pointed in his friend's direction.

"What is he wearing?" Assistant State Attorney Pam Bondi asked.

"A black suit," Jon said after looking directly at Adam.

"Objection! Were you impaired by LSD?" asked Defense Attorney Rick Terrana, jumping to his feet. His dark, short hair sprinkled with white fluttered slightly. "Did Mr. Davis consume more?"

"He had one-and-a-half cubes. I shared a half with Valessa."

Attorney Rick Terrana sprinted to the lectern and the pretty blond prosecutor stepped aside. "What you said is a total lie. Didn't you say you saw the murder? You were charged with first-degree murder? You entered a plea agreement to avoid a death sentence. Your twenty-five year plea is a lot better than a death sentence. The State allowed you to plea to five years grand theft auto and twenty-five for murder in the second degree to run concurrently."

"Correct," Whispel answered, looking down.

Terrana returned to the table and sat next to fellow attorney Charles Traina, who—with longer hair and mustache—appeared to be the younger of the two. Adam Davis was expressionless as he moved his head closer to listen to his attorneys.

With very little prompting, Jon Whispel returned to his testimony describing using LSD with Adam Davis and Valessa Robinson in Denny's restaurant. "We drank orange juice and talked about Valessa's mom wanting to send her away. Valessa giggled and repeated that we should kill her."

Jon Whispel's voice lowered. "At first we thought she was kidding. Adam suggested we inject her with heroin and kill her with an air bubble. We tried to think of where to get heroin and remembered a party."

He faced the jury. "We spent a few hours trying to score heroin, and failing, we returned to Valessa's home with a syringe that Adam filled with bleach from the laundry room. We sat in Valessa's bedroom smoking cigarettes, planning her mother's murder. She was sleeping when we entered her bedroom, but she got up and went into the kitchen in her nightgown. Adam grabbed her in a sleeper hold from behind. She tried to get away. In a chokehold, he injected the bleach into her neck." Whispel held up his arms, imitating the struggle. "I returned to Valessa's bedroom and put my head in my hands and listened to the screaming."

"Adam entered the room and said, 'The bitch won't die.'"

Jon Whispel coolly explained how he had provided a knife and how Adam had returned to the kitchen and used it to stab Valessa's mother, while Valessa sat on her legs.

"Davis came in holding the knife in his bloody hands," Whispel described. "Adam had blood on his hands and Valessa said, 'Babe, you need to go in the bathroom and wash your hands.' Again we heard Valessa's mother cry out. Adam returned to the kitchen to finish her off and then returned to Valessa's bedroom and we smoked cigarettes as we waited for her to die."

"Did you notice blood on Valessa?"

"No."

"You did on Davis?"

"Yes."

"Did Valessa go to the bathroom with Adam?"

"I didn't notice," Jon Whispel answered.

"In your deposition—middle of page twelve taken under oath on August 12th this year—"

"Objection," Rick Terrana said.

Adam's attorneys asked to approach the bench. Rick Terrana and Charles Traina were joined by both Pam Bondi and Shirley Williams. After a short conference, Pam Bondi continued.

"For the purpose of continuity, I'll read the question and your answer. About Adam's blood: Valessa suggested he go to the bathroom to wash his hands. Did Valessa go? No, she was sitting right next to me. She did not go with him to wash her hands too."

"Objection. Is it fair to say throughout the entire evening you were suffering the effects of LSD; focusing, seeing things in front of your eyes, difficulty to concentrate?" Adam's defense attorney continued. "You don't know all the details."

"I had a good picture of who did kill her," Whispel said.

"Objection."

The judge said, "Don't argue in front of the jury."

Jon Whispel continued, "We loaded Vicki Robinson's body into a garbage can we found in the garage and cleaned up the blood in the kitchen with scrub brushes, bleach, and towels. As we put the garbage can in the van, Mrs. Robinson's dog, Lady, cowered in the corner of the garage and started growling."

Attorney Rick Terrana addressed Jon Whispel. "You didn't run out or scream. You saw the blood on Davis's hands. Lots of blood. You heard Valessa say, 'Let's kill mom.' You didn't run."

"No, sir."

"Is it fair to say, when asked in your deposition about the demeanor of Adam Davis, you answered, 'I wasn't paying attention to him.'? Were you impaired by LSD? Were you personally aware of Adam's use of heroin?"

"Yes."

"On the ride to Valessa's house, you didn't hear a plan? You went to get heroin. You didn't go into the party going on and hear what Adam Davis told people he wanted to use it for? You didn't buy the syringe? When Adam didn't get heroin, you asked for your money back?" The attorney quoted from Whispel's deposition.

"Yes."

Adam's attorney questioned Whispel at length about their drug use. It was obvious that he wanted to disqualify Jon Whispel as a witness who had been impaired and was not competent to testify against anyone.

Prosecutor Bondi excused Jon Whispel, and introduced the police interview with Adam Davis to the bench. Judge Holloway asked the defense, "Any objections?"

"No, Your Honor," Adam's attorney answered.

"For the purpose of form. Did he sign? You sign?" Judge Holloway looked down at the blond prosecutor.

"Yes."

The judge again asked the defense, "Any objections?"

She began to read the multiple pages after hearing the defense reply "No."

"Miranda?" the judge inquired.

"I explained that before," Assistant Prosecutor Bondi said.

"Did Davis sign? Did you?"

"Yes."

"Did he describe where the body was? Provide a map?"

"Yes."

"Did Davis tell you on tape how he killed Mrs. Robinson? Cleaned up afterwards?"

Before putting the document into evidence Judge Holloway asked again if the defense had any objections.

"No."

Shirley Williams stepped up to the lectern to question a tall, balding, bespectacled man wearing a gray suit. He took the oath and sat down. "I'm Detective Jim Iverson with the Hillsborough Sheriff's Department. I became involved the afternoon on Monday, June 29, when a Missing Persons form was filed on Vicki Robinson."

Attorney Williams asked, "Did the Hillsborough Sheriff's Office get a call on June 27th regarding Vicki Robinson's homicide?"

"As part of a Missing Persons alert, it's a given. A teletype on June 29 referred to Vicki Robinson," the officer answered.

"Did you go to her home?"

"Yes. No one was home."

"At the house did you observe any foul play?"

"No." The detective looked down.

"That first day did you talk to anyone?" Williams asked.

"Yes. We went to Mr. Whispel's house and talked to his mother. Our investigations found that Vicki Robinson's ATM card was used on the morning of the twenty-seventh," Detective Iverson said directly to the jury.

"Where?" Shirley Williams asked.

"A local convenience store. We investigated the use of the card and contacted Linda Sales from the bank. The card was used at several locations: Ybor City and Home Depot on Dale Mabry where we were able to obtain videotapes of Adam Davis, Valessa Robinson, and Jon Whispel."

"Put on the video at Best Buy with Valessa," Attorney Williams asked the deputy running the camera.

"They took turns pushing Valessa in a wheelchair at Best Buy."

Everyone in the courtroom could see the three playfully fooling around like teens at an amusement park, tipping and twirling the chair while Valessa laughed happily. The behavior of the three young people preparing to dispose of Valessa's murdered mother suggested a celebration more than a dirge.

Vicki's family watched, visibly traumatized. They reached out to each other for comfort. Their pain radiated throughout the courtroom.

All of Vicki Robinson's family and friends were dressed in elegant black like they had worn to the funeral. Vicki's mother's graying hair was well-groomed, despite her obvious inner turmoil. She grabbed her husband's arm tightly as her body shook.

The fifteen-year-old's actions on the screen displayed thoughtless pleasure. The court emitted hushed, shocked sounds. Some coughed. It was possible to hear people draw in their breath. A few covered their open mouths with their hands to talk to the people next to them.

Whispel and Davis appeared on the big screen, facing a store clerk. Valessa was not seen.

"Which store is that?" Shirley Williams asked.

"They're at Home Depot," the detective answered.

Their purchases of shovels, cement, and garbage bags were captured by the store security camera as they paid for items with Vicki Robinson's credit card.

Pam Bondi talked to Shirley Williams, then turned and addressed the judge. "We would like to interrupt Detective Iverson's testimony to present Sheriff Bruce Wilson from Texas. His testimony will be out of order due to conflicting travel arrangements," she said.

Pam Bondi returned to the lectern again to question him, and the court settled down to listen.

"I'm sixteen years with the sheriff's office and have thirty-two years in law enforcement," Bruce Wilson said after taking the witness chair. He was a portly man wearing a gray suit. The top of his forehead gleamed stark white compared to the rest of his ruddy face indicating he often wore a hat.

"You became aware of this case after June 28, 1998?"

"There was a Missing Persons bulletin on the teletype that morning. On July 2, 1998, I contacted the Hillsborough Sheriff's Office because of a credit card used in the adjoining town. I sent an officer to look for a Florida vehicle on the interstate. I told him I was going farther ahead on the interstate. One of my officers, Larry Jackson, spotted a green Nissan minivan."

"Based on the description did you see the van?" Pam Bondi asked.

"I spotted the Florida tag and tried to stop the vehicle with overhead lights." The officer glanced toward the jury.

"Did they run another car off the road?" the attractive blond prosecutor asked looking down at her notes.

"Yes, with a man, woman, and child inside. The van picked up speed, from eighty to one hundred miles an hour. I radioed ahead that they wouldn't stop. We would draw close and they didn't even slow down. The deputy shot the right rear and then the left. They went through a barrier cable to an access road going toward Stockton. We went around and shot out front two tires."

"Judge, if you have no objections, the State would like to show State's exhibit 101, a video taken on July 2, 1998 at 11:38 A.M. The video is mounted on the sheriff's cars."

After a conference before the bench, the video in question came up on the big screen before the jury.

A dirt side road and a two-lane highway came on the screen before the van came into view. As the sheriff's car drew closer the van moved away forcing other cars off the road. The van entered the left lane to pass a big wheeler. A road sign flashed by and a police car came into view. A trooper went to next exit, while the sheriff's car with the video went under the overpass. From that perspective, a long expanse of road appeared, including a red truck and a distant rail road crossing. The green van, now wobbling on flat tires, stopped on the left, just short of the overpass.

Next a video camera mounted on the sheriff's car (or another handheld one) caught Jon Whispel lying in the road, and Valessa lying close by, prone on her stomach.

"Who was driving?" Pam Bondi asked.

"Adam Davis," Sheriff Bruce Wilson responded.

On the television screen the date 7/2/98 appeared again, as well as the time: 11:46.36 A.M. The entire harrowing scene took less than ten minutes, proof of the speed of the vehicles and the expert marksmanship of the officers.

The crowded courtroom relived the intensely emotional experience. Police said Valessa described the experience as "being in a movie."

Three officers entered the scene next to the overpass; one wearing a T-shirt and cap, another in a white shirt and cowboy-styled sheriff's hat, and a third wearing a Western hat (who appeared to be the man sitting in the witness chair). He directed his officers to put each of the teens in separate patrol cars.

Pam Bondi brought the court's attention back to the witness. "Sheriff Wilson, do you have independent knowledge of what happened in Tampa?"

"No," Officer Wilson responded.

"No further questions, but you will remain under oath," Pam Bondi said.

The judge looked at the clock. "We'll recess for lunch. Court will resume at 1:00 P.M."

The bailiff entered. "All rise."

Judge Cynthia Holloway took her place on the bench.

Adam's two male defense attorneys and the female prosecution team held an animated discussion with the judge not privy to the court. Shirley Williams called Detective Iverson. He resumed his seat in the witness chair and his testimony continued after a few minutes of questioning by the younger defense attorney, Charles Traina.

"Did you tape the entire segment of Adam Davis's testimony after reading him his Miranda?"

"Yes," Lt. Iverson answered.

Shirley Williams, the brunette prosecutor announced, "Adam Davis with Detective Jim Iverson, on tape at Fort Stockton, Texas."

Her words were repeated in print on the screen dated 98-05-03-2:31 P.M. The detective's voice said, "Go back to June 26."

Vicki Robinson and
her daughter, Valessa.

Vicki and her fiancé,
Jim Englert, before taking
a romantic cruise.

Vicki Robinson's house in the exclusive Carrollwood area of Tampa. *(Author photo)*

When Vicki and Valessa disappeared, Detective James Iverson was put in charge of the case. *(Photo courtesy of the Hillsborough Sheriff's Department)*

(Left to right) Michael Hurley, Jorge Fernandez, James Iverson, Captain John Marsicano, and John King, of the Central Bureau of Investigations. *(Photo courtesy of the Hillsborough Sheriff's Department)*

Once Detective Iverson obtained a search warrant, officers entered Vicki Robinson's house through the garage. *(Photo courtesy of the Hillsborough Sheriff's Department)*

The kitchen showed no visible evidence of the murder
that occurred there.
(Photo courtesy of the Hillsborough Sheriff's Department)

Robinson's living room appeared immaculate and undisturbed.
(Photo courtesy of the Hillsborough Sheriff's Department)

Vicki's bed was found unmade, which alarmed Englert
because she was a meticulous housekeeper.
(Photo courtesy of the Hillsborough Sheriff's Department)

Valessa's bedroom.
(Photo courtesy of the Hillsborough Sheriff's Department)

An advertisement for body piercing was found on Valessa's table.
(Photo courtesy of the Hillsborough Sheriff's Department)

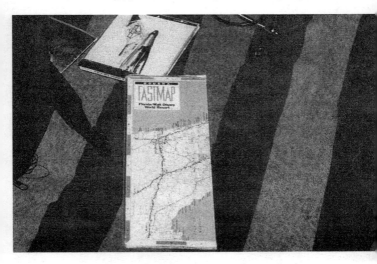

Detectives found a map on Valessa's bed.
(Photo courtesy of the Hillsborough Sheriff's Department)

Valessa's garbage can contained empty beer cans and cigarette boxes. *(Photo courtesy of the Hillsborough Sheriff's Department)*

John Whispel's house. *(Author photo)*

Detective Jorge Fernandez searched for Robinson's body in the vast area behind Whispel's house. *(Author photo)*

Searching for a body, police flew over the shallow lake near Robinson's home.
(Photo courtesy of the Hillsborough Sheriff's Department)

Valessa, Davis, and Whispel planned to dump Robinson's body in this canal behind Whispel's house.
(Photo courtesy of the Hillsborough Sheriff's Department)

At this Home Depot, Adam and John bought cement to weigh down the body in the canal. *(Author photo)*

Valessa, Davis, and Whispel were captured in Texas by Sheriff Bruce Wilson. *(Photo courtesy of Pecos County Sheriff's Department)*

Vicki Robinson's van after the shootout.
(Photo courtesy of Pecos County Sheriff's Department)

John Whispel used this ID and Social Security card to rent hotel rooms. *(Photo courtesy of the Hillsborough Sheriff's Department)*

Vicki Robinson's credit cards were in Adam Davis's possession. *(Photo courtesy of the Hillsborough Sheriff's Department)*

Detectives gathered at the double gates near Whispel's house
one week after Vicki was reported missing.
(Photo courtesy of the Hillsborough Sheriff's Department)

This plastic garbage bag contained the bloody towels
used to clean up after the murder.
(Photo courtesy of the Hillsborough Sheriff's Department)

The green plastic garbage can containing Robinson's body
was concealed by dry palm leaves.
(Photo courtesy of the Hillsborough Sheriff's Department)

When the medical examiner opened the can, Robinson's foot was
clearly visible. *(Photo courtesy of the Hillsborough Sheriff's Department)*

Pam Bondi was the assistant public prosecutor for the case. *(Photo courtesy of Hillsborough County State Attorney's Office)*

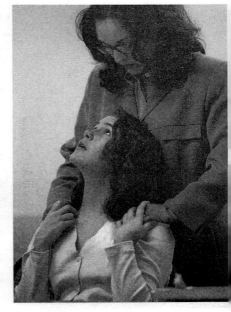

Valessa's assistant public defender, Dee Ann Athan, comforts her client. *(Photo courtesy of The Tampa Tribune)*

Athan attempted to discredit the testimony of Whispel and Davis.
(Photo courtesy of The Tampa Tribune)

Adam Davis listening
to his recorded
statement at trial.
*(Photo courtesy of
The Tampa Tribune)*

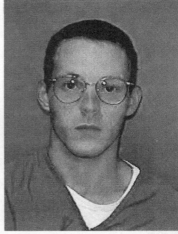

John Whispel was sentenced to twenty-five years at Calhoun Correctional Institution in Sneads, Florida. *(Photo courtesy of the Florida Department of Corrections)*

Adam Davis is on death row at Union Correctional Institution in Starke, Florida. *(Photo courtesy of the Florida Department of Corrections)*

Valessa Robinson, twenty, is serving twenty years in Homestead Correctional Institution, south of Miami. *(Photo courtesy of the Florida Department of Corrections)*

"We were sitting in Denny's; Valessa, Jon, and me. Her mom was tryin' to break her and me up. I tried to get heroin . . ."

Adam Davis watched as the state played his confession. His half-inch-length dark hair matched his black suit. He looked down at his hands and then back to the jury, fascinated with the television screen. His hair was the same color as Valessa's, but his olive skin, straight nose, and full mouth contributed to his masculine good looks. It was easy to see how the young girl could be attracted.

Answering Lt. Iverson's questions about the murder of Valessa's mother, his tone was flat and void of emotion. He appeared younger than twenty as he listened to the tape, tears streaming down his face.

"We went in Valessa's mom's bedroom. She woke up and she asked, 'What are you doing here?' She went in the kitchen in her nightgown. I followed, walked up behind her. We tried to put her to sleep."

"When you say put her to sleep, what are you talking about? You had bleach, not heroin," Lt. Iverson's taped voice asked.

"I sat on her chest. Jon brought up the knife. I don't know what was going through my mind when I did it. I was trippin' so hard, I just sliced and sliced."

"Put the knife in her back?"

"Yes."

"Upper or lower?" Iverson questioned.

"Lower. When I realized what I did I started to wig out. Got a trash bin. Put the body in. Before daylight . . ." Adam's voice got lower and raspy. "got [the] body in [the] van and shovels . . . closed garage doors. When we got out there the ground was hard. . . . Put the can with the body near trees."

"The map you drew, is it correct?" Detective Iverson asked.

"Yes. We went back to the house but then got a hotel room," Adam's taped voice mumbled. "We stayed away the first couple of nights. Then I found out I was on the news," Adam said clearly. He then indicated, in a quieter, less coherent voice, that he had bought a newspaper to see for himself.

"Did you call someone?"

"No."

"Did you and Jon discuss what you were going to do if you were caught?"

"No."

"Did you drive back to Jon Whispel's house?"

"Yes."

"Did you tell anyone about the murder?"

"No."

"12:45 a.m. Tampa time," Detective Iverson's voice said, concluding the interview. A State employee removed the tape.

Pam Bondi asked for the State's exhibits to be reviewed. The pictures of seven through thirty-eight flashed again before the jury, plus a list on the computer screen. "Any objections?"

"No. Let them be admitted."

The items pictured included the garage; one garbage can; Vicki Robinson's bedroom; her four-poster bed; the lanai area; the pool; Valessa's room; her bed, closet, and clothes; and a picture in a heart-shaped frame.

Pam Bondi asked the detective, "Whose picture?"

Detective Iverson answered, "Adam Davis."

Exhibits twenty-nine through thirty-eight included photographs of the bathroom with scalloped, ruffled pink curtains over the tub; a sink; pink towels; the doorway to the laundry room; and the living and family rooms.

A video camera in a convenience store caught Adam Davis in a white T-shirt and black cap and Whispel in an oversized lime green T-shirt and baggy jeans standing at a red counter. "June 29, 1998" flashed repeatedly throughout the convenience store videotape.

At the Best Buy entrance the security camera captured the date 6-29-98 and time 12:50 P.M. The clerk fast
forwarded the videotape through Adam and Jon pushing Valessa in the wheelchair giving it a more comedic
look. Some people in the court were prompted to
laugh. The members of the jury remained stoic.

Adam watched with his chin in his hands until a four-
way split screen showed him at ATM machines on June
30. His attorney quickly acknowledged exhibits forty-
five through eighty moving the case along.

Adam Davis stared penetratingly at the jury. He turned
toward his family sitting in the first row, who blew him
kisses but wiped their eyes when he looked away.

Pam Bondi refused to be rushed through the exhibits and introduced items including a wallet, a lighter
and a pack of Marlboros; Mrs. Robinson's mobile; a
Wal-Mart receipt; a black wallet; another lighter and
$200 in cash; and cosmetic items in Vicki's bag.

"Did Mr. Whispel have cash?" Pam Bondi asked.

"No. Cigarettes and a pawn ticket," Detective Iverson
answered. He removes more slides from a crackling
envelope. "These are the State's exhibits eighty-one
through one hundred ten."

"Where did those come from?" Pam Bondi asked.

"The van," Detective Iverson answered. "They include
pictures of a lawn edger; a hoe; a brown leather suitcase; a cooler; a keyboard; an electric guitar case; and a
carton of Marlboro cigarettes."

"Enter exhibits into evidence," she said, without in-
sisting upon showing them.

"Objections?" the judge asked.

"No objections," Adam's attorney answered. "May I
approach the bench?"

Adam held his chin watching his attorney. The detective squirmed around and looked from the jury to

the two television camera operators. The four attorneys conversation with the judge droned on.

"We'll recess for fifteen minutes; return by 3:45," Judge Cynthia Holloway said.

Most reporters escaped to meet their deadlines, leaving about twenty-five observers. Adam's small family and a few social workers took part of a row near him. Prosecutor Harry Lee Coe, a past judge, sat on the far side near Adam Davis. His presence caused murmurs of speculation. Vicki's big family and dedicated friends filled the first two rows near the jury.

The trial resumed. Shirley Williams asked Detective Iverson, "Was Valessa lacking in emotion?"

"Yes."

"Adam?"

"Yes."

"Would it be fair to say he understood the charge of first-degree murder with regard to Mrs. Robinson?"

"Yes."

"He used one stab wound in the carotid artery and wounds in her back?" the Assistant Prosecutor asked.

"He used the terms 'wigging' and 'freaking.' He couldn't understand what he had done," Detective Iverson answered. "His statement included regret."

"Mr. Davis was free to tell you anything?"

"Could have," the detective answered.

"Was there an indication of a motive?"

"Money—the van," the detective answered.

"You had the opportunity to talk to Mr. Whispel, who saw a chokehold being placed on Mrs. Robinson. And then he stayed in the bedroom until the murder was over. Is that correct?"

"Yes."

"Dismissed," Shirley Williams said.

The two defense attorneys asked to approach the bench, followed by the two female assistant prosecutors. After some discussion the prosecutors called John Marsicano.

The dark haired detective in a light gray suit said he had been with the Hillsborough Sheriff's Department for fourteen years.

"Did you accompany Detective Iverson to Midland, Texas on the Robinson case?" Shirley Williams asked.

"Yes."

"Who did you interview first?"

"Valessa Robinson."

"Do you remember the date?"

"July 3, 1998."

"What time did you contact Adam Davis?"

"5:30 A.M."

"Did you read the form?"

"Yes."

"What was his demeanor?"

"Alert."

"Did you have any trouble?"

"No."

"Were you in contact with Tampa?"

"Yes."

"Information relayed back to Tampa?"

"Yes."

"Were you present when he was questioned by Detective Iverson?"

"Yes."

"No further questions."

Judge Holloway looked toward the defense. "Court will resume at 8:30 A.M. tomorrow."

Thursday January 4: Pam Bondi called Albert Montanez to the stand. The top of his straight light blond hair spilled over onto short darker hair in a style often adopted by modern teens. He wore a dark T-shirt and jeans, and raised his right arm to take the oath.

"You worked in the Valhalla Tattoo Parlor in Ybor City on the twenty-seventh of June 1998?" Pam Bondi asked.

"Yes."

"Adam Davis came into Valhalla to ask for tattoos. Point that person out."

"Right there." He pointed to Adam Davis, who frowned at him.

"Did he get a tattoo that day?"

"Yes."

"Did he come back on two consecutive days?"

"Yes. He came back on Sunday to complete his tattoo."

"Describe it."

"He got a two-and-a-half-inch Jester. His friend chose a skull, and both got eyebrow piercings."

"How much did that cost?"

"About six hundred dollars."

"Did you hear a conversation?"

"They were going to Arizona. Davis had a new van."

"Did you make an inquiry about them?"

"Yes."

"Did you identify the tattoos?"

"Yes."

"The witness is excused."

"No questions," Defense Attorney Charles Traina said.

Shirley Williams called Jeff Brantly. The short heavyset man, wearing a white shirt and tie, took his position in the witness chair. He rolled his shirt sleeves a little higher as he waited to testify.

"You're employed at Denny's?" Assistant Prosecutor Shirley Williams asked.

"Yes."

"Do you know Adam Davis?"

"Yes, I do."

"How long?"

"A month, when he started working at Denny's."

"Did you know Vicki Robinson?"

"Yes."

"How?"

"Real estate. She showed me a house."

"Did you hear Adam Davis talk about hurting Mrs. Robinson?"

"Objection!" Traina jumped up. "Don't tell us what was said." The two male defense attorneys met the two female prosecutors before the bench, and angry words were exchanged.

Shirley Williams started again. "What did you hear Adam Davis say?"

"She's always accusing me of things. I'm going to knock her ass out."

"How long was this, in time, until Mrs. Robinson's death?"

"About a week to ten days."

"I'd like to show you the Denny's employment report."

"I object," Charles Traina called. He and Rick Terrana stood up. Terrana asked Judge Holloway, "Can we approach the bench, Your Honor?"

The two defense attorneys strode toward the judge, and Pam Bondi joined Shirley Williams in front of the bench. The conference before the judge appeared to be another argument. Judge Cynthia Holloway's head turned from one side to another as though she was watching a tennis match. Assistant Prosecutor Pam Bondi smiled at Vicki's family when she returned to her seat.

The dark-haired Traina ran his fingers over his mustache as he followed Rick Terrana back to the defense table. He slapped Adam Davis on the back before he sat next to him.

Shirley Williams returned to the lectern and faced Jeff Brantly in the witness chair. He fingered his tie nervously.

"The Denny's employment report says Adam Davis started June 21 and finished June 26. That's less than a week," the assistant prosecutor stated.

"Employees paperwork starts ten days later."

"So it doesn't change your testimony."

"No."

"How many times did you visit Vicki Robinson's home?"

"Only once. Adam and me had a huge fight after he made the threat. He didn't make the statement to Mrs. Robinson."

"Thank you. You may step down, Mr. Brantly," Shirley Williams said, moving aside to accomodate Pam Bondi, who called Robert Anders to the stand.

Robert Anders, wearing a black T-shirt that showed off a wide silver chain around his neck, took the stand. Pam Bondi covered the preliminary questions, including Anders's relationship with Davis.

"Did you know Valessa and Jon Whispel too?

"Yes."

"How long?"

"A few months."

"Did he tell you he (Davis) was caught having sex with Valessa?"

"Objection," Rick Terrana said.

"Overruled," Judge Holloway said immediately.

"Where on the night of your party was Mrs. Robinson's van?"

"In front of the house."

"Did you ever see him drive it before?"

"I'm not sure."

"What did Adam Davis want?"

"Heroin."

"How many bags?"

"Four."

"Did he say he was going to take someone's ass out?"

"Yes."

"Did you see him after the party?"

"At my mom's house. He showed me [his] new tattoos."

"As soon as you saw the articles in the newspapers about Mrs. Robinson you called the police," Pam Bondi prompted.

"Yes."

Pam Bondi looked at the defense table and said, "Cross."

Charles Traina said, "Good afternoon, Mr. Anders. There were ten people at your party, including Richard Cunningham, correct?"

"Yes. Adam came in angrily," the witness blurted.

"He talked to other people before he talked to you. Right? Were you drinking and doing drugs? There were other people. You couldn't tell what he was saying to others could you?"

"The room was small. He came up to me," Anders frowned.

"Did you get up from the couch?"

"No." Anders stared directly at the attorney.

"When you basically made a statement in this case on May 14 this year, did you remember all questions someone asked you?"

Mr. Traina shot his questions out as fast as the witness could answer them.

"Objection," Pam Bondi said.

"The question is—" the dark haired attorney tried again.

"Objection! Sidebar."

The four attorneys argued before the judge. Mr. Traina came back and continued.

"Did you not at any time walk up to Adam Davis and talk to him?"

"He was angry. He talked to me."

"Did you smoke marijuana the day of the party?"

"Probably," Anders said, and looked down at his hands.

"Was Jon Whispel with Adam?" The attorney didn't wait for Mr. Anders to answer. "You don't have any problems, do you?"

"No," Anders answered in a throaty whisper.

"That party you were talking about in your deposition—you answered that you were drunk."

"Probably was."

"You were intoxicated!" Adam's attorney shouted.

"Yes."

"You were not only drunk, but you were taking some drugs along with alcohol," Traina said.

"Probably."

"You answered 'yes'. You're under oath."

"He said 'probably'," Pam Bondi interjected.

"Objection," Mr. Traina complained. "I'm not asking. What are you trying to do? You were using drugs with alcohol. You made the observation that Adam was angry. Have you committed a felony?"

"Once," the witness responded, and squirmed in his chair.

"Did you tell people in the neighborhood that you were going to get Adam Davis?"

Pam Bondi's objection created another conference. She met Mr. Traina before the judge. Her blond loose bun bopped up and down during the animated discussion. Shirley Williams joined her. Rick Terrana joined the younger attorney. The four attorneys spoke to the judge for less than ten minutes.

"I'm finished at this time," Charles Traina said.

"Redirect?" the judge asked. The prosecution passed.

"Well, we'll have a fifteen-minute recess. It's 4:30."

Pam Bondi leaned over the wooden separation and spoke to Vicki Robinson's family during the break.

A white-haired man wearing a dark suit took the stand and told the court he was Sam MacMullen a crime scene detective from the sheriff's office. "I took photos and fingerprints for the disappearance of Mrs. Robinson. The State's exhibits were replayed for the third time. The gallon of Kash 'n' Karry bleach got more attention this time as the officer described how they lifted fingerprints from the plastic container. He explained how they took "latent prints."

"Detective MacMullen, were you asked to identify the lift?"

"It belongs to Adam Davis," the expert said, and was excused.

Judge Holloway glanced at the clock. "We'll resume tomorrow."

November 4, 1999

A casual atmosphere pervaded the courtroom as Judge Holloway administered to the lesser criminals wearing prison orange that filled the jury section. She listened to the drug offenses and parole breakers and scheduled some for trials.

Preparing for the main event an officer of the court piled paper bags of more evidence, while Vicki's family—wearing elegant, somber clothing—looked on. Her mother and father appeared to be in their seventies. Vicki Robinson's sister was beautiful with her light blond straight hair touching her shoulders. Her brothers were as handsome as their father. They exuded an air of wealth also as they sat stoic and silent among the more casually-dressed friends and families of the prisoners in orange. The T-shirt-clad group disappeared as the judge handled each of the twenty cases.

A young woman with a massive, curled blond pony tail who investigated for the defense conversed with a Hillsborough sheriff. "Remain seated and come to order. The court is now in session," a bailiff announced. "Are we ready to bring him in?"

Adam Davis entered and took a seat next to the blond investigator who whispered in his ear.

The members of the jury entered. Mr. Traina stood up, looked down at a large yellow legal pad, and said, "I want the court to go over two matters."

Judge Cynthia Holloway responded, "I have some business with the attorneys. Will the jury leave the court-room?"

As the jury filed out, Adam's attorneys put their heads together at the defense table, while Judge Hollo-way read a number of documents. Her long dark hair appeared less curly and was drawn back behind her ears. "Time's passing. I've been in this court since 5:30 A.M.," she complained crossly.

Adam's attorneys jumped up and hustled toward the bench. They were joined by the two prosecutors. An argumentive discussion ensued, after which the judge ordered, "Bring the jury back."

The jury returned for the second time in fifteen minutes. "Jurors, I'm sorry for the imposition, but a few minutes now can save hours later," Judge Holloway apologized.

Pam Bondi called Susan Kalupa. A trim woman with short blond hair sat and faced her. The State played an aerial shot. "Do you recognize that as Carrollwood?"

"Yes, I live on Cartnal Avenue, next to Vicki's house."

"You observed her dog running free early Saturday, June 27, 1998?"

"Yes, I brought Lady into my house."

"That never happened before?" the blond prosecutor asked.

"No. Vicki's van was gone too."

Shirley Williams stepped forward and called Adam Clay, while a male clerk piled cement-filled paper bags between the lecturn and the witness chair. Williams asked the young, dark haired man, "Do you work at Home Depot now?"

After he answered yes, she held a tape before him and waited while he reviewed the register and cashier numbers on the receipt.

Adam Davis's attorney jumped up to object and asked to see the tape. "Why do you remember this tape?"

"The guy's new tattoo attracted me."

Mr. Traina returned to the defense table.

"What time do you start work?" Shirley Williams asked.

"7:30 A.M."

"Anything unusual?"

"Two guys buying sacks of cement."

Shirley Williams looked toward the defense shrugged and dismissed the witness.

"The State calls Linda Fales to the stand," the blond prosecutor announced. A brunette woman wearing a tailored navy suit stepped up and took the oath. "I work at the [Sun Coast Schools] Credit Union."

"Did you come in contact with the sheriff's office about the disappearance of Vicki Robinson?" Pam Bondi asked.

"Yes. Detective John Marsicano [called] on June 30. He asked for ATM records from June 26th."

"Did your organization decide to assist in the investigation?"

"Yes, our machines have the number of the ATM used. We sent new videotapes," the bank employee answered.

"Did you produce a picture from the video?"

"Yes. We also agreed to limit each withdrawal to $100 a day so we could track where they were coming from. There was a concern the account would run out of money so the sheriff's department agreed to pay if the account ran out. We determined they were no longer in Tampa. An employee brought his laptop computer home so he could monitor the account at night. On July 2 he called at three in the morning. I immediately gave the information to Detective Iverson."

"Were they able to take money out at that time?"

"They tried at a number of locations and were denied, but we had the information. Detective Iverson called and asked for the total amount able to be withdrawn? 'I answered $1,483.00.'" Linda Fales glanced away from Pam Bondi briefly. Her eyes lingered on Adam Davis, who was staring at her with his mouth open.

"Thank you. Cross," the blond prosecutor said.

Adam Davis's attorney Rick Terrana asked, "Was her account accessible to other members of her family?"

"The account was in Vicki Robinson's name," Linda Fales answered tersely.

The attorney glanced down on his pad and ran his hand over his graying crewcut. "Thank you, Ms. Fales."

Shirley Williams took over the lectern and called Leana Hayes. "Leanna Hayes is a prisoner serving in the Orient [Point] Road Jail."

"Were you brought back to Tampa?"

"Yes, I went to Nashville."

"Do you see other people transported with you?"

She pointed, "Adam Davis."

"Describe how you were seated."

"Davis was behind the driver next to me."

"Did Davis have a conversation with you?"

"Yes."

"Did you know him?"

"No."

"What did he say to you?"

"Did I know he was a dangerous person?"

"Was he proud of it?"

"Yes."

"Did he tell you about murder for fun?"

"He said he was in headlines. He said he and Valessa were the Romeo and Juliet of the 90s."

"Did Jon Whispel contribute?"

"He had a nervous giggle. Not a ha-ha."

Assistant Public Defender Charles Traina, holding a legal pad, came forward to question the witness and Shirley Williams stood aside.

"Miss Hayes, you haven't gotten out of prison. Are you a felon?"

"Yes."

"How many times?"

"Twice."

"Is it accurate to say the transport officer could hear? They were seated in front of you. You could be heard by Jon Whispel behind you? He was far away laying across the back seat," the attorney stated imperiously.

The witness twisted her finger in her brown hair. "I don't think so. He was talking to the driver."

"You don't remember anyone being there at all. You had a terrible experience and were upset and angry. These people you met coming back from Nashville tell you about a murder? Not likely."

"Adam Davis was bragging. Whispel was giggling in a scared fashion," the young brunette answered.

"Your discussion was how many minutes?"

"About an hour."

"You had never met Adam Davis before, and he'd tell you?"

"Davis said he did it with her."

"Did he make mention of the fact he loved this girl very much?" Adam's attorney asked.

"One thing he said was that he cut her mother up."

"Was it fair to say they were using alcohol and drugs?"

"He did it for his girlfriend," Hayes said.

"Did you tell people in jail what you know about this case? You know the person who had been writing to Adam Davis, and you still have contact."

"No."

"Of all the people in this world, he chose to tell you?"

The witness raked her dark curls with her fingers and answered, "I guess he liked the story of Romeo and Juliet."

"No further questions." The attorney slapped his yellow pad on the lectern and strode back to the defense table.

Next the prosecutors presented a DNA expert, who examined blood on Davis's shoes and found a spot of Vicki Robinson's blood on the left shoe. She put on a pair of rubber gloves, and took some bloody white towels, which had been used to clean up Vicki's blood, from several paper bags.

The Medical Examiner, Dr. Lee Miller, took the stand. He described, "Vicki Robinson's body was severely decomposed from six days in the hot Florida sun as well as destruction by maggots. The putrefaction of some of her body resulted in mummifying a shoulder and arm. I could not isolate the bleach as it dissipated."

Shirley Williams asked, "Would the wound to the neck be painful?"

"Yes."

"If it was shot with bleach?"

"Yes, very painful."

The photograph on the big screen showed what detectives witnessed when they removed the cover of the garbage can. Vicki's feet and rump flashed on the big screen. In spite of the bloodstains on her nightgown, it was possible to see the original peach color. Dr. Lee Miller explained she had been thrown in head first. "Her gold cross was somewhere around her neck at the bottom of the can."

The people in the courtroom were spared the putrid odor, but were given the grim details.

"Any defense wounds?"

"I couldn't see them from decomposition."

"How long could she live after the stab wound to the neck?"

"Thirty to sixty seconds."

"Would Vicki Robinson's blood keep pumping during that time?"

"The heart stops beating after losing a liter of blood."

"Accurate to say you don't know about moaning?" Shirley Williams stated.

"Yes," the doctor answered.

The defense attorney asked the doctor, "No defense wounds at all? You found no wounds to the left hand?"

"None."

Shirley Williams announced, "The State of Florida rests its case against Adam William Davis."

His attorneys asked for a few minutes and talked to their client. They approached the bench.

Judge Cynthia Holloway addressed Adam Davis. "Your attorneys are resting your case. Do you understand? You have the right to take the stand."

Adam Davis indicated "no" by shaking his head.

"So we have no clerical mistakes, his answer is 'no.' Counsel, how long for closing arguments? Before lunch or after?"

Rick Terrana stood. "We need a short recess, Your Honor."

The jury filed out while plans were made for closing

arguments. The judge turned and stepped away through her private door behind the stand. Shirley Williams sat alone at the prosecutors table and was joined by a gray-haired man. The clerk asked the bailiffs, "Did you get the women?"

Adam's stepmother, wearing a dark green woolen sweater and black slacks, took a seat in the first row near him. His natural mother looked at Adam and smiled, but quickly lowered her head and brushed her cheek with her fingertips. She stood and pulled the bottom of her white sweater down before she bent over the low barrier to blow him a kiss. He stared at the ceiling.

The jury and the judge returned. She announced, "We'll hear the State's closing before lunch. The defense will present after lunch. I rule that 'reasonable doubt' be included in the jury's decision."

Shirley Williams recounted the State's evidence in detail, beginning with her opening statement in which she described Adam Davis as being on a collision course with a terrible, tragic destiny. She punctuated her argument with passion as she went over the murder and clean-up, which was executed before Adam Davis tossed Vicki Robinson's bloody body in a garbage can. She reminded the jury that he used Vicki Robinson's money for tattoos, and drove her van—for a joyride and flight.

She paced in front of the twelve jurors, eyeballed each one, and said, "He continued to use Vicki's ATM cards. That's how the trio got caught in Texas."

She hammered down premeditation. "Adam's friends and working associates testified he made threats hours and days before the murder. The evidence is overwhelming. 'Me, Valessa, and Jon wanted to be together.' He asked Robert Anders where he could get four bags [of heroin] 'to take someone's ass out and make it look like an accident.'"

Her most emotional, wrenching argument for the

jury was when she exclaimed: "The bleach isn't working! Vicki arms and legs were flying around trying to
get away. He got a knife and stabbed her repeatedly and
entered Valessa's room covered in blood. Vicki Robinson
was still alive on the floor moaning. 'The bitch won't
die,' he told Jon Whispel and Valessa before he went back
to finish her off. Premeditated from 11:30 P.M. to 5:30
A.M. It doesn't get any more premeditated than that.'"

After lunch, Charles Traina pointed to Adam Davis
and said, "The defense isn't contending he didn't do
the crime. Premeditated? No. Does Adam Davis fit into
premeditation? Analyze the difficulty in establishing
guilt. Who did stab Vicki Robinson? Jon Whispel,
Valessa Robinson, and Adam Davis were the only people there. We don't really know what happened. Jon
Whispel doesn't know. He brought a knife to two people, Adam Davis and Valessa Robinson, who said that
she wanted to kill her mother. Who took her mother's
life?"

Adam Davis's dark eyes appeared be tearful as his attorney described the injection of bleach and the stab
wound in her neck. "You don't know." Charles Traina
directed his comment to the jury. One woman's mouth
dropped open like she thought he was talking directly
to her.

"It's possible to believe Adam Davis took the knife
and killed Vicki Robinson. You don't know that Valessa
didn't kill her mother. The idea has to be in the mind
of the killer. Premeditation has to be in the mind of the
killer at the time of the killing."

Mr. Traina glanced toward Adam. "Three people
took LSD two hours before at Denny's. Adam Davis and
Jon Whispel thought Valessa was joking. As the LSD
took a greater hold, they went to get heroin. The State
would have you believe that this was premeditation. Did
they try to get heroin for his use? They smoked ciga-

rettes outside the house while waiting for Vicki Robinson to go to sleep. I suggest that the mother didn't know Valessa was out."

Adam Davis stifled sobs in his hands while his attorney continued. "Jon Whispel kept telling you he wasn't all there—hallucinating on three hits of acid. Isn't it possible that the drug affected all they did that night? The use of drugs releases passion and a certain mental state cannot exist."

Members of Vicki Robinson's family, who were grimacing at one another to convey their annoyance, audibly groaned. Adam Davis put his head on the desk. His shoulders moved as though he were sobbing. If he could be heard, it could only be at the defense table.

"Apply the law of premeditation. This leads more into second-degree. There's not one person acting in broad daylight. Would you trust the word of Jon Whispel? Adam didn't act alone. Who's fully responsible for the act because of drugs consumed that night? Brantly met Adam Davis two times and still heard a threat against Vicki Robinson as recently as a week before. Anders and Jim Englert did not hear anything. You can't believe Leanna Hayes, a convicted felon. The state would have you believe Adam bragged about killing Vicki Robinson for ninety minutes. She claimed to be sitting behind transport guards who didn't hear the same thing. You have to believe her testimony was a lie. The guards weren't felons."

Traina's voice rose and he began to pace. "Do nothing more than consider the young man you heard on the tape confessing his love, for whatever it's worth. She was fifteen. He was nineteen. He loved her. Would do anything for her. Did he commit premeditated murder, or did he take the blame for Valessa Robinson? If you believe that, take the whole confession—not a part of it. He said he was raging—tripping—that he didn't understand what he was doing. I'm going to ask you to do two things as evidence for second-degree. If you use that statement as a basis, use all of it. The State can't have it two ways. He either did the stabbing in an intoxicated state, or he confessed to protect Valessa."

The attorney's voice moderated. He stood close to the jury as if in confidence and said, "Jon Whispel's involved in a plea agreement to gain a second-degree charge. Did he get blood all over him? Of course he did. There was blood all over. Do what's fair here," Charles Traina said, his voice escalating. "I submit that it's unclear who took the knife and murdered Vicki Robinson. First-degree, he knew what he was doing. Second, he didn't have intent to kill on his mind. You can't bring Vicki Robinson back. This trial is now or never for three people who have made a terrible hole in this community. I ask you not to take it out on one person and bring in a verdict that is fair to Whispel, Valessa, and Adam."

The attorney turned toward the judge. "On behalf of Adam Davis, I want to thank you."

The prosecutor reminded the jury that drugs don't relieve a person of a crime. "Voluntary intoxication is not a defense."

The judge explained the perimeters of the law regarding charges and sent the jury out to deliberate.

They returned after an hour and twenty minutes. The foreman read the vote: 7-5 that Adam Davis was guilty of first-degree murder.

Judge Cynthia Holloway informed the court that on Friday, the jury would make its recommendation of either life in prison or death in the electric chair. They would hear family and specialists talk about the mitigating and aggravating circumstances.

Vicki Robinson's family and friends congratulated the prosecutors. Deborah Sartor-Englert hugged Pam Bondi and smiled. "I'm so thankful. I'm going to sleep well tonight."

Donna Davis, his stepmother, said, "I'm scared for what's going to happen to Adam now."

The families sat across the aisle from each other as though they were at a wedding. The long, wooden, polished benches did indeed resemble church pews. The black-robed judge took her elevated position on the bench.

Adam's small family of women wanted him to be set free and sat near the defense table. Vicki's large contingent of family and friends took up five rows behind the prosecution and in front of the jury, and didn't hide that they wanted a death sentence.

Judge Holloway explained that the jury's recommendation would be considered after aggravating and mitigating circumstances were considered. The more aggravating the circumstance, the greater the penalty. A mitigating circumstance would lessen the penalty, if the defendants actions were affected by them. She called Jim Englert first.

He read a statement he wrote. "Vicki Robinson loved people. She was my best friend and soul mate. She personified the Christian faith. We loved each other's heart and soul. I miss her loving smile and a portion of my life."

Blond and beautiful Deborah Sartor-Englert, wearing a tailored black suit, took her brother-in-law's place on the stand. "Her laugh made us smile. It was an honor to know her. She was living for the Lord and her family."

Deborah stopped and cried. Her voice continued with difficulty. "One couldn't imagine such an amazing woman. She will always be missed."

Tom Klug, Vicki's oldest brother, witnessed for his sister next. He was handsome like his father, who only had a few grey sprinkles to separate the years. "My sister lived her life for forty-nine years dedicating her life to family and friends. She majored in education and was employed by a head start program. She was more interested in helping children than a Master's in Education."

He cried when he talked about how she visited when his son was born with problems and how much she helped. He rambled on about vacations she shared with her family, but mentioned two weeks she had spent with Jim Englert in 1997, when his niece was in the eighth grade at Seminole Presbyterian and had chosen to stay home.

He jumped to Vicki's, finding her daughter a place at Steppin' Stone on July 7, 1998, and ended with, "We never got to say goodbye."

Before he left the witness chair he read a letter from his parents that ended, "Good-bye sweet Vicki. Mom, and Dad."

People were still tearful when Dr. Michael S. Maher took the stand.

Adam's defense provided counselors and family members, who each told the court about a young man who was devastated after his father's death. Each of the people who took him to live with them described a willing young person who captured their hearts, but ran away when pressed to perform simple tasks.

CHAPTER 22

DEATH ROW SYCOPHANTS

Circuit Judge Cynthia Holloway entered her courtroom at 8:30 A.M. on December 17, 1999, and the bailiff called, "all rise" She listened to three prisoners in orange jump suits topped with bulky denim jackets, and she quickly disposed of their cases by setting trial dates for various felonies and violations of parole due to theft and drug use. Her perfunctory duties took fifteen minutes.

One of the three prisoners, about the same age as Adam Davis, blew a kiss to a young mother holding an infant in a cuddly pink outfit. The young mother waved at him, before she tried to squeeze past two women sitting on the isle. One wearing a purple T-shirt stood and moved into the aisle. She threw out her ample bosom emblazoned with: I'M OPPOSED TO THE DEATH PENALTY. The thinner, younger brunette pressed herself against the bench, leaving enough room for the mother and baby to pass. She watched the mother and baby as they retreated from the courtroom, at the same time the three prisoners shuffled out.

The attractive brunette in a conservative navy dress reached over and tapped a man in the front row on his shoulder. "I came to witness Adam Davis's sentencing. Am I in the wrong courtroom?"

The white-haired man turned. "No, my dear. I'm here for him. I'm Bill Canals and counseled Adam Davis for five months with the prison ministry."

The pretty woman with dark hair whispered, "I'm here for Adam Davis, too." Her voice hiccoughed as she tried to choke back tears. "I wrote to him after the jury found him guilty. He wrote me back and now I visit him in jail. I'm Elena Cadrecha. Did he tell you about me?"

"We only talk about spiritual things. I've been with Prison Fellowship for fifteen years. Here's my card. Call me if you need to talk," Bill Canals said.

"I expected to see more people here. Where are his family members, or Valessa's?"

Bill Canals faced her with open, raised palms.

Adam Davis entered at 8:45 and stood before the judge wearing prison attire like the previous prisoners. The similarities ended there. In a flat tone, Judge Holloway reminded Adam Davis that the jury voted for his death seven to five, used the legal descriptions of aggravating and mitigating circumstances, and explained that the "mitigating" was far outweighed by the "aggravating."

Her voice sounded angry as she described the aggravating circumstances. She admonished the young man for the two felonies he committed and was given probation for on March 9, 1998, before the murder of Vicki Robinson. She described Dr. Lee Miller's testimony as to the cruel nature of the crime. How Davis led the victim out of her bedroom into the kitchen, called her daughter to get the bleach-filled syringe while he held her mother in a chokehold for several minutes, before Whispel handed him a knife in the kitchen.

Judge Holloway repeated Dr. Lee Miller's testimony,

describing how Vicki's throat was cut as an "unnecessary intrusion." As she narrated the prolonged, painful death by choking, stabbing, and injection of bleach, passion overtook the judge. "No one heard her cries. What would it be like to be the victim?

"Vicki Robinson's murder was cold, calculated, and premeditated," the judge continued. "You plotted at Denny's to kill Vicki Robinson with her daughter and Jon Whispel, before you returned on bicycles. While she slept and you pushed Vicki's van out of the garage so the sound of the motor wouldn't wake her on your pursuit of drugs 'to take someone's ass out.'"

The judge addressed the influence of LSD as a defense. "You've been described as nineteen and lacking in sophistication. There's no lack of sophistication in advising that if you were caught to say, 'We were stoned out'."

Judge Holloway reviewed the documents in front of her and read aloud. "Adam Davis's life was mitigating. He was born of a teenage mother who used drugs and then turned over to father and stepmother at two and a half. His father died at the age of fourteen . . . The aggravating circumstances outweigh the mitigating. Adam Davis, you are sentenced to death. So ordered here in Hillsborough County, Florida, December 17, 1999."

The fortyish woman wearing the anti-death penalty T-shirt jumped up and shouted, "He's innocent! I'm going to write a book to explain why."

She stood and proudly thrust out her ample chest, spotlighting the anti-death penalty slogan, while Adam Davis signed some papers before the television camera. He left the court through the door next to the judge's bench with the bailiff.

Outside the courtroom, Adam Davis's friend, Elena Cadrecha, talked to reporters who learned her interest in him was created by newspaper articles published since the jury recommended of death on November 5, six weeks earlier.

One female reporter asked, "He's a good looking guy, but why would you be attracted to a man the jury believed committed murder? Anyone attending the trial would agree," she added.

"He's protecting Valessa. She's responsible," Cadrecha said angrily.

"How responsible can a fifteen-year-old be?" the reporter asked. "Are you impressed with the celebrity status the media has provided the killer, or certain sympathetic movies about saving the innocent from the death penality?"

"Adam is a wonderful, romantic man, and I love him. He loves me too," Elena defended.

"I guess we'll find out during Valessa's trial," the reporter said.

"You'll find she's pure evil," Elena spit out.

One of Adam Davis's attorneys walked past to enter the elevator. "Do I ask you for permission to speak to Adam Davis?" the reporter asked.

"He has to approve you. Ask Elena. She sees him all the time," Adam's youngest attorney, Charles Traina, said casually as he stepped onto the elevator.

Elena smiled.

The reporter's face expressed surprise. "I'm amazed you attained such power in so little time. Please ask Adam when you see him that I want to interview him. Here's my card."

A man with a TV camera on his shoulder interrupted, and asked Elena to come with him to be interviewed on the street behind the building. They entered the elevator.

Vicki Robinson's fiancé Jim Englert talked to a television camera from another station in front of the courtroom's double doors. The thin, graying man wearing a colorful, striped shirt reached up and touched a piece of jewlery that hung on a gold chain around his neck. "Vicki gave me this ring. I will miss Vicki forever, but her senseless murder will separate Valessa and Adam Davis forever too."

The down elevator filled with stragglers from Adam's trial who shared their differing opinions with each other as the elevator descended: he deserved the death sentence; drugs were responsible; he was a guy madly in love, blinded by his young girlfriend; he was innocent and couldn't afford better attorneys; he was railroaded by that female bitch judge.

A television crew set up at the north end of the court building. Elena Cadrecha and her friend in the purple T-shirt with the anti-capital punishment message walked down the steps. A television reporter stopped her and asked, "What did you think of the death sentence for Adam Davis?'

"Adam's a lover, not a killer. I love him," Elena said.

The interviewer's mouth dropped open in surprise. "Why do you say that?"

"It's my private business," Elena said, and walked away.

The TV reporter called, "Wait, explain that! I'm with the Associated Press." the man chasing Elena said. "I was anxious to interview Adam Davis, but I'd rather talk to you." He removed a pad from his breast pocket.

"Adam doesn't want to grant any interviews until Valessa has had her trial."

"That makes sense. Her recent interview with WFLA-Channel 8 got canceled after the station had promoted it for weeks. The sheriff's department taped the interview too. I don't know why that was objectionable, when they could watch television along with the rest of us."

"Adam doesn't want to say anything to jeopardize his appeal. He's innocent. That girl did it. He's going to tell everyone now that he's going to death row," Elena exclaimed.

"He's said that before, but he was taped in Texas telling Detective Iverson otherwise."

"Who?"

"The homicide detective."

"Adam and I don't talk about that. He's so beautiful and romantic. I've never been so in love. When he's moved up to Starke, I'm going to relocate there to be near him," Elena said.

"You just met him. Why are you going to change your life? Are there any jobs in Starke? It's a small town."

"I work from my computer and can live anywhere. I don't expect you to understand. My family doesn't. I haven't loved anyone in years."

"Why Adam, a guy who'll be on death row?"

"He's had a tough life. His father died and he learned that his real mother had given him up as a baby. He moved from one relative to another, but it didn't change his endearing qualities. He experienced the same attraction that I did."

"Why do you think you haven't been in love for so long? You're very pretty. More attractive than Valessa."

Elena laughed. "I'm so much older. I'm thirty-one. It's been me and my computer for a long time. I don't trust many men."

"You trust the one they call 'Rattlesnake,' who just got the electric chair. How did he get that name?"

"It upsets him to be called that. He was fourteen when he wore a rattler around his neck in school. At the time, he was proud he had killed it in Arizona while on a trip with his father. The nickname hasn't served him well."

"Has he told you everything about his life?"

"Of course, he loves me as much as I love him," Elena said. "Someday we'll get married and have children. I was with a man for a few years, but he left me when I got pregnant. I had to give the child up for adoption. Adam wants a baby."

"Some psychologists and psychiatrists who have studied women who fall in love with men on death row claim the attraction is the prisoner's remoteness. They are locked up and don't present a threat."

"I've read that kind of nonsense. It doesn't represent my feelings for Adam. He's innocent. Valessa killed her mother and he took the blame. He's over that now that he's met me."

"Well, Ted Bundy managed to father a child while he was on death row. More recently, a woman from Tampa gave up her four girls to her attorney husband because she fell in love with a convicted serial killer, Oscar Ray Bolin. She worked on his appeal. Tell me you don't you think that's strange."

"It has nothing to do with us, but it makes me understand why Adam doesn't want to talk to reporters. Good-bye."

CHAPTER 23

VALESSA'S ATTORNEYS FIGHT BEFORE HER TRIAL

On Adam Davis's twenty-first birthday, Thursday, December 9 1999, Valessa's trial for the murder of her mother was to begin. When the lovers and Jon Whispel were interviewed in Texas, Valessa told detectives that she had killed her mother. Her testimony differed from that of Davis and Whispel, but each agreed they were tripping on LSD before making statements about the night of the murder. Hillsborough Circuit Judge Cynthia Holloway rescheduled Valessa's trial to February 14 after her lawyers indicated that their expert witness on the topic of LSD, John H. Halpern of Massachusetts, needed more time for evaluation. Hearing of the delay, possibly pleased that her trial was on Valentine's Day, Valessa smiled.

Monday, December 20, before Valessa could appear, Assistant Public Defender John Skye asked Judge Holloway to remove herself from Valessa's case, citing the judge's comments while sentencing Adam Davis. The attorney read the judge's words from the record. "Valessa was only fifteen . . . but the court would note

that between these two defendants, there is no signifi-
cant difference in the level of culpability."

John Skye looked up at the judge. "Given that fact, I
think it's pretty easy to see how someone in Miss
Robinson's position can say, 'Wait a minute, I've been
tried and convicted prior to having a trial.'"

Valessa's attorneys from the Public Defenders Office
won round one. Judge Holloway recused herself on
Thursday, December 23, 1999.

On Monday, January 7, 2000, Judge J. Rogers Padgett
took over and listened to the State's forensic pathologist review the wounds Vicki Robinson received. The
doctor referred to photographs of Vicki's decaying body
that had been taken five days after her murder. He described the gaping cavity at the base of the throat that
was enlarged by maggots and other entry wounds. Prosecutors asked that one photo of the stab wound to the
neck, which the medical examiner had testified had
caused her death, be shown to the jury. Valessa turned
her back away from the pathologist and put her fingers
in her ears, making her handcuffs and chains visible to
the video cameras and viewing public. She appeared to
cry before she put her face down on the desk.

Assistant Public Defender Lisa Campbell argued,
"It is our opinion that the photographs don't serve
any purpose other than to inflame the jury. Mrs.
Robinson's body was too decomposed to offer precise
evidence."

Valessa's orange prison suit shuddered as she tried to
stifle sobs. The lead Assistant Public Defender, Dee Ann
Athan, stroked her dark hair.

Judge Padgett said, "I agree to exclude the photographs, but I promise to revisit the issue during the
trial if circumstances warrant it."

*   *   *

Friday, January 21, 2000: Psychiatrist John H. Halpern testified as an LSD expert for the defense. "Valessa told me she dropped four hits of Purple Jack-in-the-Box LSD during the chase in Texas to eliminate the evidence of the drug. The dose was four times greater than she had ever taken before. She said the effect was intense; she was not able to sleep or eat and experienced 'clown-like' hallucinations."

Valessa's skin appeared like white marble, and she was as animated as a statue while she listened to her recorded voice.

Dee Ann Athan asked Judge Padgett to rule that Valessa was under the influence of drugs, in pain from a yeast infection, and had been persuaded to confess before detectives had Mirandized her.

Judge Padgett didn't rule, and told the court that he would do so after the hearing at 1 P.M. on Wednesday.

On Wednesday, January 26, 2000, Valessa appeared in court wearing her usual jail-house orange. Instead of looking down at her handcuffs, or at her attorneys, she smiled at a dapper man stylishly dressed in a navy blue jacket with gold buttons. The attractive man near the defense table grinned and waved. It was evident to everyone in the courtroom that he was her father, for the girl appeared animated for the first time and mouthed, "I love you." Her entourage of public defenders each took turns to speak to him quietly before Circuit Judge J. Rogers Padgett entered.

Dee Ann Athan's red jacket blazed bright among the gray and dark suits of the other attorneys. She made an impassioned plea to discredit Valessa's taped confession, which had been made in Texas in front of Hillsborough detectives Jim Iverson and John Marsicano. "The detectives cajoled, tricked, and coerced Valessa into making a statement. They gave lip service to getting her parents' permission. Charles Robinson, her father, did not know Valessa was a suspect in a murder investigation when he gave his permission to talk to her."

She left the lectern and paced close to it, talking directly to Judge Padgett. His white hair and beard appeared like snow, in stark contrast to his black robe. He gave the attractive attorney his full attention.

"The Supreme Court ruled that the Nathan Ramerez confession be thrown out because the juvenile's parents weren't contacted and he didn't understand his right to remain silent under the Miranda law. Ramerez's statements were inadmissible . . . Valessa Robinson's statements must be suppressed. They were obtained illegally. They were self-incriminating. She was taken from her cell at 11:01 P.M. Texas time and met with detectives at 11:29. The tape wasn't turned on for thirty-nine minutes. It played from 1:09 to 1:20 A.M."

Dee Ann Athan looked at the defense table. Valessa stared back. "Detectives said it took her three minutes to draw a map. Eight minutes are unaccounted for. The detectives—by design—failed to turn on the tape recorder until Valessa Robinson incriminated herself."

"We talked for a little bit. What happened to your mom? I want to put a little tape recorder between us," Detective Iverson said. "What I want you to do is tell us what happened? You had a little fight with your mom on Friday night?"

"Detective, by your own admission, the suspect is a juvenile with limited experience," Dee Ann Athan accused. "She was wearing handcuffs and yanked out of bed by both arms."

"Objection. No facts to prove Miss Robinson was yanked up by arms," Shirley Williams stated, with an annoyed edge to her voice.

"At no time did they suggest that Miss Robinson cancel the questioning until her parent was available. Ramerez's statement was inadmissible because there was no parent in attendance. Valessa's must be suppressed," Dee Ann Athan argued. "The officers took advantage of her physical pain. Valessa Robinson concluded the questioning because she was in pain."

Valessa looked up at her young attorney, who had long dark hair like her own and intently listened to every word. Her quizzical expression changed to one of belief and admiration.

Prosecutor Shirley Williams was equally passionate. "No one knew what happened to Vicki Robinson. The detectives went to interview Valessa Robinson not knowing if she was a victim like her missing mother."

Judge Padgett ruled that Detectives Iverson and Marsicano complied with the law getting permission to interview Valessa as a witness to what happened to her mother until she blurted out that she killed her. The confession would admitted into open court.

Adam Davis chose not to take the stand on his own behalf during his trial, but after two months on death row, he requested a meeting with prosecutors. Detective Jim Iverson complied and drove the two hours to death row in Starke, Florida to take his statement.

In his new statement he recanted his confession and offered a new rendition which was uncorroborated by his old friend Jon Whispel or other testimony. He told detectives that he became enraged when Vicki Robinson said something derogatory about his father, whom he idolized. He snapped, rendering her unconscious on the kitchen floor. He left the kitchen to find something to restrain her with when he heard thumps. He returned to find Valessa standing over her mother with a blood-covered knife. Davis claimed that he had hu-

mored Valessa into thinking that he was going to use
heroin to kill her mother because he wanted the nar-
cotic for his own use.

Prosecutors took him off the witness list for Valessa
Robinson's trial, scheduled for April 10. Hillsborough
Public Defender Julianne Holt said that his new statement enhanced Valessa's case, and that he was a controlling, manipulative young man.

On Monday March 20, Circuit Judge J. Rogers Padgett
refused Assistant Public Defender Dee Ann Athan's request for more time to review Adam Davis's new statements. He also refused her request to change venue, so
requested because of all the local publicity. She said,
"At this point, I don't see how we're going to pick a fair
and impartial jury."

Friday March 31, 2000: Dee Ann Athan again argued
to exclude Valessa's statements to Detective Iverson and
Marsicano, since the youth hadn't been told that she
was a murder suspect and that her court appointed
lawyer must be present. Athan called a Texas probation
officer who testified that Robinson was considered a
murder suspect while she was in custody. The probation
officers testimony strengthened Dee Ann Athan's argument.

Athan contested the testimony of nineteen-year-old
state witness Colleen Macklem because she hadn't been
presented to the defense until February. "The young
woman allegedly told prosecutors in October that Valessa
said, 'I'm going to kill my mom, and need Adam's help.'"

Prosecutors claimed they didn't know until February
that they were going to use her.

The judge denied all of Athan's motions except for
one. She bought a birthday cake for Valessa so that her

family could celebrate her seventeenth birthday in court. "It's not unusual for inmates to meet with family in the courtroom. We try to stay on the good side of lawyers when they make harmless requests."

CHAPTER 24
HIDDEN SECRETS

The mystery of teenage romance twisted through Valessa's life with the destruction of a cyclone. The brief time Valessa spent with Adam Davis was similar to the black cloud that sets down for mere moments, leaving devastation in its wake. He was incarcerated for most of their liaison.

Like so many teenage girls, she shared her thoughts in her diary, which her defense attorneys managed to have sealed until after her trial. Had her journal revealed her love for Adam or her hatred for her mother? Both?

Would they help people understand Vicki Robinson, who wanted to protect her daughter from Adam Davis but allowed her daughter to visit him in jail? She even drove Valessa to a rendezvous with an older female, Colleen Macklem, whose boyfriend shared a cell with Adam Davis. Did Vicki know?

When Davis got out of jail at the beginning of June, after serving a few days time due to Vicki's complaints of child abuse, she let him into her home, where he stayed overnight in the guest room she had prepared. Vicki and her boyfriend Jim Englert were always hospitable to Davis.

Vicki welcomed Jon Whispel, sometimes driving him to work so that he wouldn't be late. Why didn't Vicki worry about Jon Whispel being with the couple constantly? Would it explain how the couple managed to have a personal relationship with him sharing their room?

Did Valessa understand her mother's actions? Vicki let a man two years older than Adam, James Hardee, stay in her home for three weeks while Davis was in jail. Did she hope Valessa would be attracted to him? James told friends he enjoyed watching soap operas with Vicki and Valessa. He was charged with possession of crystal meth soon afterwards. Would Valessa's diaries explain why he was a houseguest?

Vicki surrounded herself with single people who talked about relationships and their faith. Vicki and Jim attended many weddings. Mauve pillows decorated with hearts filled her living room. Did they contribute to Valessa's focus on love and a baby? Did Valessa resent all the positive attention her mother received from everyone around her?

Even Adam Davis wrote Valessa letters from jail that told how much he wanted Vicki to like him. Would her diary reveal animosity toward her mother—or had Jon Whispel influenced others to believe that she wanted her mother dead?

Was the serious photograph of Vicki Robinson in her nightgown taken before her murder on the last roll of film developed by police? The nightgown reached her ankles. Jon Whispel's testimony about the evening of the murder described the peach nightgown as "calf length."

Jon Whispel accompanied Adam on his aborted trip to Arizona in the first stolen van. They had the oppor-

tunity to scope out Vicki's lovely home. Adam Davis
needed his buddy's driver's license to be able to rent a
hotel room.

Adam Davis's trial didn't reveal any mysteries, except
that he knew how to attract women of all ages.

Vicki's move to the gracious home in Carrollwood
her father had given her after her divorce, changed her
life and the lives of her two girls. They transferred to
public school, and Vicki gave up her job with the
Christian school and went to work selling real estate at a
RE/MAX office. Was Adam attracted to Valessa the person, or just her aura of wealth?

Christians often use the word "love" in reference to
God. The word is used by others to describe every emotion from eating ice cream to creating a child. Is that what
drove Valessa to tell everyone that she wanted Adam's
baby? She expressed her undying love for Adam to anyone who would listen.

The people in the Ybor City tattoo parlor, Valhalla,
told reporters how she lay on the couch watching him
being tattooed, talking about having his baby. In jail,
she again professed her love and tried to send him letters. She even worked out a code, hoping to keep their
communication private.

Adam Davis talked about family during his interview
with local TV Channel WFTS-28. He described Jon
Whispel as a brother and Valessa as his future wife and
mother of a possible family. He even said that he as-
pired to be a father like his own. He never explained
why, after he dumped Valessa's mother in a garbage
can, he brought Valessa to see his father's grave, where
they both prayed along with their friend, Jon Whispel.

CHAPTER 25

A MOTHER'S PASSIONATE DEFENSE

On Monday morning, April 10, 2000, Dee Ann Athan's delaying tactics failed, and eighty-one people waited to be selected for the jury in the highest profile case to ever hit Tampa. Hillsborough Circuit Judge J. Rogers Padgett asked for twice the usual number of candidates due to the publicity the case received in the press.

Valessa's father and stepmother sat in the second row behind Harvey Moore, Ph.D, known for his ability to pick a jury. The sociologist earned his money and reputation from repeated victories in civil suits. Dee Ann Athan recruited him to help *pro bono publico*.

Two rows back, her grandmother and grandfather waited with Vicki's brother and sister. Valessa entered wearing a white sweater set, black pleated skirt, white stockings, and hair that had been professionally tamed. As she walked to the defense table, her eyes searched the courtroom. She took her seat among her attorneys and leaned forward to smile at her father, then settled back, hidden in the huddle of attorneys.

Her grandmother gasped and exclaimed in a loud voice, "She never looked like that. That's not the way she wears her hair."

Valessa responded to her grandmother's voice and glanced in her direction. Her lower lip quivered.

Assistant Public Defender Dee Ann Athan addressed the judge. "I'm here with the responsibility of representing that child, Valessa Robinson," she pointed, and then walked closer, smiling and patting Valessa's shoulder. "We're here because no one protected this malleable child."

Valessa appeared transformed—not only by a new hairdo and pretty clothes, but by her attorney's evident belief in her argument that she had been an impressionable child. The girl who had dragged herself into the courtroom so many times reflected an inner light which had been ignited by her attorney. It flickered briefly every time she talked to her father.

Assistant State Attorney Pam Bondi responded to Valessa's appearance by objecting, "It's unfair to make Robinson appear less grown up."

Judge Padgett did not rule on the issue, so Dee Ann Athan continued, "That child stands accused of masterminding the murder of her mother, Vicki Robinson, a forty-nine-year-old real estate agent, by two men. One who drugged her, sexed her, and killed her mother."

The Assistant State Prosecutor, Pam Bondi, asked Judge Padgett to prohibit the defense from referring to their client as a child in front of the jury, and protested that, at seventeen, she was a young woman.

"There is much evidence coming in that's prejudicial to this child," Dee Ann Athan said, holding Valessa's shoulders. "It doesn't mean I can't call her a child. She is."

Judge Padgett denied the state's motion and called in the first candidates from the jury pool. Twenty trooped in and took up the right side of the courtroom. Valessa stood as she was directed to by Lisa Campbell, who was closest to her. At five foot two, she appeared tiny next to her trim black female attorney, who was nearly a foot taller

Judge Padgett addressed the semblance of plumbers, secretaries, teachers, carpenters, and insurance agents who passed muster from the general pool of jurors. "First the jury will decide, if it can, what happened at some other time and place. Now, you make that decision based on what evidence you hear and see, and that becomes the official version of events at some other time and place." The judge turned his attention to the whole court. "And I like to call those the true facts." He told the perspective jurors, "Your knowledge of the case isn't as much an issue as your ability to put aside opinions and render a verdict based on the evidence."

The jury selection began as Dee Ann Athan questioned each man or woman about their views on teenage sex, drugs, divorce, parental discipline, juvenile crime, and what it might mean to a fifteen-year-old minor to fall in love and have sex with a nineteen-year-old adult male. "Would it be child abuse? Would the girl be susceptible to the manipulations of the young man?"

Harvey Moore wrote notes on Post-it pads, sticking them on the podium and on his jury plan. He watched the response of each potential juror being questioned by Dee Ann Athan. Some were immediately discarded for admitting they were squeamish or sensitive.

During the breaks and lunch, Valessa was removed and prohibited from talking to anyone in the courtroom. Dee Ann Athan hugged her, smoothed her hair back, and lifted her chin up before Valessa disappeared through the rear door.

The first day passed with a struggle between Dee Ann Athan and the judge who complained that she was testing her case before the trial. Twenty more people were added to the original group of prospective jurors. Each side reviewed answers to questions to "accept" or "strike." Harvey Moore's gray hair gave the impression that he had a few years over the five female attorneys. The Tampa sociologist took his time as he studied each potential juror. The white-haired judge pulled on his short beard and tapped his fingers. Dee Ann Athan reached over and squeezed Valessa's hand, giving her a look of encouragement.

Pam Bondi frowned at Shirley Williams and shook her head with frustration. She addressed Judge Padgett, "We ask that Dee Ann Athan refrain from holding hands with Ms. Robinson throughout the trial." She raised her voice. "And conduct her questioning and opening statements from the podium, and not with her arms on Ms. Robinson."

Dee Ann Athan sprang from her chair. "Why don't we just send me out of the courtroom?"

Judge Padgett's blue eyes, already magnified by his glasses, appeared even bigger as he looked at the prosecutor. "Holding hands? Ms. Athan was holding hands with the defendant?" He blinked and looked at the defense attorney.

"I was holding her hand. I have held her hand from time to time. I view her as a child. We're in an adult court with very serious charges. She's a child. I have held her hand."

"She's also your client," Judge Padgett said. He hesitated. "I'll allow displays of affection for now. If it becomes a problem, we'll address it again." He frowned at the defense.

Some potential jurors received more attention than others, who were quickly dismissed. The prosecution favored individuals who had associations with police and military. The defense sought people who didn't read the newspapers or were tolerant of drug use and not judgmental. Only a rare person pleased both sides and had their names included on a more selective list.

"It's 5:30. Court's adjourned," the judge said.

*   *   *

The second day tussle between Dee Ann Athan's questions and the parameters set by the judge continued. She kept finding ways to ask the same questions about Valessa's use of LSD and marijuana. One female questioned responded that she saw a miserable child. "I look at her and say it's because of drugs. That's why this happened." She was dismissed.

The prosecutors asked some questions, but Dee Ann Athan hammered prospective jurors that under the Constitution a defendant is presumed innocent until proven guilty. She stood behind Valessa with her hands on her shoulders. "Valessa Robinson is innocent as she sits here today. Does everyone of you agree with that?"

Assistant Public Defender Dee Ann Athan wasn't content with a group nod, and addressed the remaining potential jurors individually. She pointed at each and repeated, "Can you agree Valessa's innocent until proven guilty?" She waited for a response before moving on, ignoring the prosecuting attorneys who appeared frustrated by the repetition. Pam Bondi shook her head and ran her hand up to touch her blond hair, as if secure her coiffure. She grimaced at her brunette partner, Shirley Williams, who raised her right hand as if to wave away any thoughts of objecting.

Dee Ann Athan continued. "Does everyone understand that I am Valessa's voice in this courtroom? I speak very loud. Does anyone have a problem with that?"

Murmurs reached her ears. "You can find me irritating, even obnoxious. That's OK, as long as you don't take those feelings out on Valessa. You can hold that against me. Not against her."

During the break, many people involved in or watching the trial commented on Valessa's demure appearance in a blue plaid and black jumper with a short skirt, and blue, little girl barrettes. Some complained about her black patent leather "Mary Jane" shoes.

Her stepmother, Vanessa, reminded some of the most vocal observers that Adam Davis appeared before the court in a black suit, like a seminary student. Chuck Robinson drew her away, and they stood alone for a few minutes. Reporters converged with questions.

Chuck Robinson broke his silence. "Vicki and I wanted to give our youngest baby girl a special name, and thought 'Valessa' was striking, not strange. Valessa misses her mother terribly. She's innocent."

One reporter observed, "She's impassive and lacking in emotion."

"Valessa comes from a family trained not to show emotions, especially when times are hard. Her sister, Michelle, hides her emotions too," Chuck Robinson said before he reentered the courtroom with his head held high.

Dee Ann Athan addressed the issue of Valessa's clothes before the prospective jurors. "Valessa wore baggy jeans and large T-shirts before her arrest. Now sitting before you, she is dressed conservatively. Do you view Valessa's make over as an attempt at manipulation by the defense? Do you think the defense is trying to put one over on you?" Dee Ann Athan asked.

One prospective juror, wearing a ponytail and gray suit, answered loud enough to be heard in the back of the courtroom, "I don't usually dress like this either." His comment evoked laughter and got a smile from the attorney.

It was the one and only laugh of the day as Athan and the prosecution queried over each and every juror. The judge kept reminding the attorney that she wasn't supposed to be presenting her case, only selecting jurors.

A little after 5:30 P.M., the judge counted the names

before him and announced, "Thirty-three remain from a potential of eighty-one. Court's adjourned until 9:00 A.M."

Wednesday morning, Valessa entered wearing a white sweater decorated with embroidered blue flowers that matched similar flowers in the material of her dress. The coordinated outfit triggered complaints and frowns from her mother's friends and family. Discussions of Valessa's clothes moved from the courtroom into the news.

Judge Padgett tapped the list of names in front of him. "I'll read a name and I want quick responses. Is everybody ready?"

The rhythm of the final decisions flowed like a well-oiled machine. The judge called out a name. "What says the State?"

"Accept," a prosecutor said.

"What says the defense?"

"Strike," an assistant public defender said.

The judge smiled when he heard two accepts. They coincided thirteen times by 11:39. Finally after two and a half days of battle, a twelve person jury was selected with one alternate before noon Wednesday, April 12, 2000. Six and one alternate were men along with six women. None appeared old enough to retire. Two huge posters of Jon Whispel and Adam Davis prepared by the defense were placed near the jury box along with an enormous chart entitled, "A Chronology of Sex, Drugs, and Murder."

Assistant State Attorney Pam Bondi outlined the state's case against Valessa in a similar fashion to the one that had been presented against Adam Davis. "The trio consumed LSD in Denny's Restaurant, where Valessa concocted the plot to kill her mother. Adam Davis suggested injecting her with heroin to put her to sleep with an air bubble that would kill her. [Unable to secure heroin, bleach was used instead.] When that failed to kill her,

Whispel handed either Davis or Valessa a knife, and one of them plunged it into Vicki Robinson several times."

Pam Bondi described, "Valessa, Whispel, and Davis dumped Vicki Robinson in a garbage can and cleaned up." She reminded the jury how difficult it was for a divorced mother to bring up two girls, and how she struggled with her youngest, Valessa, who frequently ran away and wanted to become pregnant by Davis.

She stopped to let her words sink in before she continued. "The trio partied in Ybor City with Vicki's money and got tatoos costing $600, before they tried to escape using her van and credit cards."

Pam Bondi ended, "Valessa Robinson said, 'I'm glad she's gone and now I'm free.'"

Assistant Public Defender Dee Ann Athan began her opening argument by gripping the edge of the huge poster of Adam Davis in prison orange and said, "This man was having a lewd and lascivious relationship with that child. This case is really about our failure to protect that child. With the psychological hold this guy had over that child, this child didn't have a chance." Dee Ann looked at her client. "He sexed her, drugged her, and drove her half way across the country. He was a drifter who was sometimes called 'Rattlesnake', a two-bit loser and criminal. He provided Robinson with drugs and manipulated both her and her mother, who once had him arrested."

Dee Ann Athan moved to the lectern and held it with both hands. "Davis is the spark that ignited the flame and slithered like a snake into Vicki Robinson's home."

Valessa smoothed her new sweater sleeve nervously, but her expression remained placid. She looked down at her matching flowered dress. Only she could know what she was feeling. It was lunchtime and Dee Ann hugged her before she left by the rear door.

* * *

In the afternoon, the prosecution called their first witness, Jim Englert, to the stand. Vicki's parents and friends sat behind the prosecutors. Mr. Robinson and his family sat near Valessa and the defense table.

Jim Englert, wearing a well-tailored black suit, sauntered to the witness chair. Once he sat down he stared at the prosecutor, not looking right or left. He stroked his silver and black striped tie nervously. His fingers found and held a gold chain with a cross and a topaz ring. "I gave these to Vicki," he said, glancing down at the jewelry.

The Assistant State Attorney Pam Bondi stood by the lectern. "Tell the jury how you knew Vicki Robinson."

The thin man with a full head of graying hair (kept long in the back) glanced at the jury. "I met Vicki Robinson through Single Purpose, a Christian singles group. Our first date was at the Clearwater Jazz Festival in Fall 1996. She brought her two daughters. I have three kids myself. I thought Vicki was beautiful and couldn't believe my luck." His voice was soft.

"Tell us what happened on the night of the murder."

"Vicki and I had finished dinner on the night of June 26 and were watching TV in the living room. I was sitting on the floor, and Vicki was behind me on the couch combing my hair. Around 11:30, Valessa, Adam, and another boy walked through the house. I got up to leave. It was late. Vicki told Valessa it was time for the boys to go home. Valessa said, 'Mom, the boys aren't leaving tonight.' I kissed Vicki good-bye in the garage and got in my car. I will never forget Vicki in the doorway." Jim Englert said. "I—"

Assistant Public Defender Dee Ann Athan jumped to her feet. "Objection, nonresponsive. There's no question."

"Overruled," Judge Padgett said.

"Go ahead, Mr. Englert," Pam Bondi coaxed.

"It was just a picture of her, the look she had on her face, the—" He was no longer touching the gold chain.

"Objection, Your Honor," Dee Ann Athan said.

"Overruled."

"I left her there."

"Cross," Pam Bondi said, and turned her witness over to the defense.

"You didn't agree with Vicki Robinson's style of parenting, did you?" Dee Ann Athan asked.

Jim Englert appeared surprised and took a few minutes before he answered cautiously. "I don't think any parent would agree 100 percent with anyone else's parenting style."

"But she was doing the best she could?" Dee Ann Athan said, encouraging the witness.

"Definitely, under the circumstances," he offered.

"In the summer of 1997, you and Vicki took a trip to Michigan without Valessa. In fact, she stayed alone, didn't she?"

"She didn't go with us, but I assumed she stayed around the house."

"Tell us why Valessa didn't go to Michigan with you. Tell us about that. The child was fourteen and was being left alone for two weeks."

"She had run away the day before."

"When you say that she had run away, you mean she would stay out all night, right?"

"She would stay out for days," Jim Englert responded tentatively. He looked away from his inquisitor.

"You have personal knowledge of that?" the attractive defense attorney asked, with a hint of accusation in her voice.

"I can't say I do," he admitted, looking at her again.

"What if Valessa was simply spending the night at a friend's house before leaving on a vacation? Did Vicki try to reach her daughter?"

Englert answered, "I don't know how many times Vicki may have called Valessa from Michigan."

Dee Ann Athan's voice raised. "She was fourteen

years old and told her mother, 'I'm not going on the trip.' And the next day when you came to the Robinson house, you, Vicki and Valessa's sister took off for Michigan, and left Valessa in Tampa, right?"

"Correct," Englert answered.

"And the whole time, no one called to see if she was alive. Did you?" Dee Ann Athan asked.

"I, personally, didn't call." Englert answered. "I don't know, maybe Vicki did."

"No further questions," Valessa's public defender said.

Jim Englert looked pensive as he slowly left the witness chair. Vicki's family were more unhappy than usual.

The jury filed out and Valessa stood up to leave. Dee Ann Athan hugged her. Valessa responded by clinging to her attorney.

Thursday morning, the courtroom was crammed full of visitors, voyeurs, and high school students. They were all impressed that the TV show *48 Hours* had a camera crew there to film the proceedings.

Valessa entered the courtroom wearing an ankle-length flowered skirt, white stockings, and black, low cut, strapless shoes. A blue cardigan sweater over a white blouse completed her outfit. Although conservative, no one could criticize it as a parochial school uniform. The skirt flowed as she walked to the defense table, closely followed by a deputy.

Before sitting, she raised her head and scanned the court with her eyes. She stared briefly at her grandparents, who scowled back. She looked at her father who smiled. She took her seat and cried. She looked at the ceiling as tears rolled down her cheeks. Perhaps she was asking God or her mother to help her. She didn't ball up her fists to hide the tears as she had done in so many previous court appearances. Assistant Public Defender Lisa Campbell tried to comfort her.

Valessa's tears were contagious. Chuck Robinson put his head down on the podium wall that separated him from the defense table, and his wife Vanessa wiped her eyes with a handkerchief. The judge and jury hadn't entered. Vicki's family and friends remained dry-eyed.

Everyone stood as Judge Padgett took his position on the bench. The jury followed. Assistant State Attorney Pam Bondi stood by the lectern and announced Jon Whispel. She hadn't restrained her blond hair in a loose bun today, but pulled it down and let it rest on the collar of her tailored navy suit.

Whispel entered with his hair clipped short in prisoner fashion. He wore a denim jacket and orange prison jump suit. "Prison pallor" had further whitened his skin. He took his place in the witness box and removed his glasses. He examined them and then put them back on.

The prosecutor asked him to tell the jury who he was, what his participation in Vicki Robinson's death consisted of, and about his plea agreement with the prosecution.

"The State allowed me to plead guilty to second-degree murder and receive twenty-five years in prison."

"In exchange for what?" Pam Bondi asked.

"My truthful testimony at any hearings, trials, or retrials of Adam Davis or Valessa Robinson."

"How old were you at the time of the murder?"

"Nineteen," he answered.

"How old was Adam Davis?"

"Nineteen."

"And Valessa?"

"Fifteen."

"So you were all teenagers," Pam Bondi stated.

"Yes."

"Go through the events of Friday, June 26, 1998, the day Vicki Robinson died."

"Me, Valessa and Adam spent most of the day with Vicki. She took us on errands to a shoe repair shop, and a JC Penney, and to Burger King for lunch. That night, me, Valessa, and Adam smoked marijuana in Valessa's bedroom and snuck out of the house, then bought some LSD. We sat around Denny's talking about heading back to Valessa's bedroom to trip on acid and stare at her black light. Then Valessa came up with the idea. We're sittin' around. Nobody's sayin' nothin'—all of the sudden Valessa gets all happy and says, "Let's kill my mom."

"What did you say?" Bondi asked.

"I was like, 'How could you get away with this?'" Jon Whispel held up his open palms and glanced at the jury.

He turned his head and faced Valessa. "Adam wanted to get some heroin and inject Vicki with a fatal overdose. It didn't pan out. Adam couldn't find some heroin to buy, but obtained a syringe. So we returned to Valessa's room and Adam started talking about using the syringe to inject Vicki with bleach and an air bubble."

The sound of one of Valessa's young friends crying interrupted him. He glanced around the court as if he was searching for the noise. He frowned.

"Adam got the syringe ready and then he and Valessa went into Vicki's bedroom. A few minutes later they came back and said Vicki had started to wake up. They were about to hide the syringe when Vicki knocked at Valessa's door. Adam opened the door, and Vicki told Valessa to grab her sleeping bag and come with her. Vicki headed back to her room through the kitchen, when Adam went after her."

Jon Whispel studied his handcuffs and looked up at Pam Bondi. "Valessa was still in her room when we both heard sounds of a struggle. They went into the kitchen and there was Adam with a chokehold around Vicki's neck. Adam told them he needed to get the syringe. He told Valessa to restrain her mother until he came back."

The sandy-haired young man took a few breaths before he described, "Me and Adam went to Valessa's bedroom. Adam found the syringe and returned to the kitchen. I followed and saw Vicki on the kitchen floor, struggling to get away from her daughter."

"And what was Valessa doing?" Pam Bondi asked.

"She was sitting on her mom's legs." His voice seemed to ring out in the hushed courtroom. "As she held her mother down, Adam put the syringe of bleach into her neck. Vicki saw it and asked Adam what he was doing. Adam complained that the syringe wasn't working. Valessa was still on top of her mother, hitting her in the stomach."

Jon Whispel, Davis's helpful sidekick, told the court, "I went back to Valessa's bedroom for Adam Davis's folding knife and returned to the kitchen. I gave it to either Adam Davis or Valessa Robinson. I didn't see who took the knife from me."

"Why?" asked prosecutor Pam Bondi.

Whispel removed his glasses and rubbed both eyes until the lids were red. He said, "To this day, I don't know, and I don't think I will ever know."

He put his glasses back on, as if they helped him see into the past. "I went back to the bedroom. Valessa came too. We heard the sound of escaping breath from the kitchen. Soon Adam joined us holding the knife in his left hand. Both the knife and Adam's hand had blood on them. 'Baby, you need to wash your hands,' Valessa said. Adam went into the bathroom to clean himself up and joined us in the bedroom. We smoked cigarettes and then we heard moaning coming from the kitchen."

Jon Whispel hesitated and observed the courtroom. Every seat was taken, and people standing were packed to the far walls. Some kept encroaching on the area in front of the television cameras, and were pressed back. The crushed mass of humanity were silent, hanging on Whispel's every word.

Pam Bondi said, "Please continue, Mr. Whispel."

"Adam said, 'The bitch won't die.' He went back to the kitchen. When he returned, he told us how he finished her off by stabbing her and tryin' to break her neck."

The blond prosecutor put her hand up to her mouth as though his words were affecting her. She managed to say, "Continue."

"Adam and me put Vicki in a garbage can we found in the garage and carried her to the minivan before cleaning up the blood with bleach and towels. We got Valessa and went to the woods near my house to bury her body. The ground was too hard, so we left it under some palmetto fronds. We planned to go back and use cement to sink it in the water."

The states exhibits of Vicki Robinson's house and garage flashed on the big screen as Jon Whispel pointed to areas in the kitchen, laundry room, and garage. Mrs. Robinson's unmade four-poster bed, surrounded by beautiful furnishings and french doors, flashed briefly. He pointed out the bed in Valessa's room, where he claimed that he and Valessa had waited for Vicki's death. The visuals made his story even more dramatic.

Valessa stared at her home as if she was in a trance. The pictures were clear. It must have been the first time she was seeing her house since her mother's murder. If she had spent a lot of time in her teens in a drug-induced haze, the life-sized pictures must have been awesome.

Whispel commented, "For the next few days we stayed in different hotels, got tattoos in Ybor City, ordered pizza, and bought drugs with Vicki's ATM card. Once Valessa mentioned her mother as we walked along Seventh Avenue in Ybor. She said she was glad her mom was dead. She's like, 'Well, now I'm free. I can do whatever I want."

Dee Ann Athan reached out to Valessa and held her hand. The girl's head was down, and she rested her chin on her chest.

Whispel then described their flight from Tampa. He ended with, "We was in Texas when Adam Davis saw the sheriff's cruiser. He hit the gas and cranked up the volume on the CD for a little travelin' music. Valessa lit two cigarettes: one for her and one for Adam."

Dee Ann Athan had watched his testimony without any expression, but frowned during his last remarks. She jumped to her feet to cross-examine the witness. "Why did you ignore that little detail until this court appearance? It's not in any of your depositions."

Jon looked down. "I just remembered it."

The judge observed the time and called a recess until 1:30 P.M.

Valessa had to be helped from the courtroom at lunchtime. She began the day crying, and trying to remain composed had taken its toll. She didn't turn to wave good-bye to her father.

If it was possible, there seemed to be more people in attendance in the afternoon. The benches contained no room for people's personal items. Pads, pocketbooks, and briefcases were placed under the seats. Curious onlookers lined the walls three deep. Illicit sex, drugs, and murder were everyday occurrences in contemporary America, but the religious upper-middle class consider themselves immune from such sin. It was a new phenomenon. Newspaper and television coverage of teen lovers who had been turned against one another by matricide created an intense public interest.

Dee Ann Athan stood at the lectern and said, "Good afternoon, Mr. Whispel." Her voice sounded soft and gentle. Her long dark hair appeared to have natural

waves. Her glasses, dark suit, and demeanor made a
commanding impression.

"How many hours did you spend with the prosecutors preparing your testimony?"

"Plenty," he answered.

"Wasn't Valessa a child back then? If you and Adam
wanted to go to an R-rated movie, Valessa couldn't get
in?"

Whispel appeared confused and looked at Bondi
and Williams, sitting toward his right.

"Why are you looking at the prosecutors?" Dee Ann
Athan shot at him. She left the lectern and got in his face.

"I ain't lookin' at them, I'm lookin' at you," Whispel
returned angrily. His voice raised and his white skin
flushed.

"Who scrubbed the blood from the white floor of
Vicki's kitchen?"

"Me and Adam."

"Who shoved her body in the garbage can?"

"Me and Adam."

"Who chose where to dump her. Who tried to dig
her grave?"

"Me and Adam, not Valessa." Jon Whispel testified,
somewhat more relaxed.

"Wasn't Adam always in control when the three of
you were together?" Athan asked.

"No! We all made decisions on what would happen
next. Nobody ran the show," Whispel answered, sounding annoyed.

The television camera captured his anger. Dee Ann
Athan appeared surprised but delighted. His reputation
of being a follower was promoted in the media for two
years as "The Lost Boy" or "Adam's Shadow." Athan again
tried antagonize him. "Your plea bargain was based on
you being a follower and nonparticipant. Do you deny
that was true?"

Brian Gonzalez, Whispel's attorney, squirmed in his

seat and tapped his fingers nervously. The two prosecutors didn't look any happier. Some members of the jury leaned forward and grew more attentive.

Whispel hung his head. "No," he said in a low voice.

Valessa's attorney changed her line of questioning. "You and Adam stole a van months before Vicki's murder and headed for Phoenix. You crashed it in Tallahassee, while being chased by the police, but managed to get away on foot. Valessa wasn't with you." Dee Ann Athan stated.

Before she could even ask a question, Jon Whispel volunteered, "Valessa's boyfriend Adam was with me. We . . ."

Assistant Public Defender Dee Ann Athan started to continue her line of questioning. Her mouth was open. She stopped and thought a minute. "Valessa's boyfriend? Did the prosecutors tell you to throw in her name as much as possible to get Valessa? To hurt her?"

"Ah . . . er . . . no," Whispel stammered.

Athan turned away from Whispel and appeared to be contemplating her next question. She turned on her heel and said, "In your direct testimony about the night of the murder, you said all three of you went to buy a heroin overdose for Vicki. Adam told you and Valessa to stay in the van because it might be dangerous. Why, in all the reams of depositions, did you fail to mention that conversation? You don't know if Davis scored or not. You only know what he told you."

"I . . . ah . . . er know he didn't get heroin. That's why he filled the hypodermic needle with bleach," Whispel mumbled.

"Why did he squirt it if he wanted an air bubble to kill her?" Dee Ann used a voice reminiscent of her schoolteacher days.

Pam Bondi jumped to her feet. "Objection, Your Honor."

"Let's not argue with the witness," Judge Padgett said, sounding like a gentle grandfather.

As she paced near the lectern, Dee Ann Athan decided to come at the witness from another direction. She glanced at the jury, and turned and shot her question at Whispel. "You testified that Valessa held her mother down. You're bigger than Valessa, aren't you?"

"Yeah," he said.

"While this horrible thing was going on, do you want this jury to believe that Adam Davis called this little thing to sit on her mother?" Attorney Athan pointed to Valessa, sitting at the defense table between Lisa Campbell and public defender Lyann Goudie. Her demure persona and small size was accentuated by the two bigger attorneys.

"That's right," Whispel answered. He held his head and closed his eyes.

The members of the jury looked from Jon Whispel to the slight young girl. The man wearing a big bulky prison jacket over his orange jumpsuit appeared huge in comparison. The violent images that Whispel's description of Valessa had evoked were in stark contrast to the serene girl seen in court that day, two years after the murder.

Dee Ann Athan continued to make the image clearer. "In all the pictures, Vicki was taller and bigger than her daughter."

"She was."

Dee Ann Athan pounced like a mother tiger. "If she was fighting for her life, Vicki could be presumed to be stronger."

Whispel removed his glasses again. He looked toward the prosecutors as if waiting for them to save him. "I . . . er, guess."

"Both you and Davis described Valessa as being high on LSD."

"Yes, we all were."

"You said in your deposition that Valessa was sitting on the bed next to you when Adam Davis entered with the knife in his bloody hands, but in the Davis trial in November '99, you implied Valessa was in the kitchen when her mother was stabbed."

"I made a mistake. I—" Whispel started to explain.

Dee Ann Athan reacted. "You made a mistake!"

"I was nervous. Like then I was nervous. Like now I'm nervous." Jon Whispel looked at the attorney as if he had answered her question.

"And could you be making a mistake now?" Dee Ann Athan asked before shaking her head affirmatively.

"No, ma'am," he said.

The judge looked toward the prosecutors who remained seated and then at the clock. "Court is adjourned until 9:00 A.M."

People straggled out in little groups talking about the trial while they waited to pass through the two doors. Two guys tried to get Whispel's attention, but his back was turned as he shuffled out between the two bailiffs near the judge's bench. The taller guy winked at his coworker and said, "Even Whispel knows bleach kills the HIV virus in a used hypo."

A woman carrying a pad asked, "Would you like to make a statement for the press? What's your name?"

"Me, ah . . . no," the clean-cut gentleman wearing a golf shirt said. His friend, wearing tan Dockers and Gucci loafers, laughed. "That should teach you to keep your mouth shut." They both pushed along the side of the slow crowd to get out of the room faster. The reporter followed in pursuit, but gave up when she reached the door and saw them enter the elevator.

The atmosphere on Friday morning was calm. The camera from *48 Hours* no longer caused excitement.

The division between Valessa's relatives was again evident by their seating arrangements. Her father and stepmother sat near the defense table. Vicki's family and friends settled behind the prosecutors. People squeezed together on the smooth wooden benches.

Valessa's dowdy white dress with black flowers, sporting a hemline that hit just below the knees, didn't receive negative attention from her mother's relatives, the prosecution, or the press. Even with the bulky black sweater, she didn't look like a matron. Her courtroom outfits were used only to strengthen Dee Ann Athan's contention that Valessa was a child at the time of the murder.

Whispel entered and resumed his position in the witness chair. Dee Ann Athan walked to the lectern to continue her cross-examination. Yesterday, Athan had tried to make Whispel appear deceptive by getting him noticeably confused and angry on the witness stand. He gained some composure overnight, whereas she lost some. As she went over numerous discrepancies in his testimony, he responded less hesitantly.

"Yesterday, you said Adam Davis cranked up the sound of the CD for a little traveling music when he saw the sheriff's car in Texas. You added that Valessa lit two cigarettes: one for her and one for Adam. Why didn't you bother to reveal that detail before, Mr. Whispel?"

"If I didn't, I didn't," he retorted in an loud, argumentive voice. Then, moderating it, he said, "I mean no. I don't think I did."

"Tell the jury the terms of your plea agreement to ensure you wouldn't end up on death row."

"I get twenty-five years."

"In return for what?"

"My testimony in any trials against Adam Davis and Valessa Robinson."

"All you have to do is come to court and testify against Adam Davis and Valessa?" Dee Ann Athan emphasized for the jury.

"And to tell the truth, Your Honor," Pam Bondi interjected.

Dee Ann Athan looked at the prosecutor and back to Whispel, "And who decides the truth, Mr. Whispel? Do I decide the truth?"

"Somebody who was there, seen it and knows what happened." Whispel answered.

"Valessa was a vulnerable child led into a world of sex, drugs, and eventually murder by her older boyfriend, Adam Davis," Dee Ann Athan stated. "Okay, let's focus on how Valessa was feeling in the days after Vicki Robinson's murder. Hadn't Valessa been especially pale, tired, and sickly?"

"Yes," Whispel answered.

"Had she eaten much?"

"No."

"She spent a lot of time in bed, while you and Adam were free to run errands and use her mother's credit card. Neither of you were sick?"

"No."

Jury members followed the defense attorney with their eyes. Her sincere efforts in the defense of her client were unmistakable. Lisa Campbell and Lyann Goudie comforted Valessa during Dee Ann's cross-examination of Whispel. They included Valessa in their side comments. The girl appeared to thrive on their attention. She was no longer the lonely ice princess portrayed by the press. Her teacher, Mr. Dipple, said that Valessa would defend any of her classmates if she thought they were being picked on. She and Dee Ann Athan had that in common.

After going over all of Whispel's testimony, Dee Ann Athan had to return the witness to the prosecution for rebuttal.

The Assistant State Prosecutor Pam Bondi said, "Vicki Robinson was on her stomach—with Adam Davis on her back and Valessa sitting on her legs—when you handed him the knife?"

"Yes. That's how they were."

"Had Adam forced her to get the 'A' tattooed on her hand?"

"No. She did that while he was in jail."

"Did Adam make her take drugs?"

"No."

"Did you ever see Adam be anything but sweet to Valessa Robinson?"

"That's all he was to her."

"Describe Valessa's personality."

"Sometimes she was real ditzy. You hear about people who aren't blond who act like blondes." Whispel's face turned crimson after his words escaped.

The blond prosecutor's ponytail raised off her collar as she quickly turned away from the jury to stare at Whispel. "Thank you," she said crossly.

Most people in the courtroom laughed at the blond joke. Pam Bondi didn't join them.

The prosecutor returned to the business of wiping out the inroads made by the defense. She ordered a repeat of the visuals of Valessa's house, the site where her mother's body was found, and two pictures of the body. This time the prosecution brought in the tools and real items that were recovered from Vicki's van including, three wallets belonging to Valessa Robinson, Adam Davis, and Jon Whispel.

She announced, "Davis had Vicki's credit cards in his possession. Valessa had some cash. Jon Whispel's wallet contained receipts for all the hotels they stayed in."

Whispel acknowledged them with a nod.

"Enter the exhibits into evidence," Bondi said.

Neither the prosecution nor the defense asked why Whispel saved the receipts. They were the real evidence that connected him to the crime (besides the location of Vicki's body near his house). Davis's fingerprints were on the bleach bottle. It was Valessa's mother, her credit cards, her van, and her house. If Whispel wasn't somehow emotionally attached to Adam Davis, he could have escaped punishment by betraying the couple. Of all the questions Dee Ann Athan had asked, she ignored the big one: why he stayed. Perhaps because he wanted the drugs Vicki's money bought them; or more insidiously, because he had been a participant with Davis. His attorneys had pulled the greatest coup. Even his attorney Brian Gonzalez couldn't explain why Whispel participated and stayed. He said, "He can't tell you. He doesn't know."

Pam Bondi excused the state's star witness, Jon Whispel, and called Bruce Wilson to the stand. The big man wearing a navy jacket with blue jeans and black cowboy boots strode to the witness chair with the energetic step of a man with purpose. He took the oath and told the court he had been a sheriff in Pecos County, Texas for sixteen years, and had been with the department for thirty years. The top of his forehead was whiter than his ruddy face, suggesting he often wore a hat. His badge glinted when he sat down.

The Assistant State Prosecutor Pam Bondi uttered, "Please tell the court what happened on July 2, 1998."

"I read the bulletins on the case. At 7:00 A.M. that morning, the latest teletype showed the fugitives stopped during the night at an ATM in Luling, a town 400 miles east on I-10. I went home for lunch and my secretary called that an ATM was hit in Ozona 100 miles east. It meant my deputies and I had to be on I-10 to watch for the green Nissan minivan with a Florida plate. I drove to an overpass and joined a Texas Highway Patrol trooper parked in the median, waiting for the van also. Within minutes, one of the deputies pulled up and we decided to move farther east. I got in Larry Jackson's cruiser and took over the driving. We needed to be in one car in case Jackson had to shoot. The trooper was waiting with spikes to stop the van. We waited at a curve in the highway and when a green Nissan minivan fitting the description came into view, I got behind it and turned on the lights and the siren trying to get it to stop." The sheriff looked away from the prosecutor.

"Did the vehicle comply?" Pam Bondi asked.

"No, it did not," Sheriff Wilson responded.

"We have a videotape taken by the Texas Highway Patrol officer. Describe what's happening while it's on the screen," Pam Bondi said. She gave the sheriff a penlight to point out the actions on the video.

"There's the van rushing past." The red beam in the sheriff's hand caught the Nissan minivan. "That's the police cruiser, the one my deputy and I were in. As I chased after the van, my deputy leaned out the passenger window and fired his pistol. There is the van spinning after the deputy hit both back tires."

Sheriff Wilson's slow Texas drawl sped up as he re-enacted the exciting chase. The sheriff's profile as he focused on the screen revealed he had an indentation in his hair from wearing his Texas hat. "This is the trooper here." He highlighted the red beam on an officer aiming a gun at the van. "He's shouting 'Stop! Stop! Stop!' The van spun off the highway and continued on the service road even after the deputy shot out the remaining two tires. When he shot at the fender on the driver's side and pointed the gun at the driver, the van stopped."

The visual on the screen stopped too. On the upper right corner 11:44:01 showed Texas time. The date appeared beneath it, 07-02-98. The pictures of two teens lying on their faces in the Texas dirt were frozen in the time dated video. "That's Whispel," Sheriff Wilson said, focusing his brilliant red light on him. "That's Valessa right here."

Valessa watched her own capture like everyone else in the courtroom. When she was on LSD, she told her

captors the chase was like a movie. She was stone cold
sober watching it on the television screen. The sheriff
in the ten-gallon hat on the screen was only a few feet
away in the witness chair. Adam Davis was on the driver's side of the van, and invisible.

If she was remembering her feelings for Adam Davis
after the video, only she would have known. She observed it with less emotion than most people experienced a movie.

"Sheriff, what was her demeanor when she was arrested?" the assistant prosecutor asked.

"She was mad, in my opinion," the sheriff said, looking at Valessa.

"Was she crying?" Pam Bondi asked.

"No."

Dee Ann Athan left her client at the defense table
when the prosecutor indicated that she was finished
with the witness.

"When the three were taken into custody, were they
murder suspects?" Assistant Public Defender Dee Ann
Athan asked.

"No, it was not confirmed. At the time there was foul
play feared."

"Thank you," Athan said.

The morning disappeared into multiple images of
videos, in Tampa and Texas interspersed with actual exhibits making the state's case strong.

In the afternoon, the prosecutors changed places.
Shirley Williams was six inches shorter than Pam Bondi
and wore her dark hair turned under at the ends like a
"page boy." She stood by the lectern and called Colonel
Keith Billingsley. He was young compared to the sheriff.

"I'm with the Tampa Police Department," the dark-
haired man said after taking the oath.

"How did you come in contact with Valessa Robinson?"

"Her mother reported her a runaway in May 1998. I investigated an address we had for Adam Davis and knocked on the door. He said he didn't know where she was, but there was a girl with a book bag covered with 'Valessa loves Adam.' It gave her away."

"What happened?"

"Valessa was handcuffed and placed in the back seat of the police cruiser. She began kicking at the windows when she learned Adam Davis was being arrested."

"Did she say anything to you?"

"Yes. She said, 'I don't care who it is or what I have to do. I'm going to be with him no matter what it takes.'"

"No more questions," Assistant Prosecutor Shirley Williams said, looking at the defense table.

Dee Ann Athan strode to the lectern with determination. "Mr. Billingsley!" Her voice was full of vitriolic rage. "You decided Adam Davis was the reason she wasn't in school that day, didn't you? The adult was keeping the child out of school. Right?"

"Yes, ma'am," the officer said.

The Assistant Public Defender Dee Ann Athan looked at the prosecutor triumphantly. "Again another prosecution witness proved my point. Valessa was a child. No more questions."

Shirley Williams quickly excused him and called the Home Depot clerk who had sold Adam Davis and Jon Whispel cement. She had the State's exhibit twenty-five put on the screen. Adam and Jon were caught on videotape and the state produced register receipts too. The clerk's testimony was illustrated with bags of cement, shovels, and a pitchfork.

The defense attorney asked, "Was Valessa with Adam Davis and Whispel when they bought cement?"

"No, just the two men on the videotape."

"Thank you. I have no further questions." Dee Ann went back to stand behind Valessa and patted her shoulder.

Shirley Williams called Albert Montantez. "I'm the manager of the Valhalla Tattoo Parlor on East 7th in Ybor City."

"On Saturday night June 27 and early Sunday June 28, did you see Valessa Robinson, Adam Davis and Jon Whispel? Did they come in for tattoos?"

"Yeah. They were flush with cash, excited and spinning," the dark haired man answered. "They would have paid anything we asked."

The prosecutor asked more questions about the tattoos, and she questioned more about their actions before turning her witness over to the defense.

Dee Ann Athan was prepared for him. She shook a paper in the air. "This is a consent form for minors. Only adults can legally get a tattoo."

"That's right."

"Doesn't that make Valessa a child?"

He nodded his head and said "yes" before being excused.

The prosecution's case dealt with the heinous nature of the crime, and they brought out the forensic technician, who had photographed Vicki Robinson's body in the garbage can. Dee Ann Athan opened her case by stating that Valessa was a child who wasn't protected from two adult males who had killed her mother. She jumped up just as Shirley Williams commanded, "Tell the jury what time you got there and what you saw when you arrived."

"It was the early morning hours. There was someone out there, like one of the detectives." He looked at the defense table.

"May we approach the bench briefly?" Dee Ann Athan requested. She stood by Valessa while Lisa Campbell met the prosecutors before the judge. The blond curly haired court reporter stood and listened to the conference, which the court was not privy to. Valessa and Dee Ann joined them.

The judge looked down on Valessa. "Do you wish to leave the room?"

She nodded her head. "Yes, sir."

"You have a right to be present during testimony," Judge Padgett reminded her.

"Yes, sir," she acknowledged.

"Okay, you can take her out," Judge Padgett told the defense.

The room murmured with whispered conversations about why Valessa had chosen to leave. When an aerial photo of the crime scene appeared on the screen, Vicki's parents headed for the front exit. They barely made it to the door when the photograph of Vicki's decomposed body appeared.

Donna Klug, Valessa's grandmother, sat on the bench in the lobby, clutching her pocketbook and crying. The seventy-five-year-old woman rocked herself slightly and looked small and frail. She asked a reporter why Valessa had been allowed to leave the courtroom. "She should be made to take it. She should sit there and watch what they did to my daughter."

Another reporter asked, "Why do you believe that Valessa is a monster who wanted her mother dead?" The grandmother turned toward her husband and didn't answer.

On Monday morning, April 17, 2000, Valessa entered the courtroom looking like a mother's dream, in a white sweater set, a short, navy blue plaid skirt, white stockings, and navy shoes with straps that matched her skirt. Her outfit was more like one that newspaper writers claimed good little school girls wore to Sunday school.

The State called Linda Fales. She had short dark hair and worked for the Sun Coast Schools Credit Union, where Vicki Robinson banked and owned an ATM card.

"Did you have contact with the sheriff's office about the disappearance of Vicki Robinson?" the prosecutor asked.

"Yes, on June 30. Her account was accessed on the twenty-sixth for $58.57—by July 1st it had been accessed many times."

"Did you decide to assist in an investigation?"

"Yes, we sent new videotapes to all our machines and allowed the used tapes to be examined."

"Did you produce a picture from one of the videos?"

"Yes, ma'am."

"Did you agree to limit withdrawals to $100 a day?"

"The sheriff's department asked us to and to monitor the account. One of our employees volunteered to monitor it at night and brought his laptop computer home. He took a call in the early morning hours of July 2, and I called Detective Iverson."

"Thank you, Ms. Fales."

Dee Ann Athan took over at the lectern. "You testified your company put new videotapes in your machines. Did they produce any pictures of Valessa Robinson?"

"No, just Adam Davis," the bank employee answered.

"Thank you, no more questions." Dee Ann Athan went back to the defense table and smiled at Valessa.

After the morning break, Shirley Williams called Lieutenant John Marsicano. He was an attractive man in a well-tailored gray suit. His dark hair was full, except for a thinning patch in the front. After taking the oath, he told the court that he was heading the investigation of Vicki Robinson's murder. He and Detective Iverson had hopped on a plane for Texas as soon as they heard that the three teens were being held. They had arrived just before midnight on July 2, 1998, then drove to the juvenile center in Odessa.

"A nurse at the center said Valessa complained about being ill earlier, but was well enough to be questioned.

We interviewed her in the conference room to ask her about the disappearance of her mother."

"What did she tell you?" Assistant Prosecutor Williams asked.

"She said she had no idea where her mother was. Iverson and I continued to question her. When she said her mother was dead, she admitted being involved in a homicide." The detective glanced at the jury and back to the prosecutor. "She told us what happened and then we went over her Miranda rights with her. She drew us a map showing where her mother's body could be found."

"Did you take a further statement from her?" Shirley Williams asked in a perfunctory way.

"Yes, we did," John Marsicano said equally deadpan.

"And was that statement tape-recorded?" The prosecutor's voice was flat.

"Yes, it was, ma'am." He watched as the tape recorder was placed on the defense table.

"This is the State's exhibit 103," Assistant Prosecutor Shirley Williams said as she held up the tape. She passed it on, to be placed in the stereo recorder.

An older man's voice announced he was Detective Jim Iverson. Marsicano said, *"We're in the Juvenile Detention Center in Odessa, Texas to question Valessa Robinson. It's 1:09 A.M. Tampa time."*

Marsicano's voice continued. *"What I want to do is place this recorder down on the table in front of you so that you can talk into it. Just talk clearly so it will pick you up. What I want you to do is to go back to Friday night, when you, Adam, and Jon had been partying a little. You had done some acid. It was late Saturday or early Saturday (Sunday) morning. You came back into the house and apparently woke your mom up. You got into an argument there in the kitchen of the house. If you would just go from there and tell me what happened."*

Valessa's voice started. *"From what I . . ."* She made a little cough like clearing her throat.

The person who seemed to be the most surprised in the room at the sound of her voice was Valessa. She put her hand up to her mouth in embarrassment. She acted like so many people do when hearing their voice on tape. Every man and woman on the jury stared at her.

"From what I guess I could say recall, I was on acid. I remember I stabbed my mother once in the throat, and it released a lot of blood. And she wasn't dead yet, and I stabbed her again twice in the back, and then I couldn't handle all the blood and everything and I panicked. And I went to my room and I had Jon and Adam clean up the blood and put her body in a trash can."

Either the recorder had a problem or Valessa had trouble making her voice clear. It cracked slightly. *"We took my mom's body down past Jon's house . . . down a dirt road. And we were going to bury her, but there were a couple of problems, so we just stuck the body there. We were gonna go back an bury her, but then I found out that there was like reports that I was missing, and my mom was missing, so we had to leave and get out of Florida, and we left."*

Her hands in her lap, Valessa picked nervously at the sleeve of her new white sweater. It occupied her and kept her eyes lowered. Dee Ann Athan put her hand on her shoulder and patted her. She smoothed Valessa's hair back making her face more visible.

"You left taking your mom's van?" Iverson's voice was strong.

"Yes." The small female voice came from the recorder on the prosecutor's table.

"When y'all left Florida you came across Interstate 10 towards Texas. How much money did y'all take out of her account?"

"I seriously don't know."

"You used her credit card. You used her Visa card?"

"Yes."

"You used her Mobile gas card?" Iverson continued.

"Yeah. I used two other of her credit cards, too. I just don't know what they're called."

The girl's voice on the recorder sounded cooperative. The detectives took turns, continuing to focus on the money issue, and moved to the map she had drawn for them.

"You said you stabbed your mother with a knife. What did you do with it?"

"I don't know. Honestly I don't remember where we tossed it." She answered and as though they weren't happy with her response. *"I was so high. Oh man, we went so many places. I don't remember where."*

"What kind of a knife was it?"

"It was a pull-out knife about a foot in length. I got it from a friend named Danny."

Marsicano asked, *"Where did you stab your mother?"*

"The kitchen," Valessa answered.

"It all took place out there in the kitchen."

"Yes."

"Was it closer to the sink or the refrigerator?"

"It was closer to the sink."

"Did she hit her head on the floor when she fell?" Iverson's said, dominantly.

"I pinned her down before I like stabbed her. I had to pin her down."

"Were y'all fighting before this happened? I mean like physically fighting before you pulled out the knife?" Iverson asked.

There was dead silence except for the sound of the tape whirring.

"You're shaking your head. You have to say yes or no," Iverson told her.

"Yes."

Marsicano's voice came in. *"What clothes were you wearing, Valessa? Do you recall?"* He sounded gentle.

"I don't know."

"How was your mother dressed?"

"In her nightgown."

"How was she dressed in the garbage can?"

Iverson came in. *"What color was it?"*

"Peach."

Marsicano jumped in. *"Did the knife go through the night-gown?"*

"I don't recall." Valessa paused. *"It should have when I got her in the back."* Her voice was less clear as she stammered and paused during her answer.

"Okay." Marsicano continued. *"And Adam and Jon were in the bedroom there?"*

"They should have been. I don't remember them coming out." Valessa's voice sounded strained and confused.

"Was the door open or closed?"

"I don't know. That's all I'm going to say."

The detectives stopped and a few turns of the tape whirred. *"Are you saying you don't want to say anymore?"* Marsicano asked.

"No, 'cause my stomach's really getting hurt."

"Okay," Marsicano said.

Iverson took the head detective's lead. *"All right. We're going to conclude the interview. It's now 1:30, Tampa time on the third of July."*

As the State prepared another exhibit, Donna Davis, Adam's stepmother, moved from her rear seat to a space behind Valessa's father and stepmother. For her first appearance in court since his trial, she was wearing a black dress with white flowers. She put her head on the back of their seats and stared past them at Valessa, hanging her head.

The big screen lit up with a television news clip of Valessa the day after her mother's funeral, when she was moved from the juvenile center to the adult jail. In response to reporters asking her why she had done it, she entered the police van and retorted, "You'll find out later."

John Marsicano was still on the stand. Assistant Prosecutor Shirley Williams had asked him questions before Valessa's confession and the more damaging TV clip. Valessa's appearance on television was visual evidence of her defiance. Williams let the image have an impact on the jury and then turned toward the defense table and said, "Cross."

Dee Ann Athan hugged Valessa and then took over the lectern. "When you interrogated Valessa, didn't you consider her a murder suspect?"

"No, not at first," Marsicano answered. "We were not sure Vicki Robinson was dead."

"Were you aware Valessa had taken LSD before being taken into custody?"

"She seemed coherent."

"What about Valessa's father? Was he notified that you planned to question his daughter?"

"Yes, I called Chuck Robinson and talked to him before the interview."

"Was he told that she was a murder suspect?"

"We didn't use the word suspect with her father."

Chuck Robinson leaned over the wall separating him from his daughter and the defense table, and hung his head.

Donna Davis, sitting behind him, said, "I hope she gets the same justice Adam did." Her loud voice carried her message to more than Mr. Robinson. Some members of Vicki's entourage smiled in approval.

Donna Davis made wry faces at Dee Ann Athan as the prosecutor tried to destroy the impact of Valessa's confession. People in the jury watched. It was unlikely that they knew who she was.

Chuck Robinson kept focused on his daughter. When Athan pointed out inconsistencies regarding the

young girl's naïve attempt to accept responsibility for
the actions of the two older, bigger men, Donna Davis
groaned audibly.

The tape took nineteen minutes to play, but Dee
Ann Athan dissected it for an hour and a half. Lieutenant John Marsicano began to act like he was being
personally attacked after the first hour of cross-examination. He remained professionally polite, but his tone
of voice included anger. His expression broadcast dis-
dain.

If Dee Ann Athan noticed, it didn't daunt her verbal
sparring with the detective. It may have encouraged it.
He was testy when asked about the girl's right to be represented by a juvenile advocate, and if an attorney were
due her under Texas law. His defense for questioning
her without a parent or anyone else present was that
she was not a suspect. Dee Ann Athan gnawed at his testimony, trying to shred it like a lion ripping food off a
carcass to keep her cub alive. Her tenacity for her
young client couldn't be questioned.

It angered Donna Davis and Vicki's friends and family. The only reason could be that they feared the Assistant
Public Defender gained points for Valessa. As Athan's
questions went on, Valessa's father sat up and smiled at
his daughter. He was one who appreciated the defender's
efforts.

At the break, Donna Davis rushed from the courtroom. The woman who sat closed-mouthed at her stepson's trial talked to everyone with a pad or a camera. "I
want to see she gets justice," she repeated in a shrill
voice, entering the lobby. Her anger and demeanor attracted reporters. She orchestrated her own little press
conference. "Adam didn't introduce Valessa to drugs.
He wasn't the mastermind. Valessa participated in the
death, and celebrated afterwards. Adam got a death sentence. She can only get life. It isn't fair. She gets special

treatment. She got to celebrate her birthday in court. We have to fight to see Adam for fifteen minutes."

Chuck Robinson and his wife Vanessa stood on one side, and Vicki's family and friends were a few yards away. All could hear Donna Davis's complaints. If Vicki's family recognized that Davis's misgivings were similar to their own, they didn't join her. Instead they joined the Robinsons, shook hands, and acted like old friends reunited.

Reentering the courtroom, the family separated as usual. Vicki's sat near the prosecution and the Robinsons near Valessa and the defense. Adam's stepmother had accomplished her mission and didn't return.

The State called Colleen Macklem. A woman appearing to be in her twenties took the stand. She was attractive with little makeup and her light brown hair pulled back, revealing her ears and tiny earrings. Her high, severely plucked eyebrows gave her a perpetually surprised look. The suit she wore was conservative, even with a short skirt.

Shirley Williams asked, "How do you know Valessa?"

"My boyfriend shared a cell with Adam Davis and asked me to drive her to jail to visit him," Colleen said. "Valessa's mother drove her to the Kash n' Karry where I picked her up."

"How long was the ride?"

"About twenty minutes. At first Valessa didn't talk much, but I got her talking about Adam. Then she started complainin' about her mother and how she wouldn't let her do what she wanted. She said her mother was the reason Adam was in jail on child abuse charges."

"What else did she tell you?"

"And she was like, all of the sudden her exact words were to me, 'I'm gonna kill my mom and I'm gonna get Adam to help me.' I tried to reason with her, but she cut me off."

"How did she do that?"

"She's like, 'You'd better be nice to me or I'll kill you too.' She's like, 'You don't know me. You don't know my mom. You don't know our situation.'" Colleen Macklem glanced at Valessa. "When we got to the jail and she walked into the visiting booth, where Adam waited, she changed. When she saw Adam she was a ray of sunshine; a totally different person."

Valessa stared back at the witness with an incredulous look on her face. Her attorneys presented her as a child. When she listened to the testimony, she appeared to be a youth that just found out there was no Santa Claus. If she thought Colleen was a friend and confidant, her testimony proved how mistaken she was.

Dee Ann Athan charged up to the lectern when the prosecutor turned over the witness.

"How many times were you convicted of a felony?"

"Twice." Colleen answered. She looked more alert as she waited for the attorney's next question.

"Why did you wait more than a year to divulge this damning evidence?" Athan asked.

"I had personal problems."

"Didn't you ever say, 'I could kill my mother,' in anger and not mean it when you were a teenager?"

"Well, yes, mothers sometimes make you want to scream."

"No more questions." Dee Ann Athan turned and went back to the defense table and comforted her client with a loving pat on the shoulder. Valessa looked up at her attorney.

The Assistant State Prosecutor Shirley Williams called Dr. Lee Miller. The balding, white haired Hillsborough Medical Examiner wearing a gray suit and maroon tie took the oath and outlined his credentials: 6,000 autopsies and testimony in hundreds of trials.

Vicki's brother escorted his parents from the courtroom. Some family members and friends remained seated behind the prosecutors. Valessa's father and stepmother held their usual position—as close to the defense as they could get. Valessa leaned forward and acknowledged their closeness with a nod of appreciation.

The doctor began to describe that the needle marks on Vicki Robinson's neck were so obliterated by decomposition that it was impossible to tell the presence of bleach in her system. He testified that the two disturbed areas in her lower back were impossible to define as knife wounds, but he pointed to an area on his own neck to show the jury where she had been stabbed. "She could have lived a minute or two afterward."

"Would Vicki Robinson have been conscious during that time?" Shirley Williams asked.

"Yes, for most of it anyway," the doctor answered.

"The official cause of death?"

"Homicidal violence, including a stab wound of the neck, penetrating the left carotid artery and jugular vein."

Chuck Robinson's body shook. He watched his daughter ball up her small fists and press them into her eyes. His wife clutched his shoulder.

"Did you observe any type of defense wounds on her hands or arms?" Shirley Williams asked, and looked toward the jury.

"No. There were no such wounds," Dr. Miller answered, also focusing on the jury.

If the implication was that Vicki trusted her attacker, it wasn't verbalized. The members of the jury stared at Valessa.

Valessa dropped her head on the table, and her father lifted himself out of the seat as if he was going to jump over the wall, but he eventually regained his composure and sat down.

Shirley Williams offered the witness to the defense.

Dee Ann Athan stated, "You pointed to the left side of your throat and said Vicki Robinson suffered a fatal stab wound to the left side of her neck through the carotid artery and jugular vein. Valessa told detectives that she stabbed her mother in the throat, when in fact she was stabbed in the side of her neck?"

Shirley Williams jumped up. "Objection, Your Honor!"

Dee Ann Athan retreated to return and fight another day.

"The State rests, your Honor," Shirley Williams said.

The press hounded Athan to find out if Valessa would testify.

"That will be up to Valessa."

Tuesday, April 18: the defense attorneys were visited at the defense table by a number of other attorneys, who then left quickly. Valessa had entered, wearing a blue plaid jumper and big black sweater. She talked seriously to her three attorneys.

Assistant Defense Attorney Lisa Campbell walked to the lectern and called the defense's first witness, Dr. John Halpern. His wild, curly, dark hair circled his receding hairline, giving him the appearance of an aging hippie in a dark suit. Small, wire-rimmed glasses added to the image. He told the court that he was a Harvard-trained physician practicing psychiatry in Boston.

Lisa Campbell was so tall that she had to lean down on the lectern. She encouraged the doctor to describe his specialty, LSD.

"Lysergic acid diethylamide is a chemical compound extracted from ergot alkaloids, used in the study of schizophrenia and other mental disorders, and as a psychedelic drug; it produces hallucinations, delusions resembling those occurring in a psychotic state. Messenger compounds can produce psychotic breaks. It's been my specialty since it escaped from the laboratory in the 1960s," he said.

Lisa Campbell chuckled, and most of the others in

the courtroom too laughed. The doctor appeared to enjoy the reaction, as though he was used to it.

"Doctor, how long does LSD last?"

"One hit of LSD lasts from eight to ten hours. Time and space distortions are common. A person can experience anxiety and bliss at the same time."

"Is judgment impaired by the drug?" Lisa Campbell asked.

"Emotional reactions can seem indifferent. You can say that judgment is impaired," the doctor responded.

The Assistant Public Defender stopped short of asking him to give direct testimony about Valessa. She went back to the defense table and conferred with the other two attorneys. They must have decided it was too dangerous to ask him about Valessa for fear that it would prompt the prosecutors to ask that Valessa's private journals be revealed.

Lisa Campbell didn't return to the lectern, but thanked the doctor from the defense table. The black attorney sat next to Valessa and whispered in her ear.

Assistant Prosecutor Pam Bondi asked to approach the bench. All the lawyers met for the sidebar. Pam Bondi reminded the judge about how the doctor had talked about indifference. "Reading the journals, she's a very indifferent person, based on her past."

Lisa Campbell protested. "He hasn't testified or given anything at all on Miss Robinson."

The jury was protected from the information and the judge ruled the journals would remain sealed.

The defense called Corey Simone. A long lanky skeleton of a man took a seat in the witness chair. He told the court he worked as a tattoo artist at 'Valhalla Tattoos' on 7th Avenue in Ybor City. He resembled a living billboard. When he rubbed his shaved head, he called attention to the words "Murder Junkies" at his virtually nonexistent hairline. The intricate blue tattoos on his arms appeared like a lace extension from his short sleeve denim outfit trimmed with white embroidery.

The numerous ring piercings on his nose, ears, and lips jiggled as he answered the defense attorney. "Yes, I inked Adam Davis and Jon Whispel the weekend after the murder."

"What about Valessa? What was she like?" Dee Ann Athan asked him.

"She looked really sluggish. Sickly, I guess you'd call it. Like she was comin' down from a bad drug high."

The members of the jury stared at him. Some showed shock by leaving their mouths agape. Others appeared stiff as they tried not to reveal any expression. One juror covered her mouth with her hand. The guy with the ponytail smiled.

The prosecutor asked, "Did you see the 'A' Miss Robinson had tattooed on her hand?"

"No," Corey said, shaking his head. The rings swung in the opposite direction.

"Thank you, Mr. Simone."

Dee Ann Athan called Jennifer Larsen. A beautiful young girl with shiny, long, dark, hair took the stand. She smiled at Valessa, who smiled back. The only jewelry visible was a cross on a chain around her neck.

"You are a friend of Valessa's?" Dee Ann Athan asked.

"Yes, we've been best friends, starting during the second grade at Seminole Presbyterian and continuing through the ninth grade."

"Is she still your best friend?" the defense attorney asked.

"Yes, she is." Jennifer Larsen again looked toward her friend at the defense table. Her voice was strong and clear.

"Jennifer, have you ever said, 'I wish my mother was dead?'" Dee Ann Athan asked.

"Yes I have," Jennifer Larsen answered, glancing at the jury.

"When you saw Valessa on television news being transferred to the adult jail shouting, 'I love Adam!' what did you think?"

"She was trying to stand tall; acting tough," the young girl answered.

"Is that the Valessa you knew?"

"No. She was usually more happy and carefree."

"Thank you, Jennifer. I'd like to call Robert Larsen, Jennifer's father."

The father patted his daughter's arm, affirming their warm relationship, as they exchanged places on the witness stand. He had a short beard and thinning hair, but there was a remarkable family resemblance between father and daughter.

Dee Ann Athan smiled at Robert Larsen. "You and your wife must have known Valessa well, since you bought her all the new clothes she has worn to the courtroom."

"Yes, she accompanied us on family outings to Disney World and car races. She was like a member of our family since she was a little girl," Mr. Larsen said.

"When you heard her voice on the confession tape, did it sound normal?" Dee Ann Athan asked.

"No, she sounded lethargic and down—not Valessa."

"Thank you, Mr. Larsen," the defense attorney said.

The first witness from Texas, Pyote Wickett, testified that the runaway was suspected of murder. He knew her father lived in St. Louis, but he didn't have an address or phone number. He stated, "Valessa seemed scared while in custody."

Corey Williamson, the intake officer from the Odessa Juvenile Center, testified, "Valessa complained of pain in the pelvic area."

Sandra King, a juvenile probation officer who handled Valessa's case in Texas, said, "Knowing what she was suspected of doing, I thought she was very calm."

Susan Black, a secretary and bookkeeper who

worked in the probation department in Pecos County, Texas, testified, "I saw Valessa curled in a fetal position, playing with her belly button."

Dee Ann Athan asked, "How long had she been playing with her belly button?"

"Approximately five to ten minutes. She began to ask questions while she was being driven to another facility. She asked what happened to the two gentlemen who were with her. She was asking if they were okay and if we knew what was going on with them."

Dee Ann Athan called Jim Iverson from the Hillsborough County Sheriff's Office. She brought out a model of Vicki Robinson's house—complete with pink countertops in the kitchen and a replica of Valessa's bed, including the doors and the direction they faced open and closed.

"Do you agree that this is an exact model of Vicki's home?" she asked, placing the model in the detective's hands.

He observed it and turned it. "I'm not sure about the angles of the walls, but it's fairly accurate." He answered like a careful detective.

"Do you see how when Valessa's bedroom door is open, the wall obstructs the view of the kitchen?"

"Yes."

Dee Ann took back the model and then said, "When you interviewed Valessa in Texas with Lt. Marsicano you talked to her a long time before turning on the tape. Your questions revealed that you already knew what her response would be. You played fast and loose with the teenager's rights, and tricked her into confessing. Didn't you tell her about her right to remain silent only after you already knew what you and Lt. Marsicano wanted to know?"

"No, ma'am."

"You were supposed to read her Miranda from the beginning, weren't you?" She stood near the lectern and reminded the detective, "You talked to Valessa without parental consent and violated her rights."

He removed a folded paper from his pocket. "This is a consent form." He pointed to the bottom of the page. "This is Valessa's signature."

"Her Miranda should have been given to her before you questioned her." The attractive defense attorney looked from the detective to the members of the jury.

Again he reminded the defense attorney that Valessa wasn't a suspect until she admitted to killing her mother.

The attorney pointed out that Valessa admitted the crime, but got confused on the details. "She was taking the blame for Adam and Whispel. She said she stabbed her mother in the throat. Yesterday, Dr. Miller stated that she was stabbed in the carotid artery on the side of her neck."

"Objection, Your Honor," Shirley Williams interrupted. "The only definition of throat is not this witness's."

"May we approach the bench?" Athan countered immediately and marched up to the bench and was joined by Lisa Campbell and Lyann Goudie. The word 'mistrial' was on everyone's lips.

Some jury members watched the sidebar carefully as if they were trying to hear what was being said. Others tapped their fingers or uneasily stared at the ceiling. Everyone in the courtroom had to guess what the attorney's arguments were. "This witness's definition of throat is not the only one," meant to the defense that the prosecutor was saying only Valessa could testify to that opinion. It was said in front of the jury. Would Valessa have to testify?

The judge called a recess for lunch. Instead of the usual stampede out of the courtroom some of the onlookers sensed there was drama happening. The television crew from 48 Hours continued filming. Attorneys huddled around the defense table. Valessa was removed through the customary door in the front of the room, but her father was escorted in right after her. Trial watchers whispered they were going to talk about her testifying. The courtroom was electric with anticipation.

Mr. Robinson returned to the seat next to his wife in about fifteen minutes and whispered in her ear. She was the only other person who knew what was said during the father and daughter conversation.

People who took the lunch break filtered back in. The television camera operators caught Valessa returning to her seat. Judge Padgett returned about 1:15 P.M., while the jury was still out. The Assistant Public Defender Lyann Goudie stood up quickly. Her gray-streaked, shoulder-length hair bounced. "The defense moves for a mistrial based on the comment Prosecutor Shirley Williams made before lunch."

Judge Padgett hardly looked at her when he said "Denied."

Goudie glanced at the other attorneys on the defense team. "The defense has an announcement to make regarding Valessa."

The judge looked up.

"She's not going to testify."

Judge Padgett addressed Valessa. "Okay, Miss Robinson, your attorney tells me that you don't plan to become a witness in this trial. Is that true?"

"Yes, sir." Valessa stared at the judge with wide eyes. Her voice was strong, almost militant.

"You understand, of course, you have a right to testify if you wish to do so?" The judge spoke softly.

"Yes, I do," she responded, without taking her eyes off him.

"Have you had the opportunity to discuss this decision with your attorneys?"

"Yes, sir, I have." She sounded less tense.

"And with your father?" the judge said gently.

"Yes, sir."

"It is your decision not to testify?" the judge asked again.

"Yes, sir."

"And you are not going to hold that decision against me, or Ms. Athan, or Ms. Campbell, or Ms. Goudie, at some time in the future?"

"No," Valessa said, quickly adding, "No, sir."

Once Valessa decided that she wasn't going to testify, the defense brought out a picture of her on the day she was taken into custody in Texas. Dee Ann Athan held up an enlargement of Valessa's face. "Do you see that her eyes are dilated from her use of LSD?"

Dr. John Halpern, a Boston psychiatrist, took the stand as an expert witness on the effects of hallucinogens. He viewed it and siad, "Yes, Valessa's eyes were dilated. She was under the influence of LSD when she made her confession."

The prosecution asked for a short recess. The courtroom emptied. Some people took the opportunity to use the restrooms.

Chuck Robinson and his wife Vanessa stood by as Jim Englert hugged his daughter, Amber, who was a year older than Valessa.

She told reporters that she didn't know Valessa well even though their parents were dating, but she remembered Vicki well. "She was a nurturer; a bright ball of walking fire." Amber added that she was praying for Valessa, and that she harbored no anger or judgment.

"I wrote a paper for my psychology class in St. Petersburg Junior College to explain my theories on what led to Vicki's murder." The pretty brunette clung to her father, Jim Englert. "It included the influence of the media, the effects of video games, and the consequences of making the wrong friends. Why did this happen? I have no idea. I'm totally lost when it comes to figuring out why."

The bailiff opened the doors, and everyone in the lobby reentered. Dr. Craig Munger took the stand as a witness for the prosecution. He was wearing blue scrubs and his feet were wrapped in surgical baggies. His attire suggested that he was a last-minute emergency witness.

The Assistant Prosecutor Pam Bondi asked,"Are you familiar with eyes becoming dilated?"

"Yes, ma'am," the doctor answered.

"Would someone's eyes be dilated approximately twelve hours after the ingestion of LSD?"

"No, ma'am, it's unlikely."

Judge Padgett dismissed the court, telling the jury they were to hear closing arguments at 9:00 A.M. Wednesday.

During the trial, Valessa's clothes were a focal point from day one. For the closing arguments, on Wednesday morning, she wore a pink sweater set and looked especially pretty. The pink reflected a blush on her translucent white skin, and set off her dark, curled hair, held back with tiny barrettes. She was wearing a black pleated skirt, white stockings, and the 'Mary Jane' shoes so many had complained about.

Before sitting down, she waved and smiled at her father. "Happy Birthday," she said. Then Valessa saw her sister sitting next to him. It was her first appearance in the courtroom. She appeared to beam with pleasure as she waved to Michelle. Michelle smiled back. Valessa wasn't the surly teen portrayed on TV. Something during the trials had changed her.

Vicki's family retained their separation from Chuck Robinson and his wife, Vanessa. Who would expect a stepparent to have almost the same name as his daughter? What was even stranger was her resemblance to Chuck. They both had very dark hair and turned-up noses, and could be taken for brother and sister (if their obvious closeness wasn't so evident). She appeared to suffer for Valessa also. With Michelle, they looked like a family.

The prosecution must have taken a hint from the defense, and for the closing argument placed a poster size picture of Valessa, in her gray juvenile detention garb, in front of the jury. The gigantic poster dwarfed Assistant Prosecutor Shirley Williams.

Shirley Williams stepped up to the lectern and said, "There is no more serious crime in the eyes of the law than the deliberate taking of a life of another human being. That's why you're here." She recounted in detail the day the police officer found Valessa as a runaway, hiding with Adam Davis when he was arrested. She repeated Valessa's own words, "I'm going to be with Adam Davis no matter what it takes." The prosecutor emphasized her statement by taking a few steps and pointing to the large poster of Valessa.

Shirley Williams went back to the lectern and reminded the jury of the young woman who had driven Valessa to the jail to meet Adam. She repeated the testimony like they were Valessa's words. "I'm gonna kill my mom, and I'm gonna get Adam to help me." Williams drove the point home by saying, "And lo and behold, less than a month later, Vicki Robinson is dead on her kitchen floor.

"Adam Davis is on death row because of her. She's the instigator of this entire thing. She had Adam Davis wrapped around here." Shirley Williams held up her pinky finger.

"Jon Whispel is doing the next twenty-five years of his life because of her."

She informed the jury that premeditation was the most important part of the State's case, and the principal theory. She defined the legal concept as: someone who intended for the crime to be committed and did something to incite, cause, encourage, assist, and advise another person to do the crime is just as guilty. She asked, "Hadn't Valessa been a principal player in Adam's crime, and therefore equally guilty as if she had done it with her own hands?"

Dee Ann Athan took Valessa's face in her hands, stared into her eyes, and appeared to be pledging to do her best before making her final argument. Her action was so intense, almost prayer-like. Lisa Campbell and Lyann Goudie jumped up to arrange the defense displays.

When Dee Ann left the defense table she carried the reproduction of Vicki's house that she had shown Detective Iverson the previous day, and placed it in front of three huge posters: one of Adam Davis, one of Jon Whispel, and one entitled "The Chronology of Sex, Drugs, and Murder" that defined her case and took up one entire side of the room.

She began to speak to the jury with the same intensity she had staring into Valessa's eyes. "I hope I haven't offended anyone with my zeal during the trial." Dee Ann Athan pointed to Valessa. The girl hadn't taken her eyes off her attorney. "I am Valessa's voice in this courtroom. I don't want to let her down. I can't let her down.

"Valessa is innocent. What is she guilty of? She's guilty of being too young, too immature, and too inexperienced to call 911. She's not guilty of first-degree murder," Athan told the jury.

She tapped the big poster of Adam Davis, and the sound reverberated. "This man used that naïve child. She was impressionable and was sucked into an association with these guys." She had to take a few steps to hit the poster of Jon Whispel. The picture shook and almost fell off its easel.

She went back to Davis. "This man purchased an $84.00 ring at Wal-Mart after her mother was killed." Dee Ann Athan pointed to Valessa. "That little girl looked up into this face." Athan scowled at Adam's poster with her chin pushed forward. "She asked him,

'What does this mean?' He said, 'What do you think it means?' She answered, 'We're married?' He let her believe it."

The attorney's voice grew increasingly angry. Most members of the jury followed her every move from the posters to staring at the young woman in the pink sweater set. The prosecution had removed the sad picture of the fifteen-year-old Valessa in the juvenile detention uniform.

"Jon Whispel lied to save himself from the electric chair. This is a model of Valessa's bedroom and Vicki's kitchen." Dee Ann Athan tipped the model upward to show the jury. "Looking at the angle of the walls, he couldn't possibly have seen the attack on Vicki Robinson from his vantage point on the bed. I suggest to you ladies and gentlemen that he wasn't in the bedroom. He was out in the kitchen sitting on Vicki Robinson's legs, where he now wants to place Valessa Robinson."

She put down the model and walked toward the jury. "Davis had illegal sex with an underage girl—who he had marked with an 'A' tattoo on her hand, and who he had bewitched with an $84 ring he had bought at Wal-Mart with her dead mother's money.

"Whispel lied and they know he lied." The defense attorney pointed to the lawyers at the prosecution table, then to the posters of Davis and Whispel. "These men murdered her mom and now they want to blame her. I'm not afraid of the facts in this case. They are up there for you to see." She pointed to the enormous poster and reviewed all the facts printed on it. It took an hour. "The charge is murder. But the case is really our about failure to protect that child."

The court clerk tapped her pen on the table to inform the attorney her time was up. Dee Ann Athan looked at her and accelerated her delivery. "Valessa Robinson has been waiting for almost two years for twelve people to do the right thing in this case." Dee Ann Athan appeared desperate, as though it was her child who was on trial. "She didn't kill her mom and she is not guilty."

Judge Padgett called a recess.

Dee Ann Athan walked slowly back to the defense table to comfort her client. Her fellow attorneys walked the distraught attorney to the back of the room. When she reached the hallway, she removed her glasses and cried. Valessa and the jury didn't experience seeing her emotion.

The prosecution had their final opportunity to rebuke any of the defense's closing statements.

"I hope you don't expect that I'm going to walk over to the defense table and point my finger in their faces and accuse them of putting on evidence they didn't believe in. I couldn't be that rude," Shirley Williams said sardonically.

All three defense lawyers jumped to their feet.

"Objection, Your Honor, improper comment," Dee Ann Athan said.

"Overruled," Padgett said.

Williams slowly and methodically reviewed the State's case against Valessa: the power struggle between mother and daughter; the plan to kill; Vicki Robinson's romantic dinner with Jim Englert that was interrupted by Valessa and her two male friends. She reminded the jury that Jim Englert offered to take Adam Davis and Jon Whispel home. She repeated Valessa's statement testified to by Jim Englert. "The boys aren't going home tonight."

She went over all the testimony about Denny's and the murder in graphic detail, and then showed a movie of what was visible from Valessa's bedroom in the kitchen. She ended with the video of Valessa entering the police van saying, "I love Adam."

Judge Padgett turned to the jurors and said, "You may now retire and consider your verdict."

CHAPTER 26
EMOTIONS RUN HIGH

The trial was over and the jury would decide if Valessa was the child her defense attorneys claimed or an adult who, in colusion with two adult males, orchestrated her mother's death. The prosecution tried to present Adam Davis and Jon Whispel as innocents who were manipulated by the devious fifteen-year-old. Yet at no point did any of the attorneys mention that all males over the age of eighteen had to register for the Selective Service making them eligible for the military. The laws in the United States labeled eighteen-year-olds adults, and gave both males and females the right to vote.

The whole trial hung on Jon Whispel's testimony. He was the only one of the three who came within two months of graduating from high school, and was the one with a driver's license that allowed him to rent a hotel room. Adam was lost without him, but the press labeled Whispel "The Lost Boy." Vicki Robinson's body was left near his house. He was the only one of the three with a supportive family, at least until Valessa's father and stepmother came to her aid.

Although Whispel's testimony changed, he managed to be the authority in Adam's case as well as Valessa's. Her testimony, considered a coverup for Adam Davis, was used against her when she came to trial.

Adam's second testimony, the one that Detective Iverson had driven to death row to record, wasn't used in Valessa's trial, but got considerable exposure in the newspapers and local TV beforehand. Adam Davis claimed he wanted heroin for personal use. He admitted knocking Vicki Robinson down in the kitchen. He claimed she got him angry by saying something negative about his dead father. Then he stuck it to Valessa, stating that she had driven the knife into her unconscious mother. The prosecutors brought him from death row—located in Starke, Florida, an hour's drive north of Tampa—to a cell near the court. They never called him to testify.

Vicki's family retired to the prosecutors' office, and the Robinsons were with the defenders. Vicki's friends from Single Purpose lined the walls on the benches in the lobby. Bonnie Smith and Theresa Goscinski, Vicki's good friends, clung to one another. They told reporters Single Purpose no longer existed, but they belonged to Sisters in Christ.

"What do you think the jury will decide?" one reporter asked.

"Valessa killed Vicki. She deserves life in prison," answered Bonnie Smith.

Theresa agreed. "When I met Vicki, she was such a wonderful person. She knew I was new and shy. She helped me feel a part of the group. I will always miss her. I love Valessa, but she did a terrible thing."

Byron "Gibbs" Wilson confided that he had been on the board of Single Purpose, and met Vicki. They dated a few times. "She had a pool party on Labor Day 1995. It was the first time Deborah Sartor and Jim Englert met

Vicki. I dated Deborah before she met Ralph Englert. I even encouraged their relationship."

"It sounds like a singles club," a female reporter said.

"The club ended December 31, 1998. We ran short of money. The executive director was no longer getting paid. The singles ministry wasn't working. Christians divorced at a rate that was two percent over the national average. I remember a special time in 1996 when Vicki took part in a skit about marriage and divorce. She was a good actress."

"What about Valessa? I guess she was like her mother, since she sang in a band," the reporter offered.

"Vicki was concerned about her daughter doing drugs. Valessa blamed Vicki for divorcing her dad. They had problems," Gibbs said. "In the summer of '97 Valessa was fourteen and she drove Vicki's van. She ran away rather than go home. She started running away at thirteen. Her father wasn't in the picture."

"How tall was Vicki?" the curious reporter asked.

"She was average; five-five, maybe five-six. Deborah's five-nine. Vicki was a type 'A' personality; outgoing, personable, talkative. She reached out to people. Vicki and I remained friends through my title company and her real estate," Gibbs related. "I bought Vicki tickets in the front row for *Joseph and the Amazing Technicolor Dreamcoat*. She glowed and retained the playbill as a keepsake. She enjoyed going to the Ice Palace in March of '98 and was inspired by Colin Powell and Christopher Reeves. We had VIP seats to see the top motivational speaker, Zig Ziglar." Gibbs appeared happy remembering Vicki.

He, like all Vicki's friends, needed to talk about her. It was difficult to get much information about Valessa, even after the trial. "Doesn't anyone here think that Valessa was overwhelmed with two grown men?" the female reporter asked. Most of Vicki's friends looked at her like she was speaking a foreign language.

"Don't any of you think Valessa's attorney scored a bull's eye when she asked Jennifer Larsen and Colleen Macklem, both on opposite sides, if they ever said, 'I could kill my mother?' They answered, 'Yes.' Some parents threaten children with, 'If you do that again, I'll break your neck.' They don't mean it."

Bonnie Smith cried again and then blubbered, "Valessa could have called 911." Her voice got stronger. "That attorney of hers was so unprofessional, hugging her all the time."

Carlton Huff spoke up, "I visited Valessa in jail. We talked about spiritual matters. She told me that she wanted her mother to be proud of her. I wish I had encouraged her to do the right thing and tell what happened."

Deborah Sartor-Englert walked by and smiled. She took a seat on the other side of the room and talked to *St. Petersburg Times* reporter Ann Hull.

The group decided to pray. It was already 3:00 P.M., and the jury was still out.

Before the members of the jury were sequestered at 7:00 P.M., they sent a note to Judge Padgett asking if a person considered a "principal" to a crime was also guilty of the crime? Their note started rumors that they were considering Valessa as guilty as Adam Davis.

Chuck Robinson expressed his concern to reporters. He told both local newspapers that he believed his daughter was innocent of killing her mother. "My wife Vanessa and I both heard it from her lips, but when Michelle asked Valessa, 'Did you kill Mom?' and Valessa answered 'No,' I was sure. Vicki was murdered in the summer prior to Michelle's senior year, when she lived in St. Louis with us."

On Thursday morning, April 20, Chuck, Vanessa, and Michelle were the first to arrive. Soon they were surrounded by reporters, all clamoring for new story information to feed the voracious public. The fact that the family had eaten a quick breakfast of peanut butter and blackberry jam on toast before yesterday's trial was salient enough personal information for some newspapers to include. Vanessa had added another insight they reported: "While we were driving here, I picked up my book of religious meditations and it fell open on page 112 that said, 'Be not afraid, stand firm and you will see the deliverance the Lord will bring you today.'"

Valessa's small immediate family were pleased that the press included Chuck's statement that Vicki wouldn't want their daughter to spend her life in prison. He reiterated his belief in his daughter's innocence on Thursday. Vanessa and Michelle followed his lead.

The family was aware that anything they said would appear in print. Chuck Robinson walked a thin line between Vicki's family and his two daughters, who had lost the mother they both loved. When he told reporters he was upset that Vicki had left Valessa alone for two weeks—and he then tried to get custody—he was viewed as an ex-husband unfairly criticizing his defenseless ex-wife.

He was never called by the defense to testify regarding the information detectives had given him before they interviewed Valessa in Texas. He told reporters how he felt she wasn't given the protection she was due under Texas law for a guardian and an attorney, before they talked to her.

He must have realized his daughter had Public Defenders who were fighting for her life better than any he could hope to afford, but he kept that to himself. His actions showed that he appreciated Dee Ann Athan's dedication to his daughter, and he worked hard to make the press realize that he was a caring father who believed in his daughter's innocence.

Dee Ann Athan entered the lobby. She embraced Chuck Robinson and shook hands with his wife, Vanessa, chatting with Michelle before she joined the

defense team sitting on the benches across the room.
She fingered the Catholic rosary beads in her hand
while she talked to the other attorneys.

Vicki's family wasn't waiting in the lobby. The big
rumor now circulating was that Assistant Prosecutor
Shirley Williams had brought Jon Whispel into her office in the courthouse to apologize to them. The buzz
was substantiated when a stampede of reporters headed
for the elevators.

Chuck and Vanessa Robinson couldn't imagine what
Whispel could say to comfort Vicki's family, who seethed
with anger at Valessa.

They pondered why reporters had disappeared from
the lobby. The couple followed Dee Ann Athan to the
Public Defender's office to try to find out where everyone had gone. Dee Ann Athan came out of her office
and shook her head in disbelief. "Jon Whispel admitted
providing the knife, cleaning up Vicki's blood, helping
dump her body, and using her money for drugs, tattoos, hotel rooms, and food," Athan said. She stomped
to the television set hanging in the hallway next to her
office, and complained with every step. "He accompanied Adam when he went to Home Depot to buy cement, while Valessa was left, helpless, in a hotel room. It
explained why she was in a wheelchair in the Best Buy
video. He rode around in Vicki's stolen van and left
Tampa with the two people he claimed were murderers,
and headed for the same destination he and Adam had
tried to reach in another stolen van, without Valessa."
She turned to face Chuck Robinson, Vanessa, and
Michelle. "Vicki's family are going to appear on television with him," the attorney announced. She put her
arms around Michelle and stroked her hair in the same
way she had tried to comfort her sister in the courtroom. Her kind gesture brought Michelle to tears, but
she quickly wiped them away with the back of her hand.

The noon news program answered the scuttlebutt

about Whispel. Valessa's father, stepmother, and sister stood in front and looked up at the flickering screen. They saw Assistant Prosecutor Shirley Williams comment, "Jon Whispel asked to speak to the family after the trial was over. I knew what he wanted to do, but I didn't say it out loud. I told Vicki's family. They thought about it, and finally said yes. I arranged for Jon Whispel to come to my office from jail for the private meeting."

TV cameras caught him entering the building, wearing his orange prison jump suit, at 10:30 A.M. The voiceover explained, "The family told reporters they forgave Jon Whispel because he was truly sorry for what he did."

Vicki's brother, Kirt Klug, said, "He wanted to apologize to us family members in person. That took courage on his part. Throughout my life, I've heard people apologize, and this was as sincere as it gets. The meeting was emotional and tearful. My mom really wanted to know if he told the jurors the truth. He said he did. What makes it really tough is that my sister didn't die easily. To relive that here has been really tough." Vicki's brother then added, "I worry what will happen if my niece is set free. If she gets out, if she doesn't get any psychological help—I mean real psychological help— she could be dangerous. She was a problem child who was content when she got her way, and ruthless when she didn't. Every once in a while she gets this demon look on her face. Knowing what happened, it sends a chill down my spine."

Deborah Sartor-Englert, Vicki's longtime friend, talked to the camera about Jon Whispel. "I'm glad he made the gesture. Maybe this will give him release and let him move on. I think it was real refreshing for the family." She disclosed, "Jim Englert, my brother-in-law and Vicki's fiancé, received a letter from Adam Davis and read it to the Klug family. It was touching. We'd like to hope it was truthful." When pressed by the interviewer, she refused to share the total contents, but reminded the reporter that Davis implicated Valessa. The television news reporter turned to the big news story from Miami about Elian Gonzalez, whose mother died taking him to America in an inner tube.

Chuck Robinson watched Sartor-Englert talking about how guilty his daughter was while she repeated how refreshing it was for Vicki's family to forgive Jon Whispel. He grimaced like he had been punched. "The prosecutors didn't wait for the jury to come in," he said, glancing away from the television screen.

The defense attorney's pretty face drooped, drained of the flamboyant color it had maintained during her fight in the courtroom. She shrugged her shoulders and raised two open palms. "There's nothing I can do now."

Vanessa, his wife, and Michelle appeared equally traumatized. The family needed to leave the building and went out to lunch.

When they returned at 3 P.M., the benches along the walls were filled. Vicki's big family and many friends stood together ignoring Chuck, Vanessa, and Michelle until she went to hug her grandmother who coldly offered her cheek. Michelle shook hands all around, but quickly returned to her father and stepmother.

The people waiting had their minds made up. Chuck Robinson planned to take his daughter and the rest of his family to a new and better environment once this ordeal was over.

If Vicki's friends and family had their way, she would spend the rest of her life in prison. They resented that her age at the time of her mother's murder precluded her from the death sentence. It was fortunate that the groups stayed separated, reenforcing their own opinions and avoiding the heated arguments mingling might cause. Valessa's few supporters would have taken it on the chin.

Most participants grew tired of waiting and assumed that the jury was in the midst of a major battle. The defense attorneys were encouraged by the length of the deliberation and shared their optimism with Chuck Robinson. By 5:00 P.M., the bailiff heard a knock from the jury room and opened the door. He took the note he received to the judge.

Without any loud announcements, people gravitated to Judge Padgett's courtroom. The judge entered and read the jury's note to the crowd gathered.

"Judge, we are currently deadlocked, and the foreman is claustrophobic and needs to get out of the room for awhile." Assistant Prosecutor Shirley Williams suggested the judge invoke the Allen Charge to speed up the jury.

Lyann Goudie jumped up. "No, Your Honor. Sequester the jury another night or grant a mistrial."

Judge Padgett read the note again to himself. "My inclination is to let this jury deliberate for as long as possible. You can't catch a fish without a hook in the water."

The blue-eyed defense attorney retorted, "I hope it is not a guilty fish we're trying to catch."

He looked at the defense attorney in the gray suit with matching collar-length hair, and frowned. "I'm going to sequester them for the night." He sent the bailiff for the jury.

"I'm going to send you to a hotel for the night to sleep on it, let you think about it, and maybe cool off a bit." He looked from Ms. Goudie to the prosecutors, and then addressed the jury again. "Whatever it takes. We'll bring you back in the morning. We'll deal with this, OK?" he encouraged.

Valessa sat at the defense table and watched the jury walk out. She turned to her father and said, "I love you." Her voice was loud. She mouthed, "I love you," to her sister and all the members of her mother's family before she was led out of the room.

* * *

On Good Friday, Judge Padgett talked to the attorneys about a note he had received from the jurors on Wednesday asking that, if someone was determined a "principal", was that person guilty of the crime? He sent them back with an explanation of the Principal Theory without answering the question directly. In a moderate tone he said, "I want to answer that question straight out. If they believe the defendant was a principal, then yes, she was guilty. These people are entitled to a meaningful answer."

The defense attorneys argued that if he were to do that, the jury would come in with a verdict of first-degree murder and send Valessa to jail for the rest of her life. Again they requested a mistrial.

The judge looked down on Lyann Goudie and into the eyes of the tall, statuesque, black attorney Lisa Campbell, and calmly denied their objections. He told the bailiff to bring in the jury. Goudie scowled up at the judge, shrugged, and stamped away. "At this point we should all go home." Her voice revealed anger. She glanced toward Dee Ann Athan, holding Valessa's hand.

Lisa Campbell sat down next to them.

Judge Padgett's mild manner disappeared. He ordered the bailiff not to bring in the jury before he admonished the defense attorneys. "You know better than to say something like that with cameras rolling. Who said that? You, Ms. Goudie?"

She turned back to the judge defiantly and answered, "Yes, I did."

"Do you want me to hold you in contempt?"

"Judge, it's your prerogative," she responded.

"There will be a contempt hearing later."

"That's fine," Lyann Goudie spat back. The young attorney with frosted collar-length hair and a tailored white suit appropriate for the Easter parade marched back to the defense table and slammed herself down in her seat.

When the jury was allowed in, the judge explained the Allen Charge and instructed them to keep trying for a verdict. To help them with their deliberation he suggested, "Take turns and tell fellow jurors of any weaknesses in your position. Don't interrupt until everyone has had a chance to speak. After all that, if you still can't reach a verdict, I will declare a mistrial."

The prosecuting attorneys didn't appear happy hearing the judge use the word "mistrial." When he started to elaborate more on Wednesday's question about "principal," the defense attorneys squirmed in their seats. The judge held the jury's question, written on a piece of a yellow legal pad, in his hand. "Now, if you have considered each of the instructions and if you have weighed all the evidence in accord with those instructions, then the answer to this question is yes."

One hour into their deliberations, the jury requested the transcripts relating to testimony that Valessa had restrained her mother. Judge Padgett informed them there were no transcripts available, and that they had to rely on their collective memory.

An hour later, the jury's note asked the judge.

You said, "Rely on our collective memory." Must we rely on our own personal individual collective memory of all the evidence or do you mean we rely on a majority memory of the collective group as a whole? i.e., If eight members remember something one way and four remember another, are the four obligated to abide by the memory of the eight, suspending any doubts they may have?

The judge called the jury in and told them, "You must rely on your own personal collective memory." Members of the jury looked puzzled, but they returned to the small room that had been their prison for three days.

The rules restricting Valessa from communicating with her family were relaxed, and she talked to her father and sister in hushed tones. They leaned over the separating wall and her chair faced them. At 12:20 P.M., the jury informed the bailiff that they had reached a verdict.

Donna Klug entered, holding a pink rose that she told everyone represented Vicki, who loved roses. The rose quivered in her shaking hands. Vicki's family remained as close to the prosecutors as they could get.

Michelle, Vanessa, and Chuck Robinson leaned back in their seats after Valessa's chair was moved back to the defense table. Dee Ann Athan held Valessa's hand and waited. Lyann Goudie paced near the wall as Lisa Campbell sat and reviewed some papers in front of her.

Judge Padgett admonished the people assembled in the courtroom before he recalled the jury. "At this point in the trial which is seen by people as either a victory or a loss, and it is not the way those of us who work here look at it, but I think that's the way other people do. This case will be seen by some people as a major loss or a victory. Please refrain from emotion or disruption."

Silence greeted his statement, but everyone looked around, not knowing which side was being asked not to be emotional. Was he worried that the defense would openly break down? Was he concerned that Vicki's friends and family would cheer? The anxiety was heightened because everyone involved, including common onlookers, knew that representatives of CBS News program *48 Hours* were present. All eyes went to the video camera.

The jury entered and the judge addressed the foreman. "Mr. Siering, has the jury reached a verdict?"

"We have Your Honor."

"Hand it to the bailiff, please."

The clerk read the slip of paper. "The State of Florida

versus Valessa Lyn Robinson. We the jury find as follows to count one of the indictment: The defendant is guilty of murder in the third degree."

The clerk's words took a few moments to be understood. The only sound was the tape rolling through the television cameras until a scream came from one of Vicki's friends, Bonnie Smith.

"We, the jury, find as to count two: The defendant is guilty of petty theft."

"We, the jury, find as to count three: The defendant is guilty of grand theft of a motor vehicle, as charged."

The judge set sentencing for May 30.

Despite the judge's warnings some people grumbled "third-degree." Vicki's friends clustered together to console Bonnie Smith, who was crying hysterically. Vicki's mother, clutching a rose, walked out of court, followed by her family.

Chuck Robinson sat, immobile. If he had been expecting to walk out with his daughter, he was disappointed. If he was pleased that she had escaped murder in the first degree, he hid it. He watched his daughter being handcuffed. He reached out to Michelle in a protective, fatherly way. His wife, Vanessa, patted his arm.

Dee Ann Athan held Valessa's face with both her hands while she spoke to her. Her intensity for her client didn't diminish with the apparent success of the third-degree verdict. She followed Valessa as the bailiff led her out of the court.

Lisa Campbell talked to the Robinsons and encouraged them by saying, "Good Friday was a good day for Valessa."

Outside the court room the impact of the verdict on Vicki's friends was evident. Bonnie Smith stopped crying and was still being comforted by hugging friends.

The trial hardened her spirited conversations about the Lord Jesus Christ. She didn't even mention Him on Good Friday.

Bonnie Smith and Deborah Sartor-Englert blamed Valessa's clothes for the jury's verdict. "I wasn't fooled by Valessa's demure behavior in court. You can dress a monkey in a suit and it's still a monkey," Bonnie Smith spit out angrily. Deborah complained, "Pink sweater, white tights . . . She looked like a little girl. I never saw her in soft colors. She preferred the rough look," she sighed. "It does show you what Valessa could have been."

CHAPTER 27
DEATH ROW ATTRACTION

The dull, tan room adjacent to Florida's death row contained some large tables surrounded by chairs. To the women who chose to romance men sentenced to death, it had become a congenial place to spend three hours every weekend, high on love. They welcomed seeing men in prison orange jump suits shuffle in like they were the sun rising in the east.

Visitors lined the outside of Union Correctional starting at eight A.M. to obtain clearance for three P.M. seating. The regulars waited with a large group of women and a few men to enter at three o'clock on Easter Sunday, April 23. The special day was a reason to wear flowing skirts. On other visiting days they were worn without panties in case the guards got careless and looked away long enough for a prisoner to cop a feel. It was against the rules to sit on a prisoner's lap, but some got lucky before attracting attention. Once that rule was broken, the woman could be banned from the visitor's roster.

Rosalie Martinez—who had divorced her Tampa at-

torney husband, Victor, and married Oscar Ray Bolin, a
serial killer—waited with all the visitors to gain access to
her husband. Rosalie Bolin had written a book about
her experience and visited many radio and television
talk shows to tell her story. The mother of four girls garnered a lot of criticism from telephone callers and studio audiences, but she found acceptance among
women who claimed to love a man on death row.

After she organized them to oppose a plan to stop
touching visits in the community room, they idolized
her. The plan was announced in December 1999, when
Adam's new love, Elena Cadrecha moved from Largo to
be near him in Starke, Florida. She was furious that
after finally getting her name on his visitor's list, her
ability to hug him might be curtailed. While waiting for
the day's clearance, she complained to a bald, leather-
jacketed man behind her.

He sympathized and asked, "Do you know that
woman with the brown hair in the front of the line?" He
stroked his clean-shaven chin.

"Yes, I see Rosalie Bolin on visiting days. She married
Oscar while he was on the phone," Elena said.

"She's been on television explaining why she divorced her attorney husband, Victor Martinez. Did you
know that she has four little daughters?" the man asked.

Elena nodded. "She knows Oscar Ray isn't a serial
killer. She worked on his defense case," Elena reminded.

"Two of his murders were overturned by the Florida
Supreme Court because of his ex-wife's testimony, but
he was sentenced to death on his retrial for one murder, and might still be for the other two."

Elena's eyes widened with shock, wondering if the
man might not be visiting a relative. "Rosalie's an inspira-
tion to all of us. She organized a hunger strike among the
men on death row. It didn't last long, but so far there's

no partition. She goes on television so she has power."
Elena reached out her hand. "I'm Elena Cadrecha."

"I've never seen that name in the press. Why?" The
man removed a pad from his breast pocket.

"Adam wants us to keep our plans to marry secret,"
Elena said.

"Adam. You mean Adam Davis? You're his girlfriend?"

"Is that so impossible to believe?" Elena said, sounding annoyed. "I may be older than Valessa, but I didn't
ask him to kill my mother."

"I'm here to write the story about the governor's
plan to separate prisoners with a shatterproof window,
but tell me what you think about Valessa receiving murder in the third degree?" The reporter got out his pen.

Elena grabbed her head and then rubbed her face in
her hands in anguish. "Don't say anything about Adam
and me, but I'm irate with the jury's decision. Adam
didn't get to testify even though he waited in jail in
Hillsborough County. I thought his testimony to Detective
Iverson should have been used against Valessa in her
trial."

"He said he was in the kitchen and knocked Vicki
down, because she said something about his father. It
gives him a motive."

"No, he said Valessa killed her while he was trying to
find something to tie her mother up with. Valessa
stabbed her mother."

"He said he lied to Valessa about the reason he
wanted heroin. It could explain why he filled the hypodermic needle with bleach."

"All I know is that Valessa killed her mother, and
Adam's family hasn't been there for him," Elena countered.

"His mother, stepmother, and aunt were in court
during his trial. His stepmother talked to reporters dur-

ing Valessa's trial. They gave Adam more support than Valessa's mother's family gave her."

"I'm the only one who visits him in jail," Elena said.

"His stepmother said that she has tried, but was only allowed fifteen minutes visitation."

"He wants to keep a good line of communication with her, so I won't say anymore," Elena said.

"Oh, come on. Your voice implies something else."

"You don't want to hear about how Adam was abused. It can't help him now. He needs his stepmother's support until his appeal is heard."

"Doesn't that prove that he uses women?"

"Of course not. He's a sweetheart. I'm going to marry him."

"Are you the woman from Tampa who told reporters she produced his child?"

"No, but Adam told me about her. She's nothing but a topless dancer he had sex with. He's not sure it's his son, but when we get married, he wants me to take care of the child. She and I talked. She told me she gave up custody when Adam got the death sentence."

"You were willing to bring up his child?"

"I'd do anything for him. I love him so."

The reporter stopped writing and stared at the pretty woman. "You don't think much of his girlfriends."

"I suppose Shana Clark was okay, but I only read her name in the paper. He has me now. He doesn't need anyone else."

The door to the prison opened and the line of visitors pushed forward. Elena turned away from the reporter and joined the throng of her new friends rushing toward a romantic interlude.

CHAPTER 28
VALESSA'S VIEW OF THE WORLD

Valessa's attorneys spoke for her in court. Once the jury came in, her diary no longer needed to be concealed and was released on April 24, 2000, more than a month before her scheduled sentencing. Writers who wanted to understand the girl in the courtroom had to labor over the small handwriting that was a little clearer than the coded message she tried to send to Adam Davis in January 1999. That message—*Don't worry be happy! I'm in love with Adam William Davis!—True love always finds a way.*—was confiscated and remained in the files until it appeared in the *St. Petersburg Times* on the first day of her trial, before the jury was chosen.

Since she didn't testify, her diary was her only voice. The *St. Petersburg Times* made her complete diary available on the Internet. The public was introduced to highlights of the diary in the newspaper. Part of her first entry on February 27, 1995, when she was eleven years old, was quoted: *"Dear Journal, Hi! It's me, Valessa. I am waiting for the TBBC to start. My mom always drops me off early."* The article informed readers that TBBC meant the Tampa Bay Children's Choir. The fact she was dropped off early by her mother didn't interest the news writers. They quoted Valessa's diary about a boy in the group who seemed to like her. "*I never really talked to him but during chorus he always looks at me. I think he's just too shy to talk to me.*"

The little sixth-grade girl poured her heart into her diary waiting to sing with her choral group. She played Pogs and collected them. In April, her mother let her stay at a girlfriend's house for two days as payment for cleaning her room. The family later took her to Adventure Island. She must have followed her mother's instructions and cleaned her room. It was a happy entry.

The seventh-grader was concerned about how the boys she liked were never the ones who liked her. Her innocent ramblings weren't newsworthy, but every normal teenage girl would identify with that painful transitional period. Their mothers could too.

On May 27 1996, thirteen-year-old Valessa told her journal her feelings about becoming the lead singer in a band called the Dead End. If she had had her own band, she would have called it "Gepeto." She thought Dead End was just that, but complained her mother wouldn't let her quit or practice at home.

She confided to her journal that she listened to a local pop music radio station, and liked the music of Boyz II Men and Michael Jackson. She dreamed of becoming a famous singer, actor, or lawyer—careers that belied her teachers' descriptions of a solitary girl who shuffled along with her head down at Seminole Presbyterian. Many stated Valessa was a depressed child; apparently she was one with big dreams.

Valessa once told her diary that she had saved $300 for an electric guitar. Shortly thereafter, she confided that Vicki and Michelle went shopping in the mall and Vicki bought her sister fifty-one dollar jeans, which Valessa thought was expensive.

Valessa's love of music was a frequent theme in her diary. Her tastes grew to include harder acts such as the Red Hot Chili Peppers, Korn, NOF, Garbage, and Rancid.

She told her diary about a boy she wanted to date, but if it meant she had to have sex with him, she didn't think that she would because she was too young.

She followed that with complaints that the television show *My So-Called Life* was taken off the air. She confided to the diary that she identified with a character named Angela who dated boys and appeared tough.

Valessa began to sprinkle her diary with words like "pissed off," "suck," and even a few "fucks." She wondered what sex would be like. On April 23, 1996, the thirteen-year-old wrote that her girlfriend wanted to be included in Valessa's diary. *"She's a b_____, who obsesses over (blanked out) Now they want to have sex. This is how they do it. People get naked and then 'INJECTION.'"*

Most of the entries in what she called "Book One" were not happy ones. She once described her life as "HELL," and then complained she went to a dance where her pocketbook was stolen.

"Book One" also included an incident that occurred when Valessa was visiting her grandparents in Michigan on the Fourth of July. A boy Valessa was with threw a firecracker into a shed that caused it to burn down, but Valessa was the one blamed for the mischief. She did confide that she had enjoyed vandalizing some of the mailboxes in the neighborhood, but added that she and her friends weren't responsible for all the damage the ensuing newspaper article had claimed.

"Book Two" began when she entered junior high at Ben Hill. Her words reflected a new interest in making friends and she even bragged she had made fifty of them within the first week. Like most teens, she was exceptionally concerned with being popular. She wrote that she was spending much more time on the telephone, and was still frustrated about not being able to quit Dead End.

Valessa described a new girlfriend that she had met at a rave club as an *"interesting people person."* Valessa admired her belly necklace and the fake tattoo on her breast, but by this time Valessa liked baggy clothes and a chain on her wallet that let it hang down past her knees.

For the first time, she claimed to hate school, and said she would like to *"move out of her fucking house."* The one constant message in her diary was that she was alone. She listed friend's names (that were later blanked out when the diaries went public), but confided over and over how she wanted a steady boyfriend. She lamented that most of her relationships only lasted two months, but older boys liked her because she was at their level of thinking. The dates she had had with younger boys hadn't gone as well. Once a boy deserted her after their date at the beach.

She was so proud that in her drama class she was given the largest role in *Hello Shakespeare*. She bragged to her diary that she got to speak on every page of the script except one.

Her journal in "Book Two" was more optimistic, as she described happy experiences at concerts, but she also discussed experimenting with drugs. She was worried that older boys would try to take advantage of her while she was "fucked up." She thought being passed around at a rave club "mosh pit" was fun.

In February 1997, she went to the Gasparilla parade in Tampa and was exposed to people who carried guns. That didn't interest her as much as her continuous search for a real boyfriend.

She wrote on April 5 about the fun she had had at a concert. She was disappointed there was no mosh pit. She continued to say that she was no longer a virgin. On March 27th, her mother left her with her sister and her sister's boyfriend, and Valessa writes that she started to make out with him, and "one thing led to another" and they had sex. The next day was her party, which "kicked ass." She notes that some people thought she might be pregnant.

Her next entry was a day later at 11:27 P.M. on April 6, 1997. Valessa gave more details about the Bush concert where she and friend tried to get close to the band and attracted a security guard. She described March 27, when she lost her virginity, as fun because she took a risk. Although they still had their shirts on, their pants were off. The boy neglected to use a condom, even though Valessa had one nearby. She used the diary to relive the experience. *"It was incredible . . . He was DARN good. He was experienced at fucking."* She said that even though she lost her virginity to a guy she wasn't dating, it was still something she would always remember. She wrote that her party was fun, and toward the end, four girls and two boys ended up in her bed. She concludes by listing her presents: a pass to Busch Gardens and Adventure Island, a necklace, two pairs of jeans, and a beeper.

This statement proved that Vicki was in the house while her fourteen-year-old and her male and female friends shared Valessa's bed.

On July 20, 1997, the fourteen-year-old discussed a big fight she had had with her mom. Valessa wrote that she ran away. Her mom paged her and they talked, and Valessa said there was no way she was going to Michigan. On Thursday, her mother, sister, and a third person left for Michigan, leaving Valessa alone for two weeks.

In the beginning of "Book Three," Valessa, still fourteen, related another gun-themed story that took place at the mall on August 7. She titled it "Mall Madness." She had heard that her friend had been threatened with a gun while she was in Smoke N' Stuff. She learned the aggressor was eating in the food court, so she followed the guy and confronted him. *"Why the fuck did you pull a gun on my friend?"* He responded by saying, *"Get the fuck out of my face."* She claimed she jumped up and smacked him and left a red welt on his face.

The prosecution would have used this entry against her, but the defense was successfully able to withhold the diary from the jury. They would have been able to show her as a leader. Her behavior was consistent with an observation made by her teacher, Mr. Dipple. He said that she would defend anyone she felt was being picked on. The defense might have used it as an example of how naïve Valessa was.

Valessa admitted to her diary that she wasn't proud of being caught shoplifting. The fourteen-year-old divulged it all, including taking hits of acid. On one page, she mentions thirteen names of teens involved with her. All remain anonymous.

When her mother called the police after she ran away, Valessa doesn't mention that any of the other teens parents notified the law. A few pages later, she tells of a girlfriend who wants to run away and Valessa has advised her not to unless she wanted to stay away forever.

On Sunday, October 7, 1997, she met Davis and Whispel. On Monday, he and another person visited her home. She had to leave for her counseling session and was thrilled to find them waiting for her when she returned. The fourteen-year-old left them alone in her house.

(Adam's name appeared for the first time. The name of the person with Adam was blanked out. Adam's name was the only name among her friends included in one-hundred and eighteen pages. Apparently the prosecutors who released the diary, blanked Jon Whispel's name out.)

On Tuesday, Adam visited again and asked her out. Six days later she ran away, planning never to return.

Valessa writes, *"Adam and two [blanks] are all running away with me. We're leaving Tampa and going out of state."* She continues, describing her plan to find a job and a place to live, and reflecting on how her friends will help her out. She concludes by declaring her love for Adam.

If Valessa knew that Jon Whispel and Adam Davis had left Tampa together and were heading for Phoenix in a stolen van, she did not tell her diary.

Valessa's defense attorneys couldn't possibly explain how needy and naïve their client was. Within days, Adam Davis and his anonymous friend, Jon Whispel had convinced Valessa that they were her knights in shining armor. From almost the moment they recognized her vulnerability, they filled her head with visions of a life of independence from her family, especially her mother.

Valessa described in her diary how Adam and Whispel were arrested for drinking and because Adam was a homeless runaway orphan. The police didn't press charges. Her sympathy went out to Adam and his friend for being punished for taking refuge in an empty house to escape the rain. *"They hadn't gotten much sleep the night before so they took a nap in an empty house and were awakened with guns pointed at their heads."* She recorded the date and time as: October 27 at 11:00 A.M. when [blank] called her from the Orient Point Jail on October 28.

(Since Jon Whispel was arrested with Adam Davis and Adam's name was never blanked out, reporters have to presume the blank was Jon Whispel. The entry about Jon and Adam sleeping in the empty house was confusing because they were in jail for stealing the taser gun on the day the story was set.)

They weren't charged for stealing the van because the owner dropped the charges. Jon Whispel confided in his deposition, how lucky they were after they deserted the van in Tallahassee, they bought bus tickets back to Tampa with stolen checks and weren't charged

for that either. Valessa either has no clue, as to the devious nature of her friends, or she doesn't want to admit
the whole truth even to her diary.

*"I had to go to Savannah to visit my dad. When I get back
to Florida I have to go on a camping trip with my mom."*

On Sunday, November 16, 1997, she tells her journal
that she and Adam have been going out for one month.
She wrote him five letters in jail and received two from
him. Since he was in jail, 'going out' had to mean something different to her.

Valessa records on the same page that she received a
certificate from her Y.E.S. class and attended the movie
Bean with her mother in the evening. Afterwards, they
met members of her mother's group Single Purpose at
the teen hangout Joffrey's.

December 4, 1997: Adam and Jon, both blanks in the
diary, pleaded not guilty for charges they claimed never
happened and had to go to trial on January 5, 1998.
Valessa told her diary, *"I got to talk to Adam tonight. He's
out of money and will have to spend his birthday, Christmas
and New Year's in jail."* Her biggest worry was getting a
ride to see him on December 10.

On Monday, January 5, Valessa went to the court to
see Adam and Jon appear. She told her diary that Jon
was bailed out before Christmas but Adam was moved
from Orient Point to the Morgan Street Jail for "getting
into too many fights."

The fourteen-year-old then mentioned a college student she's attracted to.

On February 24, Valessa told her diary she had a tattoo on her ankle touched up and added a new one on
her right hand between her thumb and second finger.
*"It's an 'A' for Adam and Aries. I'm dating another boy but ex-
pect to see Adam at his trials on March 5th and 9th."*

Her entry on March 2 told of the fun she had in Ybor
City where she used two hits of acid. She anticipated,

"Adam will be going to prison and I'll have to break up with him or ruin my life. It really sucks because I cared for him."

She included a passage about a twenty-year-old male friend and described, *"He's fun and likes hanging out with me even if I'm only fourteen."* She drifted into more about her love for Adam and conflicted feelings about the male friend who stayed in her house. His name was blanked out. *"I still love talking to him and enjoy his company."*

The friend she shared thoughts with came to stay at her house. She does not explain why, when, or who allowed him to stay. She reported that they had gone to Joffrey's to hang out on Friday, and went bowling and watched *The Wizard of Oz* on television on Saturday. On Sunday they went to church. She said she had fun but added, *"Yesterday was me and Adam's 5 month anniversary."*

On March 17, she told her diary it was only two weeks until she'd be fifteen. She related that on March 9 when she went to court to see Adam and learned he would be released. She was thrilled he took a plea bargain and with time served he would be free on April 15.

On May 11, she wrote that Adam was released on April 15. *"I was wrong about* [blank]. *I never loved him. My one and only love is Adam William Davis."* She then writes that she is trying to get pregnant by Davis, because she wants a baby "*so bad.*"

The fifteen-year-old listed a number of her friends who were pregnant or hoped to be. Then she lamented that Adam was going back to his old ways of drinking alcohol, stealing, and smoking weed. She promised her diary to write more later.

On May 18, Valessa wrote that she and Adam had had their seventh anniversary two days earlier. *"He brought a me a ½ dozen roses. I'm going to see him again tomorrow. She can ground me for a month, that won't stop me from seeing him."* She repeats that she is trying to become pregnant, then says her mother is planning on putting her on birth control—which Valessa does not want.

June 7, 1998: Valessa explained to her diary, *"If you haven't noticed the 5 pages that were ripped out of my journal, you know now. The reason for that is my mom read my journal and made copies of the 5 pages."* She explains that while she used to trust her mother with everything, she could not do so anymore. She also writes about how Adam decided they should wait on having a baby, as Valessa was still a minor. She concludes by reflecting that Adam was arrested for child abuse for "hanging out" with her, but that he'd never hit her in his life.

Valessa's diary gave an insight to Adam Davis that wasn't included in both trials. Davis was so violent in jail, he had to be transferred for fighting. She was concerned the he returned to his old ways of drinking and stealing. The last page was dated June 5, where she wrote that she would be going on a summer vacation. In less than a month, her mother was dead, and her mother's family blamed her.

CHAPTER 29

PICTURES ARE WORTH MORE THAN WORDS

After the diaries were released, the videotape of Valessa and Adam dancing in her bedroom was distributed to the television stations and the press. She was a head shorter than Adam, staring up in his eyes. In the background, Jon Whispel reclines on her bed, watching the couple like a phantom. He's dressed in black like his buddy Adam, except he is hatless. The prosecutors didn't censor him like they did his name from Valessa's diary.

The footage is very revealing. It shows the couple ignored Whispel as if he was an extra poster on the wall. Could it explain how the couple could sustain an intimate relationship with him hanging around? No one had yet accused him of being a voyeur. Did the couple hang Whispel in the closet? Was he devoid of emotions? Did Jon and Adam share a priority relationship that included each using females for their own notion of eroticism?

After serving time in jail, Jon Whispel reconnected with Adam Davis and followed him like slavishly, but told the world he's innocent of Vicki's murder because he was seen lying on Valessa's bed in the videotape.

Jon Whispel's words weren't questioned by prosecutors. They didn't explore why Whispel continued to be Adam's constant companion. They hoped people would perceive Jon Whispel as a considerate, honest, young man under Davis's spell.

Assistant Public Defender Dee Ann Athan tried to discredit Whispel's testimony by presenting a reproduction of Valessa's room, including a pink bedspread. Only Superman, with his X-ray vision, could have seen Vicki on the floor in front of her sink. Not even Detective Iverson could twist the reproduction to make the area visible from Valessa's bed.

Whispel had to admit that he had entered the kitchen and handed a knife to Adam or Valessa. He had already testified at Adam's trial that he had handed Adam the knife being hidden in the bedroom, along with the glass of bleach and hypodermic needle.

Prosecutors tried to infer that the reproduction wasn't an accurate miniaturized duplicate of Valessa's room, but apparently the jury wasn't impressed. Whispel was impressed with Valessa's South Tampa neighborhood, and the opulent house in which she lived.

He told prosecutors how he ingratiated himself with Vicki, and how she drove him to work. She never included him in complaints to her family about her fear for her daughter. He said his fear of Davis prevented him from stopping the murder.

Defense attorneys asked Whispel why he didn't just escape, instead of sticking around, renting hotel rooms and sleeping in the same room with the couple. Whispel was shrewd, crafty, and cunning enough to convince cynical attorneys and news writers that he was merely Adam Davis's pawn.

He was wily enough to get away with saying he provided the knife used to kill Vicki. If his testimony is to be believed, even Valessa trusted him. She told him extremely personal details about her life. Whispel suggested that it was Valessa who had first suggested they kill Vicki. In his version of the events, he was on Valessa's bed when he saw her sitting on her mother's legs. After handing one person a knife, he washed the kitchen and helped carry the body to an area near his house. He then nonchalantly entered, and left some money for his mother.

Because of Whispel's testimony, headlines screamed about a daughter having murdered her mother. If it wasn't for Assistant Public Defender Dee Ann Athan's defense of Valessa, Jon Whispel's changing depositions wouldn't have been challenged. The jury heard it and responded to it.

CHAPTER 30

IMMEDIATE REACTION

The Kathy Fountain Show, a television call-in program, promoted its April 27, 2000 episode as "Vicki Robinson's Friends Speak Out!" Ed Philips and Deborah Sartor-Englert smiled at Kathy Fountain while she introduced them. Ed Philips told her he was a hospice counselor and had met Vicki at the singles group Single Purpose. Deborah Sartor-Englert described herself as Vicki's best friend. Her face was as familiar to the Tampa Bay area as Vicki's Robinson's, for they had both been in the public eye for the almost two years since the murder.

Deborah complained, "We were not able to testify at Valessa's trial, and we suffered a crushing blow when the verdict was read. I still can't believe what happened to my close friend."

Kathy Fountain said, "Vicki Robinson was to have been in your wedding party?"

"Yes, we were very close. She was dating my future brother-in-law, Jim Englert. Vicki had been threatened by Valessa who said, 'I have friends who will harm you.'

I had a premonition the day Vicki turned up missing when she was supposed to be fitted for a bridesmaid dress. I called and left many messages on her answering machine."

A picture of Vicki Robinson and Jim Englert that Deborah had provided appeared on the screen as Deborah said, "Vicki was warm and hospitable. She was twenty years older, but like a sister to me. She was a woman of joy. She was so positive, a wonderful listener and a caring friend that I hoped to have for a lifetime."

"Do you think the verdict honors her memory?" Kathy Fountain asked.

"No," Sartor-Englert and Philips answered simultaneously.

Kathy Fountain took a call. "Chris, what do you think of the verdict?"

"From what we know, I feel shock, numb, angry. I didn't understand where the jury was coming from. She was so involved in the act itself."

The second caller added, "She initiated the idea, and was physically involved."

"Linda from Tampa, do you have an opinion?" Kathy Fountain asked.

"The jury should be hanging their heads. Valessa got slapped on the wrist. Vicki was a working mother, like most of us."

Kathy Fountain turned to her studio guests. "Vicki's parenting was on trial. What kind of a parent was she?"

"She loved her children. She loved the Lord. It's hard to be a parent," Deborah answered. "It's discouraging. The defense portrayed Valessa as a victim. Vicki was the victim. For the defense attorney to claim Valessa was dragged across the country is ludicrous. If I hear the word 'child' in relation to Valessa Robinson one more time, I'll throw up. She was a teenager. She also defended Bernice Bowen, whose husband killed her child and three police officers."

Kathy Fountain's program was near its end. She focused on Ed Philips, who told her he was involved in the Vicki Robinson Foundation to help parents with problem children. "It's 20-20 hindsight, but for parents listening: Don't let pride or ego prevent you from getting help."

Letters to the editor of the *St. Petersburg Times* and *Tampa Tribune* reflected anger about teenagers out of control who needed to be taught a lesson. The Internet contained e-mails from fearful parents who were afraid of their own teens, and worried that the third-degree charge given to Valessa made all parents more vulnerable.

The one-year anniversary of the massacre at Columbine High School contributed to the hysteria. People who dared agree with Dee Ann Athan that Valessa was too young to control two grown males were attacked on the Internet for their views.

One woman who called herself Mary wrote, "I applaud the jury in the Valessa Robinson case. Did first-degree murder fit this crime—NO!" Mary speculates that Valessa will rehabilitate and go on living, and she concludes that our legal system "does work."

Mary managed to enrage her critics enough that they questioned her age, sanity and education. Some were angry enough to forget Valessa and for a while they focused personal attacks on Mary.

The more creative critics suggested that Valessa should be adopted by Patsy Ramsey. One explained that O.J. Simpson's jurors retired in Florida.

CHAPTER 31

A FIGHT TO THE END

At 9:15 on Tuesday, May 30, (the day after Memorial Day), Valessa entered the courtroom in her orange jail uniform and scuffed white sport shoes. Handcuffs and shackles completed her outfit. She smiled at her father, sister, and stepmother before sitting down next to Dee Ann Athan. She became as serious and anxious looking as her attorney.

Dee Ann's black suit matched her mood. She scowled, reviewing the judge's instructions given to the jury on April 19 regarding "principal," and on April 21, regarding the Allen Charge and stated they were modified and improper. She quoted previous decisions regarding a deadlocked jury.

She repeated Jon Whispel's sentence of three charges to run concurrently, resulting in his twenty-five year sentence. She went over previous testimony regarding Valessa's arrest. "First paragraph . . . Female suspect taken to Pecos County. The Texas sheriff testified she wasn't a suspect. If she was, Valessa should have had counsel and juvenile protection due her under Texas law."

Judge Padgett frowned. "Anything else?"

Dee Ann Athan went over Valessa's prior record for petty theft and said, "Vicki Robinson was notified. Valessa wasn't arrested. Her economic statistics were drawn from school records while she was in jail." The attorney's voice began to sound strained, objecting to discrepancies she found in the file. "The probation officer lists several letters concerning Valessa's sentence. I've seen missives from her father, stepmother, and sister. There are several others that I have not yet reviewed."

The judge called a recess to give the attorney time to read the letters he had received from Vicki's family. The television cameras whirred as Dee Ann Athan shared some of the letters with Chuck Robinson and Michelle. A handwritten one brought tears to Michelle's eyes; another piece made Dee Ann shake her head in disbelief. Michelle held her hand over her mouth as she read it. Chuck Robinson bowed his head after he passed them back to the attorney. Dee Ann Athan gave the handwritten one to Valessa and came back to confer with Michelle and Chuck Robinson.

Valessa's hands shook as she read the letter. With tears streaming down her face, she looked at her grandparents, who had just returned from the recess.

Dee Ann Athan called Brenda Spivey from the Department of Records. "Did you write this report?" Athan's asked angrily.

"Yes," Brenda Spivey answered, while straightening her body and pulling her jacket down self-consciously.

While the young woman answered the attorney's questions, the defense lawyers passed Vicki's family's letters around the defense table. Lyann Goodie's head bounced back with enough shock to shake her long pageboy hairdo after she read the first one. Lisa Campbell reached out and covered Valessa's small, white, chained hands with her larger black one and whispered in her ear.

"In this report, you determine Valessa's character by a series of crimes. What crime? What date? Based on what?" Athan queried.

"Based on information we received from the State that she was a violent felon and young drug user," the young woman from the records department answered, shifting her weight from one foot to another.

"Did you consider forced violence third-degree murder?" Dee Ann Athan asked.

"No. It was Valessa's idea. She assisted in all ways. She put her mother in a container," Brenda Spivey answered.

"Where did you get that information?" Athan asked with a raised voice.

"It's common knowledge."

"The jury didn't believe that," the brunette attorney reminded.

The judge sounded impatient. "She was just doing her job. I don't want to argue."

"She's making a statement based on erroneous information," Dee Ann Athan responded.

"That's not important," Judge Padgett said. "Okay, one at a time," he relented.

"The offense was committed in a heinous manner," Spivey offered.

"What facts prove that?" Dee Ann moderated her voice and looked up at the judge.

"She was holding her mother down," the young woman announced.

"Stabbing?" Dee Ann Athan's eyebrows raised above the frames of her glasses. She took a few steps toward Spivey.

"Yes," Brenda Spivey said, standing firm.

"When did you get that information for your conclusion?" Dee Ann Athan asked. "Not at Valessa's trial," she offered, shaking her head.

"I don't want to argue," Judge Padgett again interceded. The bright lights in the courtroom bounced a glare off his glasses that made him appear expressionless.

"Information is not wholly based on the trial. She saw television, news reports, and detectives' reports," the attorney said, before she turned back to Spivey. "Do you know who authorized those reports?"

Pam Bondi jumped up. "Objection. She gave her opinion."

The argument continued over the recommendation that Valessa should go to an adult facility. Dee Ann Athan continued to fight for her client to be treated as a juvenile and be sent to a juvenile facility.

The judge said, "Her recommendation is covered in the statutes."

Brenda Spivey defended her recommendation. "Valessa will get more help in an adult facility."

"What help will she receive in an adult facility?" Dee Ann Athan asked.

"Education and psychiatric help," the young woman answered.

"Are you aware—" Athan started, but was stopped by the judge.

"You covered that."

The two women bantered back and forth about how much time would be enough for rehabilitation. The young woman testifying claimed Valessa needed thirty-six months, which she wouldn't receive in juvenile.

The judge chastised Dee Ann Athan by saying, "It's based on what she thinks and not what you think. What else do you have for us?"

"I think Valessa can take the stand to answer some of the allegations in the letters," Dee Ann said.

"The letters are opinions," Judge Padgett said.

Dee Ann Athan gave the judge an angry look and called Michelle, her sister, to testify on Valessa's behalf.

Michelle stood up and walked to the center. Before facing the judge, she smiled at her grandmother, who was sitting behind the prosecutors holding a pink rose. The grandmother looked at the rose in her hands and ignored the friendly gesture. Her angry face said the battle lines were drawn and Michelle was on the wrong side.

Michelle's hair, although straight, was the color of her mother's. Of the two girls she looked more like Vicki, but the trial didn't give her many opportunities to smile. Her mother was dead. Her sister was facing prison. She had a huge responsibility for a nineteen-year-old. "Because my mother is not here I feel it is my duty to be her voice. Valessa loved my mom very much." Michelle's voice sounded strong and clear. "I want my sister to get help. I know that in an adult facility, Valessa will get minimal or no psychological help. Let's start now to give her the help she needs in a juvenile facility. I have serious fears that Valessa will be physically harmed otherwise. Despite what the media has suggested, my sister is not a criminally sophisticated person. She trusts people. My sister has already proven that she is easily influenced by older people," Michelle's voice wavered.

She stared long and hard at Valessa while she recovered from her emotions. "Give her the treatment she needs with young people her age. That was the point I was trying to make, Your Honor."

Dee Ann Athan held the handwritten letter in her hand. "There is an allegation that when Valessa was a young child she would call the dog and then try to slam him in the door. Was she cruel to animals?"

"No."

"Another allegation was that when Valessa was in the fourth grade, she drove the lawn mower through a tulip bed to run over the family dog—"

Michelle instinctively exclaimed, "No, that is not true! I used the lawn mower."

"In the second grade, did she write a poem about killing her mother?" Dee Ann Athan asked.

"No, ma'am," Michelle responded in a loud voice.

"You were close to your sister. Did you ever see Valessa act violent toward your mother before she died?"

"Violent as in 'going to kill?' No." Michelle shook her head.

"Do you know the kind of music she listened to?" the attorney asked, looking down at the typewritten sentencing letter.

"What any normal teenager would."

"Do you listen to the same kind of music?"

"Yes."

"Thank you, Miss Robinson," Dee Ann Athan said before she called Vanessa Robinson, Valessa's stepmother, to testify.

Vanessa Robinson passed Michelle walking to the lectern. She reached out and patted Michelle's shoulder, as if to comfort the tortured girl.

Michelle sat next to her father and bit her fingernail nervously as she stared at Valessa. She didn't try to hide her worried look.

Valessa communicated her approval and shook her head and Michelle turned to watch her stepmother testify.

"How long have you known Valessa?" Dee Ann asked.

"Five years," Vanessa answered. Her dark hair was stylishly short. She was trim and pretty, and bore a striking resemblance to Chuck Robinson.

"You've written a letter?" Dee Ann Athan asked.

"Yes, I believe Valessa has been through a lot and I don't think Vicki would want her daughter to spend more time in jail," Vanessa answered. Then she addressed Valessa, sitting at the defense table. "I love you a lot and I want you to know that."

Dee Ann Athan asked, "You would take her into your home?"

"Of course," Vanessa answered but continued to focus on Valessa. "She needs to be with her sister, father and me."

"Have you had contact with her in the last few months?"

"Yes," Vanessa said, and gave the attorney her full attention. "Every month."

"Your letter is true and accurate?"

"Yes. Charles Robinson is a good man."

Dee Ann Athan then called Valessa's father and asked him if his letter was true and accurate too.

"Yes," he said as he gripped the sides of the lectern. The brass buttons on the sleeves of his navy blue jacket were the only sound in the hushed courtroom. He talked to the judge about his daughter in a conversational tone. "She's young and can be a productive citizen. I really believe that. She was a person who was obviously in way over her head. She feels remorse and has shed many tears. She lost her mother and is grieving too. She isn't prepared for prison." Chuck Robinson hesitated for a second and took a deep breath. "After reading Vicki's journals it's clear that she didn't have much time for the girls. Her work schedule was full and so were evenings and weekends. I do know Vicki would not want Valessa in an adult prison."

Dee Ann Athan ignored the groans coming from Vicki's family. "You were living at home when Valessa was nine years old. Did she ever hurt the dog? Did you ever see physical injuries?"

"No. She never did anything to hurt the animals."

"Did you ever know Valessa pushed a lawn mower through a flowerbed to attack the dog?"

"No. She couldn't, she was in the second grade. I was living at home."

"What about the allegation that her hateful grandfather put her on a plane back to Florida?"

"She spent two months in Michigan. I was told she had done very well," Mr. Robinson answered. "She spent two months in Michigan and two weeks in Atlanta with me."

Dee Ann Athan questioned in detail Chuck Robinson's knowledge of his daughter's personality and how much time she spent with him after the divorce. He admitted he refused Vicki's request that he take both girls together, because he wanted them one at a time. "Vicki said she couldn't cope anymore. She picked an institution located out of the county."

"Was Valessa living at home when she picked Steppin' Stone?"

"Yes, but her 'running away' was going to a friend's house. Most times, Vicki knew where her daughter was."

"Have you maintained contact?"

"I work for a large conglomerate. I had to wait for a transfer. I went from St. Louis to a small corporation in North Carolina before moving here."

"Since she has been incarcerated do you see her?"

"Yes, once or twice a week and telephone calls."

"Would you have any reservations about taking her into your home?"

"Absolutely not. We're prepared to give her what she needs in counseling now or three years from now."

"You sent a letter to the judge?" Dee Ann Athan asked.

The father looked up at Judge Padgett and pleaded for him to let his daughter come home. He repeatedly described how she has cried in jail about how much she missed her mother.

When his voice began to crack, Dee Ann Athan excused him and called Heidi Hamlin.

The young woman gave her credentials. She earned a Master's in Rehabilitation Counseling in 1988. She went on to say she spent time with Valessa. She addressed allegations in Jim Englert's letter to the judge. His claim that Valessa had cried for the first time in court in front of a camera wasn't true.

"Did she cry at some time when you saw her?"

"Yes. They criticize Valessa for not showing emotion. She did break down many times but not in front of a camera. During the time I worked with Valessa, she was still expecting her mother to walk into the courtroom. When the medical examiner testified, she realized her mother was dead. After she showed emotion, she said, 'I shouldn't let those people know.' I suggested she write her mother a letter. Valessa said, 'She wanted her mother to be proud of her.' She is courteous and polite . . . She's not typical of my other juvenile clients. She's motivated. Got her GED in jail and wants to go to college. I believe she can be rehabilitated. She has a supportive family. She's not mature and streetwise or hardened by the system."

Dee Ann Athan asked, "Did you consider murder in the third degree in your recommendation?"

"Yes, I did."

Dee Ann Athan called Jennifer Larsen.

The young girl with long dark hair walked to the lectern and smiled at Valessa.

"How do you know Valessa?"

"We've been friends since she attended Seminole Presbyterian with me."

"You are still her friend?"

"Yes."

"What did you think when you saw her on television being put in the police van, when she yelled at the press, 'I love Adam!'"

"She was acting tough."

"Is that the girl you knew?"

"No, but Valessa liked to hide her feelings."

Dee Ann Athan asked Jennifer's father to join his daughter. "I want to thank you both for providing Valessa's clothes for the trial. It shows how much your family cares for Valessa."

Mr. Larsen looked up at the judge. "I'd like to make a heartfelt plea that you consider Valessa a juvenile. She was always welcome in our house, but I kept my daughter from visiting Valessa's home due to the unsupervised conditions."

An audible moan came from Vicki's mother, and the pink rose in her hands quivered. The camera from *48 Hours* focused on Vicki's family and caught grimaces on their faces.

"Thank you, Mr. Larsen." Dee Ann Athan relinquished her position to the prosecution.

Assistant Prosecutor Pam Bondi placed some papers on the lectern. "I'm going to read some passages from Valessa's journal. After what she described as a 'niger' hit her on the back of her head, she began carrying a knife to school to protect herself. She admitted removing flags from mailboxes, and having sex and using drugs before she met Adam Davis."

Pam Bondi read excerpts of "Mall Madness" where Valessa claimed she confronted a nineteen-year-old for threatening a friend with a gun. The prosecutor described that the diary relates a sexual escapade with James Hardee that took place while Adam Davis was in jail. Pam Bondi joined Shirley Williams at the prosecution table.

(Valessa's entry in the diary describes a more ethereal relationship; one of mind over body. James Hardee ~~scribed~~ to reporters that Valessa had mentioned that ~~expected~~ her mother to appear in the courtroom during ~~jail~~house conversations, thereby reaffirming ~~Marlin~~'s testimony. Both witnesses experienced ~~distorted~~ view of reality once her mother was

The real fight began when the prosecution called Vicki's brother Tom Klug, an attorney, to testify. He pointed at Dee Ann Athan, walked toward her, and spit his words at her like they were missiles. "Well, Public Defender, I have news for you. You will never replace my sister as Valessa's mother." The three public defenders looked up at him as if expecting blows.

The silver-haired man, in a gray suit, returned to the lectern and looked up at the judge and softened his voice. "I want to tell you about Vicki. We did everything as a family."

He calmed down and went on to paint a picture of the perfect American family. He started when she was born, cycling through childhood sports, church, Sunday dinners, home movies, Vicki playing the clarinet and sailing on Michigan Lake. "We piled into the station wagon and it was like a home movie."

Vicki's brother turned from the lectern and faced the defense table including his niece and changed back to the angry voice. "My sister's body was turned upside down and left in ninety-degree heat to rot in the sun." He reminded the defense attorney, "My sister was criticized for not protecting Valessa, when it was Chuck Robinson's duty as a father to protect her. On one summer visit he shipped her home after just a few days."

Tom Klug again unleashed on Valessa's attorney. "You produced a dog and pony show. You got personally involved and bonded with Valessa like a surrogate mom." He asked, "What's going to happen to Valessa in five years, when you're busy with other cases?"

He informed Valessa's public defenders and the judge, "She never seemed remorseful about saying, 'Let's kill my mom.' She's never been remorseful to about holding her mother's legs down. We want Val to get the maximum penalty."

Kirt Klug acted calmer. "I feel that all the evid this case shows that my niece, Valessa, planned rible murder of her mom." He repeated parts of his parents' letter to the judge before he said, "I hope and pray that you can make her stay in prison for at least forty years, like the time of life she took away from her mother and my sister."

Dee Ann Athan fought a good fight for more than four hours. She had won a great victory for Valessa by convincing the jury that Valessa couldn't control two grown men who were involved in stealing a van only months before the murder. That act alone shot holes in Whispel's testimony, and the jury responded with their third-degree sentence. Yet Athan couldn't overcome either the vengeful letters or the overwhelmingly negative publicity that Vicki's friends and family had wrought in their attempts to discredit Valessa.

Judge Padgett announced his sentence only seconds after the last testimony was rendered, and gave Valessa the stiffest sentence he could under the law: fifteen years for third-degree murder and five years for grand theft auto, to run consecutively for a total of twenty years. His pronouncement didn't make either side happy.

Valessa's father, stepmother Vanessa, and sister Michelle, clung to their Christian notion of forgiveness. They expressed the belief that Valessa was innocent of her mother's murder and Vicki was a good Christian who would absolve her daughter for being young and foolish.

Vicki's Christian family seemed to be more influ-
~ed by the Old Testament, particularly the story of
and Eve and a snake in the Garden of Eden. The
~ake Romeo," Adam Davis had slithered into
~alessa's lives—and as in the Bible, Eve was
sin that cast the couple out of the Garden.

CHAPTER 32

CONCLUSION

Vicki Robinson's diary explains more about Valessa's dedication to Adam Davis than any other document in the huge files. Her love for Jim Englert appears on every page. She celebrated each month of their union, something Valessa tried to imitate with Adam.

True, Vicki didn't use some of the street language her daughter did, but she put Jim's needs ahead of hers. She even mentioned his children more than hers. In more than one entry, Vicki tells her diary how proud she would get when he would introduce her to his friends.

Like her daughter, Vicki was impressed by the people who surrounded her. Valessa shared the same values, but by a young age heavy metal musicians and drug dealers had become her primary role models. Adam Davis elevated himself by selling LSD. Jon Whispel, who came from a caring family in flux, gravitated to Adam as the leader for providing drugs he wanted. The social status of a drug dealer superseded his ability to provide a license and for a brief period a car. Jon Whispel, a high school dropout, was the most educated. Adam Davis excelled in street smarts from surviving from the age of fourteen without any parental guidance. His father died, but apparently Jon and Valessa were as vulnerable.

Adam's family tried to assist him but came to his aid too late to save him from the death sentence. Jon's family helped him too. Valessa's father, stepmother, and sister stood by her.

Vicki's Christian relatives and friends condemned her attorneys for reminding the jury that Valessa was fifteen when Adam Davis murdered her mother with a knife Jon Whispel admitted he provided.

Adam Davis wanted one of his female friends to write a book about the crime entitled *Why?* Vicki's diary doesn't provide the answer to why her family held such animosity for Valessa from the age of nine. The grandparents who provided a letter to the judge at her sentencing trial that described the child deliberately tried to hurt an animal with a lawn mower. They didn't live with Vicki, Valessa, Michelle, or Charles Robinson at the time. Michelle and her father testified in court that the event never happened. While she was still missing, family in-laws and cousins described Valessa to reporters as a happy, energetic child. They didn't write letters to the judge.

Vicki's murder would anger any parents, but why would they focus on a fourth grader who couldn't be expected to mow a lawn? Did Vicki begin to complain about Valessa to them, when she attended grammar school? They believed Valessa burned down a building on a Fourth of July when she visited their home at thirteen in spite of her protests the boy she was with did it. That cataclysmic incident caused Valessa to refuse to return to her grandparents, as her mother, sister, and Jim Englert had the year that Vicki left the fourteen-year-old home alone for two weeks.

Assistant Public Defender Dee Ann Athan dared to mention the two weeks to attack Vicki's parenting. The mother of three young girls embraced Valessa in court and reminded the jury that Valessa was a child, when her mother was killed by two older men who wanted her money and vehicle and used Valessa to get them.

The jury used the facts to reach their verdict of murder in the third degree. Vicki's family and friends united against Valessa's public defenders to prove Vicki's parenting wasn't perfect, but her child was an evil seed.

Valessa's grandparents participated by submitting the letter detailing Valessa's cruelty to animals at the age of nine. That fact alone would justify Valessa's feelings of alienation toward the adults who surrounded her mother. After her parents divorced, she lost the one adult she could turn to.

Teachers in Valessa's Christian school noted her depression at the loss of her father. Mr. Dipple noted that Vicki was only concerned about her grades dropping.

Parents of teens experience difficulties when their children imitate their peers. Unfortunately for Vicki, Valessa reached out to the only quasi-adults who befriended her: Adam Davis and Jon Whispel.

The family and friends' vindictive attacks were exacerbated by making public statements that they forgave Jon Whispel and Adam Davis during her sentencing trial.

Valessa serves her twenty-year sentence in Broward County Woman's Correctional near the southern end of Florida in Fort Lauderdale far from Jon Whispel at the northern end in the panhandle at Apachee Correctional in Sheads, Florida where he traded his testimony for twenty-five years. Adam Davis is on death row in Starke, Florida almost the center of the state.

His influence over women has continued in spite of incarceration or because of it. He has benefitted from the phenomenon of female attraction to men sen-

tenced to death like serial killers Ted Bundy, Oscar Ray
Bolin, and Danny Rolling who all married women after
sentencing. Ted Bundy produced a child before he was
executed.

Adam Davis collected three admirers once he was
sentenced to death. Elena Cadrecha expected to marry
him, but he married Jennifer L. Chardella. His wife has
been barred from seeing him due to a breech of inti-
macy rules in the visiting room.

On September 11, 2003, the Florida Supreme Court
in Tallahassee upheld the twenty-four-year-old's death
sentence for the murder of Vicki Robinson.

AUTHOR'S OBSERVATIONS

Murder is a tragedy that affects all human beings—not only the people involved. It strikes fear in our souls when people considered sane and normal are revealed as murderers. Youth, thought to be fun-loving and free, presents a greater quandary.

The rave clubs that catered to children as young as twelve were not on trial. Nor were the parents who allowed their children to slam dance in them. After all they saved their children from being exposed to adults who drank alcohol or smoked cigarettes in taverns.

For generations, teens received their rite of passage into the adult world by sneaking into bars. Parents seem to be according their teens increasing degrees of freedom. According to our contemporary value system, Vicki was a perfect parent who provided every comfort her girls needed, and luxuries too.

While I was taking notes and getting copies of information from the records, I met a woman doing research for attorneys. She observed what I was working on and said, "My son went to school with Michelle. He followed that case in the papers. He told me Michelle was a smart girl, but she sometimes appeared to be high in class."

"Really," I said. "I knew she had a record for breaking and entering. In talking to some of her friends, they inferred that she had some of the same problems Valessa did."

The woman shook her head. "It's such a shame. I feel sorry for the whole family. Other working mothers like me must be as terrified."

I wondered why Vicki didn't share her problems about Michelle with her friends and family like she did Valessa's. Teens who knew both girls observed that Michelle had improved since moving in with her father. Was he the one who saved his first daughter? Was Valessa the scapegoat child who was blamed for all Vicki's problems with her two girls? No one could say.

During the time I observed Valessa, she responded positively to the people who believed in her, including her dad and sister.

Many members of the press and general public were confused by Valessa's actions and condemned her. A woman at the trial tapped my shoulder and said, "I identify with Vicki, because my daughter attended Seminole Presbyterian and got involved with drugs at a very early age attending rave clubs. It opened her to associating with older drug dealers. This public crime may have saved me from Vicki's fate." She gave me her name and told me to call and talk to her daughter.

A soft young voice got on the phone. The daughter made me promise not to use her name. "I'm afraid of retaliation from the dealers if they knew I spoke to the press. You notice they can testify without getting arrested. Valessa was like so many of my friends who got involved with drugs at the rave clubs, being cool."

"You know some of the people who testified?" I asked.

"Yes, but I can't tell who. My mother shouldn't talk about this. She could have put you in danger too if she gave you any names."

"She didn't."

"Good, throw our telephone number away," the soft voice said.

Another girl I met at the trial joked that kids in the youth club at Idlewild Baptist Church were angry with Adam Davis and Valessa for giving LSD a bad name. She wouldn't give her name either.

I especially wanted Bonnie's input. I considered her a kind, loving person from our numerous talks. We hugged and she said, "Valessa should have been sentenced to life in prison."

Valessa's trial changed both of us. I agreed with Dee Ann Athan that in this true story there were two snakes. The second one was Jon Whispel whom the family forgave in their statements to the press. None of them thought his skull tattoo had any significance or connection to Vicki.

In either case, Valessa's journal condemned her. I believe Vicki was being a responsible mother when she read her daughter's diary. Nothing explains why she tore five pages out to show others. Who would dare to doubt a mother's observation? Why did she need the pages to confirm her belief that Valessa was in trouble for wanting to produce a child with Adam Davis?

From the day Valessa's jury pronounced murder-in-the-third degree, there was tremendous public outcry against their decision. Many observers did not blame the parents, but cited laws against corporal punishment, the courts, religious schools, and counselors for not doing their jobs.

Others believed the absence of a strong father figure corrupted Valessa. Single mothers like Vicki Robinson garnered the most support and empathy. She exemplified the heroic effort so many women have to make after getting divorced.

Some sympathetic to Valessa mentioned that drugs, violence, and sex—all exploited by the contemporary music played in rave clubs—had influenced her. They were parents of troubled teens who wanted to remain anonymous.

In October, local talk hosts and the newspapers in the Tampa area announced that the season premiere of *48 Hours* would be focused on the murder of Vicki Robinson. Some complained it was biased in Valessa's favor. The show included interviews with Valessa, who denied killing her mother and who provided information not mentioned in her trial. Dan Rather introduced the program, entitled "The Enemy Within," which condensed two years for the nation and contained video scenes of Adam Davis and Jon Whispel using Vicki Robinson's credit cards and being captured in Texas.

Vicki's fifteen-year-old-daughter, Valessa Robinson, wasn't a suspect until she appeared in Texas fighting to defend her two captors. The sheriff and his deputies observed the five-foot-two brunette in big denim pants and realized she was too young to be sent to an adult facility with her compatriots. She was a juvenile.

After the program, I made an appointment to meet with Valessa's stepmother to discuss the reactions of her family. She and I had begun communications after Valessa's sentencing. I found her to be compassionate. Vanessa and Chuck Robinson not only maintained a relationship with Valessa, but made a home for her sister, Michelle, as well.

Truth is stranger than fiction may be a cliché, but the day I planned to meet Vanessa, Valessa's stepmother in Tampa, she had to cancel. A few hours later I ran into Deborah Sartor-Englert at the Raymond James Stadium.

At first I didn't recognize the excited blonde who grabbed my arm. Her hair was loose and hanging straight, unlike the tamed way she wore it in court. She appeared younger.

"Joy Wellman, I just talked about you. I hoped you were the writer who left an e-mail on the *48 Hour* Web site criticizing the program," Deborah said.

"It wasn't me. I thought they did a superb job of condensing the complicated story to one hour. I didn't read the e-mails."

"Athan presented Valessa like a child. I know her. Vicki told me Valessa threatened her, saying that her friends would harm Vicki if she tried to break up her relationship with Adam Davis."

"I know. Bonnie told me that too. We had that conversation before I read Valessa's diary. Tell me why Valessa wrote that her mother wanted her to stay in the Dead End band."

"Not true."

"Valessa didn't like the group's name. She confided if she had her way, she would have her own band and call it 'Gepeto.' That seemed appropriate for a girl of her age."

"I don't know about that."

"Valessa's diary isn't a secret. It's on the Internet."

"You don't know Valessa. She was cruel to animals. Her grandparents said she mowed down tulips trying to kill their dog."

"That was used by Vicki's brother in her sentencing. Her father and sister denied it. Why did she care enough for her ferret, Slick, to take his picture with Adam?"

"I don't know, but her grandparents said she squeezed the dog in the door."

"Accidents happen, but I have a personal problem. I think families protect one another. Adam's two mothers and his aunt stood up for him."

"Doesn't that prove he was used by Valessa?"

"No, I might think that if he and Whispel hadn't stolen a van and started for Phoenix without Valessa."

Deborah stared at me as if she hadn't heard that testimony in court. "So it doesn't prove Valessa didn't plan to kill Vicki like Whispel said? Adam confirmed it was Valessa's idea."

"To me, the last day at Valessa's sentencing was almost as ugly as Vicki's murder, with her friends and family uniting to subject a child to the stiffest sentence possible."

"Valessa wasn't a child. Dee Ann Athan created that image by dressing her like a schoolgirl," Deborah said.

"You didn't complain that Adam's defense attorneys dressed him like a priest at his trial. His clothes didn't impress his jury. They listened to the facts and found him guilty of murder. Why did Vicki let a drug dealer stay in her house when Adam Davis was in jail?"

"She didn't do that," Deborah exclaimed.

"James Hardee was arrested a few months after Vicki let him stay in her house, while Adam Davis was in jail. He described how she watched TV with himself and Valessa, and how she made delicious raisin bread for the two of them."

"That's the way Vicki was. She loved everyone. She never told us about that guy. Valessa's father didn't help her. He didn't pay his child support and refused to help Vicki take care of her daughters. He sent Valessa back after having her for two days. Vicki had a right to have time alone to create to focus on her personal life," Deborah explained.

"True, Vicki Robinson was only one parent. She wasn't responsible that her gracious home attracted two predators to her daughter. Jon Whispel had a father who left his mother with breast cancer and she lost her house. Adam Davis had a drug addicted mother who gave him

up to his motor cycle father who died. Valessa and Vicki
were innocent targets."

"Vicki was innocent! Valessa planned her mother's
death," Deborah stated. "I entertained the female reporter from *48 Hours* at my house and she ignored
everything I told her also. The media wants to believe
Valessa."

"I'm sure you tried your best to convince them otherwise," I said, trying to keep indignation from overtaking
my voice.

After my conversation with Deborah, I read the e-mails
48 Hours posted from fans regarding the program. The
ones from Vicki's family and friends condemned *48 Hours*
for what they perceived as sympathy toward Valessa.
Many were critical of Valessa's father and included intimate facts that they heard from Vicki. The show also
plugged the web site established in her name to help
troubled parents.

The most poignant letters posted came from single
parents, both mothers and fathers who were struggling
with recalcitrant teens using drugs and having sexual
relationships with controlling older men. They identified personally with Vicki Robinson.

Vicki's family and friends remain committed to the
belief that Valessa wanted her mother dead. Were they
listening to the same testimony as the jury? Their statements painted a dark picture of Valessa. Did they get
their opinions from her mother? Vicki wouldn't be the
first mother who used her child for attention. Medical
doctors are accustomed to seeing cases of Munchausen's
Syndrome by Proxy, in which mothers make their children sick for attention. The mothers appear to be caring and centered on the sick child.

Valessa complained often that her mother wanted
her to continue with the Dead End band when she
wanted to leave it. Valessa even wrote that she wasn't

happy when some of the band members attended the same school, because her friends didn't like them.

Vicki complained that Valessa was uncontrollable.

Yet Vicki drove Valessa to practice with a band she claimed she didn't want her daughter to be in. Via Valessa's diary, Vicki knew of her daughter's drug use and experimental sex. Vicki also drove her to meet a felon, Colleen, who then took Valessa to meet Adam Davis in jail. She allowed grown men to stay in her house, including Adam Davis.

Vicki wasn't responsible for her own death. She wasn't responsible for the drug dealers who prey on the young and naïve in every generation to sell their poison. She wasn't responsible for the rave clubs with their mosh pits that filled the void for teens, left to their own devices while parents pursued fulfillment in work and new relationships. Vicki Robinson was successful in the adult world that expects teens to do the right thing without much supervision or guidance.

Like a lot of parents, she relied on schools, the church, counselors, and police to change her child once she realized Valessa was in trouble. Her last effort, Steppin' Stones, was too late.

The caring mother expressed reservations about committing her daughter, but she took the advice of friends who convinced her to take the hard line. In my mind, they are the same friends who wanted the courts to treat Valessa the same way.

As an adult trying to relate to Valessa's thinking in her diary, I turned the pages back to the time she invited Davis and Whispel to her house for the first time. She was so pleased they waited for her to return from her counseling session. She left them in her home alone. It was in October when she first met Adam Davis and Jon Whispel.

Immediately they included her in their plans to leave Tampa for Arizona. She told her diary that she had no money. She didn't associate that fact, when Adam and Jon left without her. She never mentioned their first venture of stealing a van and checks, or that they abandoned it in Tallahassee. If she knew about their aborted flight, she didn't tell her diary. Both Adam Davis and Jon Whispel avoided being jailed for that escapade because the owner didn't press charges. Dee Ann Athan included that flight without Valessa to prove that the two men only used her after they killed her mother. They used her mother's stolen van and money on the same trip they started without her.

Valessa was too young to understand the implications of her actions. The one opinion I was left with was that the adults who could have saved the child considered her a full-grown adult. I couldn't believe they forgave Jon Whispel. In my mind, he was as guilty as Adam Davis. He was bailed out of jail by his father before Christmas, and linked up with Davis as soon as the latter was released on April 15.

Despite the prosecution's claims, Valessa was involved with drugs and sex before she met Adam Davis and Jon Whispel. The diary indicated she was aware her drug use made her vulnerable to be used by older males. She expressed fear of what could happen to her if she passed out. Her drug use eventually led her to two criminals who latched on once she brought them into what Whispel termed her "big expensive home."

In the time she spent with Jon and Adam after her mother's death, she was used as their source of drug money as well as their meal ticket. She also tried to cover for them. I consider her as much of a victim as her mother. Both of them weren't street smart like Adam and Jon.

Whispel used the system to his advantage and even manipulated the prosecutors who put Valessa's diary in the public record with his name blanked out. He had a skull tattooed on him after Vicki's murder. He even used that for sympathy. The prosecutors didn't read Valessa's diary carefully, or Shirley Williams would never have asked the tattoo artist if he watched Valessa have an "A" tattooed on her hand after her mother's death. Valessa recorded her tattoos in her diary while Adam was in jail and her mother was alive.

I was attracted to the disappearance of Vicki Robinson because one of my daughters was a divorced realtor with two young daughters attending a Christian school. I identified with her problems of juggling a business while pursuing romance as a single mother. My thirty-year marriage ended when I was forty-eight and still had three teens at home. Vicki, was forty-nine when she was murdered.

As I sat among the mourners at her funeral, I realized that, "There but for the grace of God go I." My seven children and I were fortunate that rave clubs were nonexistent when they were as vulnerable as Valessa.

ACKNOWLEDGMENTS

I'd like to thank Detective James Iverson for his cooperation in providing the background material and pictures that allowed the Tampa Sheriff's Department to reveal some of their personal perspectives.

Assistant Prosecutor Pam Bondi provided her photograph and the exhibits that made her case. I'll always be grateful.

Sheriff Bruce Wilson sent me his picture from Texas. He told me that Larry Jackson who was the sharp shooter that brought Vicki Robinson's van to a halt without loss of life or injury has since died during a heart operation.

Pictures of Valessa Robinson, Adam Davis and the court scenes with Assistant Public Defender Dee Ann Athan were made available courtesy of the *Tampa Tribune*'s photograph department.

Jim Englert, Vicki's Robinson's fiance, provided her pictures as a memorial to her.

Joy Wellman